BALANCING ON THE MECHITZA

BALANCING ON THE MECHITZA
Transgender in Jewish Community

EDITED BY NOACH DZMURA

North Atlantic Books
Berkeley, California

Published by
North Atlantic Books
P.O. Box 12327
Berkeley, California 94712

This is issue #66 in the *Io* series.
Cover photo © iStockphoto.com/Rich Seymour
Photo for "*Opshernish*" © Charissa Tolentino
Photos for "self-portrait as *pshat*" © Thea Miklowski
Photo of Noach Dzmura (back cover) © Aaron Strickler
Cover and book design by Suzanne Albertson
Printed in the United States of America

Balancing on the Mechitza: Transgender in Jewish Community is sponsored by the Society for the Study of Native Arts and Sciences, a nonprofit educational corporation whose goals are to develop an educational and cross-cultural perspective linking various scientific, social, and artistic fields; to nurture a holistic view of arts, sciences, humanities, and healing; and to publish and distribute literature on the relationship of mind, body, and nature.

North Atlantic Books' publications are available through most bookstores. For further information, visit our Web site at www.northatlanticbooks.com or call 800-733-3000.

Library of Congress Cataloging-in-Publication Data
Balancing on the mechitza : transgender in Jewish community / edited by Noach Dzmura.
    p. cm.
    Summary: "While the Jewish mainstream still argues about homosexuality, many transgender and gender-variant people sit in the congregation, marry under the chuppah, and create Jewish families. Balancing on the Mechitza gives voice to this movement in Jewish culture"—Provided by publisher.
    ISBN 978-1-55643-813-4
    1. Transgenderism—Religious aspects—Judaism. 2. Jewish transgender people—Religious life. I. Dzmura, Noach.
    BM729.T65B35 2009
    296.086'6—dc22
                    2009052064

1 2 3 4 5 6 7 8 9 SHERIDAN 14 13 12 11 10

Dedicated to those gentle beings
murdered for their gender expression
while this book was being written, and to
the gender-variant children whose
parents allow them space to become

Acknowledgments

'd like to acknowledge everyone who submitted essays for inclusion in this volume. Thank you all for sharing your stories, and, to the contributors, for trusting me to edit your work. This has been a labor of love; together we are parents of this child.

Thanks to Lindy Hough of North Atlantic Books for the courage to publish a first-time editor on the strength of a single recommendation, and to Naomi Seidman, Director of the Richard S. Dinner Center for Jewish Studies of the Graduate Theological Union, for the recommendation. Thanks to Elizabeth Kennedy and Susan Bumps of North Atlantic for providing answers and options.

Thanks to Gregg Drinkwater, Executive Director of Jewish Mosaic: The National Center for Sexual and Gender Diversity, who cut me some slack in my duties to complete this project.

I am grateful to the LGBT Alliance of the Jewish Community Federation of San Francisco, the Peninsula, Marin and Sonoma Counties for funding my attendance at Nehirim West in Petaluma, California, a true spiritual retreat when I needed it most. Thanks to Reverend Sally Hamlin, MaryAnn Zapalac, and Reverend Suzanne Semmes for finances and food when the cupboard was bare.

Thanks to my mentor Rachel Biale for helping me navigate the Bay Area Jewish community, and to the Kol Tzedek collective for collegial activism and peer support. Thanks to Hollen Barmer, Rabbi Julia Watts-Belser, Gregg Drinkwater, Jay Michaelson, and Rabbi Rebecca Alpert for comments and/or editorial assistance. Finally, thanks to my family for an injection of lifesaving Dzmura humor, and to MaryAnn Zapalac and Deborah Cohen for friendship and unflagging support.

Contents

Foreword

Stringing the letters L-G-B-T (and increasingly I and Q) together as an adjective that modifies the noun *Jews* has become more and more common in the past decade. It reflects a commitment to these sex and gender identifications that Jews have become increasingly comfortable with—we are not only thinking about lesbians and gay men, but also bisexual, transgender, intersex, and queer/questioning people. We want to embrace the many varieties of sexuality and gender differences through the language that we use. Yet more often than not, in spite of reciting this litany of letters, the conversation is still focused on gay men and lesbians and issues of figuring out how to include us in (or sometimes exclude us from) Jewish life. *Balancing on the Mechitza* will change that.

The transgender movement is a gathering place for expressions of gender that are outside the traditional rubrics of "male" and "female." It includes those who know that their physical bodies do not match their self-perception and seek to align their bodies with their self image; those who alter how they present external manifestations that are coded by gender, like hair, clothing, and makeup, either sometimes or all the time; and those who refuse the two-gender system's insistence on using pronouns and segregated public spaces (like bathrooms and clothing stores) to circumscribe their gender identity. The transgender movement can also include people who are often labeled transsexuals, cross-dressers, butch lesbians, and girly men, or who self-identify as drag queens and kings, transmen (FTM), transwomen (MTF), and genderqueers.

Transgender is a powerful way to question the two-gender system, a strategy for putting on notice those of us who identify as men and women pure and simple that, well, it's just not so pure or simple. This book gives voice to that challenge in a Jewish context. Here you will read the stories of those who have often met with love and support for their trans selves within the Jewish community and those who have not. You will encounter new rituals (and surprising variations on old ones) that will make Jewish life possible for transmen and transwomen and will also enrich Jewish life. And you will learn from scholars and teachers, (trans and not), who are reimagining Jewish law, language, and communal practices through a transgender lens.

For readers who identify as transgender, Noach Dzmura has woven together a broad vision that makes a place within the Jewish world with which I hope you can identify and where you can feel at home. For non-trans readers, welcome to the dizzying universe of transgender Jewry where nothing about gender (or Judaism) will ever seem the same. For Jews, a people whose story is about questioning and wandering, that should fit us to a T.

Rebecca Alpert
May 2009

Introduction:
The Literal and Metaphorical *Mechitza*

> Since my transition, I have repeatedly tried to access Orthodox
> space to be able to engage as a Jew in the community and tradi-
> tion in which I was raised. One rabbi stated that in his shul, he did
> not feel that I could sit on either the women's side or the men's
> side of the *mechitza*. He also did not feel that his congregants
> would be comfortable with constructing a third section to seat me.
> This led me to wonder if Adam, the first person, who was created
> possessing both male and female sex characteristics, would be
> accepted into today's synagogues and communities. I recently
> found a progressive Orthodox shul in my hometown where the
> rabbi is supportive. I have attended a couple of times, and it's hard
> to describe how wonderful it is to be able to have a safe and wel-
> coming space where I can engage as a Jew. It is also so hearten-
> ing to find people who are supportive and accepting and who
> realize that although my gender has changed, I am still the same
> person they knew and loved.[1]

Mechitza is the Hebrew word for a barrier that separates men from
women in an Orthodox synagogue. It can take the form of a floor-to-
ceiling built-in wall or a partition erected temporarily, but a clothesline
stretched from one end of a room to the other, or a balcony at the rear
of a synagogue, can serve the purpose just as well.[2]

Along with this first conception of the mechitza, which exists in three-
dimensional space and separates men and women in an Orthodox synagogue, another mechitza stretches across our lives. It resides in the
intangible realm of thought, of Western culture and of Jewish tradition,
and separates the human population into male and female kinds. In the
quotation above, Nicole Nussbaum describes the challenging position
of a transsexual woman who determines to bring her whole self to synagogue, when the physical mechitza provides no category of seating for
a woman with her origins. When her rabbi suggests that congregants

"would not be comfortable" creating a third space, he is invoking the second mechitza, the intangible mechitza of the mind. A third space is not something that we *do*.[3]

Gender difference is not an evil or an illness that endangers the Jewish world; it is a vital and healthy Jewish variety. This book presents an invitation to encounter gender diversity intimately, safely, and within the very heart of our tradition. Written to and for gender-variant Jews, this anthology affirms the vibrancy and vitality of trans Jewish life, and provides resources, encouragement, and support to transsexual, transgender, gender-variant, and genderqueer Jews, wherever they locate themselves in Jewish space. For non-transgender allies, this book provides support and instruction about the transgender world.

If gender difference presents an obstacle to the system of human recognition, this anthology sets apart as *kadosh* the moment of ambiguity (rather than certainty). If gender difference interrupts traditional forms of communal identification, the stories in these pages propose the opportunity and the means to negotiate alternatives. If gender difference obstructs whole-bodied participation in Jewish life, this anthology shares techniques others have used to gain access.

My hope is that the stories in this book will also help readers develop compassion for human differences so that a first encounter with a transgender person can provide an opportunity for a courteous greeting rather than a cause for discomfort or embarrassment. Reading these essays can minimize the human fear of difference, especially those phobias categorized as "transphobia."[4] As readers who are unfamiliar with the transgender experience follow these Jewish lives as they go to shul, approach Torah for an *aliyah*, or shop for Shabbat at a local supermarket, gender variance will begin to seem less strange than it might once have appeared. Insight gained from these pages begins the process of Jewish reeducation and resocialization to an updated gender norm. As a result of open-hearted efforts in Jewish communities, this valuable dialogue ensures that eventually, no part of a person's gender identity need remain hidden in Jewish space.

It is my fervent prayer that gender identity and expression no longer

Beck, ed., *Nice Jewish Girls: A Lesbian Anthology;* Angela Brown, ed., *Mentsh: On Being Jewish and Queer;* Daniel Boyarin, Daniel Itzkovitz, and Ann Pellegrini, eds., *Queer Theory and the Jewish Question;* Rebecca T. Alpert, ed., *Like Bread on the Seder Plate: Jewish Lesbians and the Transformation of Tradition;* Rebecca T. Alpert, Sue Levi Elwell, and Shirley Idelson, eds., *Lesbian Rabbis: The First Generation;* Steven Greenberg, *Wrestling with God and Men: Homosexuality in the Jewish Tradition;* David Shneer and Caryn Aviv, eds., *Queer Jews;* and Gregg Drinkwater, Joshua Lesser, and David Shneer, eds., *Torah Queeries: Weekly Commentaries on the Hebrew Bible.* For literature of gender transgression, see Judith Butler, *Gender Trouble: Feminism and the Subversion of Identity,* and other works; Kate Bornstein, *My Gender Workbook: How to Become a Real Man, a Real Woman, the Real You, or Something Else Entirely;* Leslie Feinberg, *Stone Butch Blues* and *Trans Liberation: Beyond Pink or Blue;* and Susan Stryker and Stephen Whittle's first-of-its-kind *The Transgender Studies Reader.*

17. There is one exception: Rabbi Margaret Moers Wenig's piece concerns the spiritual journey transition represents; it's by a non-transgender person, but it's certainly a paean that belongs in this chapter.

Hall's statement acts for me as a reminder, one that I need to hear or read over and over. For I forget it constantly. I strive to forget it, under the pressure of a puritanical society, which demands that we detach ourselves from our bodies. Society will accept us changing our social genders and even our bodies so long as we present ourselves as pathetic and disturbed people desperate for help. If we acknowledge, or claim proudly, that we made these changes as a life-giving act of passion, we risk losing the moral authority given to victims. But victims have no power. Victims can never celebrate their lives.

When I came out I understood above all else that the knowledge of myself as female rested in the deepest places of my being. I understand now that that means the body. The body of a trance-sexual woman desires to become female, recognizes herself as female. The body desires to change her outer form. Crossing sexuality is not a concept imposed on the body by a detached mind at odds with reality. I never thought of myself as trapped in the wrong body, nor did I hate my body. When I was trying to live as a male, I hated, or rather feared, what my passions were leading me to do. When I stopped resisting my desires I did not hate my body's masculine form, but saw myself as female, whatever my shape.

Desire leads us to revelations, such as the very knowledge of ourselves in our true gender. What else but desire would lead us to do what we do? We take strong drugs to alter the shape and function of our bodies. We face the contempt and ridicule of society, friends, and even family. We take risks of imprisonment, enforced hospitalization, and torture in the form of electric shock and other kinds of "therapy." We run the danger of being beaten or even murdered if discovered at the wrong time by the wrong person. And finally, we undergo, we seek out, surgery on our genitals. Think of the power of a desire which can lead us to do such things. Most of us have experienced this as desperation. As long as we see only the desperation, as long as we cling to it for the dubious permission it gives us, we remain victims. When we start to recognize the driving force as passion, we allow ourselves the possibility of our own truth, of a life based on joy rather than pity.

Passion answers the challenge put to us in so many different forms, sometimes openly, sometimes subtly: "How can you claim to be a woman?" We do not claim anything. We know our gender as a revelation.

The trance-sexual woman sacrifices her social identity as a male, her personal history, and finally the very shape of her body to a knowledge, a desire, which overpowers all rational understanding and proof.

HOOWAHYOO?

Kate Bornstein

Editor's Note

The everyday exchange of gender identity information is a process that goes on continuously, with every human encounter. A transgender person may interrupt the ordinary course of such exchanges. Bornstein's story is crucial to this project because it begins to demonstrate how both the broadcasting and the recognition of Jewish identities must change in order to adapt Jewish social situations to trans reality. An instant, subconscious appraisal is no longer sufficient for the recognition of gender identity.

Ms. Bornstein explores the central question of the story in a way that might be familiar to many Jews who celebrate Passover. In her story, Bornstein telescopes a single narrative moment—a woman greets the author at her mother's funeral—to encompass the past, present, and future until that single moment is the right size and shape to accommodate a complicated gender identity. Past, present, and future all contain the same changing-yet-unified "I" that ultimately responds to the woman's inquiry.

The Passover Haggadah (story) commands the participants of a traditional seder to tell the story of slavery as though it were their own bodies that experienced the oppression and hardship of that long-ago age, and simultaneously the Haggadah asks that participants project their thoughts forward to a future time when no oppression exists on the planet. Seder participants experience those moments in the present. Present-day Jews who celebrate Passover know simultaneously the experience of slavery, the experience of liberation, and the experience of helping to liberate others from bondage. A transgender body narrative can tell its story in the same way: never losing sight of its sex and gender of origin, enduring or celebrating the present moment of transition by turns, and living toward a hoped-for Jewish-inclusive future.

Kate's tale of a son who becomes a daughter yet acknowledges identity in between male and female constructs an unfamiliar Jewish identity in a manner that is recognizably, perhaps characteristically, Jewish. Between the moment of slavery and the moment of freedom for all is the moment we live in now, an ambiguous time when "none of us are free while one of us is still chained," a world in which our work is necessary to manifest freedom from all human bondage and suffering.

"Who are you," asks the third blue-haired lady, peering up at me through the thick lenses of her rhinestone cat glasses. Only it comes out in one word, like "Hoowahyoo?" I'm wearing black; we all are. It's my mother's funeral service after all, and the little old ladies are taking inventory of the mourners. Me, I have to take inventory of my own identities whenever someone asks me who I am, and the answer that tumbles out of my mouth is rarely predictable. But this is my mother's funeral, and I am devastated, and to honor the memory of my mom, I'm telling each of them the who of me I know they can deal with.

"I'm Kate Bornstein," I answer her in this quiet-quiet voice of mine, "Mildred's daughter."

"Daughter?!" She shoots back incredulously the same question each of her predecessors has asked, because everyone knows my mother had two sons. That was her claim to fame and prestige among this crowd. No do-nothing daughters in my mother's family, no sir. Two sons. That was her worth as a woman.

"Mildred never mentioned she had a daughter." The eyes behind those glasses are dissecting my face, looking for family resemblances. When I was a boy, I looked exactly like my father. Everyone used to say so. Then, when I went through my gender change, those same people would say, "Y'know, you look just like your mother." Except I'm tall.

Nearly six feet of me in mourning for the passing of my mother, and I'm confronting this brigade of matrons whose job it seems to be to protect my mother from unwanted visitors on this morning of her memorial service down the Jersey Shore.

"You're her daughter? So who's your father? It's not Paul, am I right?"

Now there would be a piece of gossip these women could gnaw on over their next mah-jongg game. "Mildred had another child," they'd say after calling two bams, "a daughter no less! And Paul, God rest his soul, he never knew."

My mother had told only a tight circle of friends about my gender change. She knew that spreading the word meant she'd be torn to shreds by the long pink fingernails so favored by the arbiters of propriety of the small town she lived in. She was raised in a nearly Orthodox household, my mother was. As a young girl, she would wake up every morning just in time to hear the men and boys wake up and utter the phrase, "Thank God I was not born a woman." She lived her life placing her self-worth on the presence of the men in her life. Her father, a successful merchant, died a year before I was born. Her husband, a successful doctor, died a year before I told her that one of her two sons was about to become a dyke. She preferred the word *lesbian*. "My son, the lesbian," she would tell her close friends with a deep sigh and a smile on her lips.

My mother was there the night the rabbi asked me who I was. I was a senior in college, a real hippie: beard, beads, and suede knee-high moccasins with fringe hanging down past my calves.

I was home for some holiday or other, and my parents thought it would be nice if I came to synagogue with them. They wanted to show off their son who was going to Brown. I'd always enjoyed Friday night services. There's something lullingly familiar about the chanting, something comforting in the old melodies and the Hebrew which I never ever understood but had down phonetically.

But when the rabbi gave his sermon, I was incensed. To this day, I don't remember what I was so outraged by, any sense of my anger having been eclipsed by the events that followed. But there I was, jumping to my feet in the middle of the rabbi's sermon, arguing some point of social justice.

My father was grinning. He'd never been bar mitzvahed, having kicked his rabbi in the shins the first day of Hebrew school. My mother had her hand over her mouth to keep from laughing. She was never very fond of our rabbi, not since the time he refused to make a house call to console my father the night my grandfather died. So there we were, the rabbi and the hippie, arguing rabbinical law and social responsibility. We both knew it was going nowhere. He dismissed me with a nod. I dismissed him with a chuckle, and the service continued. On the way out of the synagogue, we had to file by the rabbi, who was shaking everyone's hand.

"Albert," he said to me, peering up through what would later be known as John Lennon glasses, "Hoowahyoo? You've got the beard, so now you're Jesus Christ?"

I've done my time as an evangelist. Twelve years in the Church of Scientology, and later, when I'd escaped Hubbard's minions, four or five years as a reluctant spokesperson for the world's fledgling transgender movement. But somewhere in between Scientology and postmodern political activism, I found time to do phone sex work. My mother never knew about that part. It was one of the who's I'd become I knew she couldn't deal with. So I never told her of the day I was standing in line in the corner store in West Philly, chatting with the woman behind the counter. From behind me, a deep male voice says, "Excuse me, who are you?" And I turn to see this middle-aged yuppie peering up at me through tortoiseshell glasses.

"Stormy?" he asks me. Stormy was the name I'd chosen for the smoky-voiced phone sex grrrl who did erotic dancing on the side and had a tattoo on her thigh. "Stay on the line with me a little longer, sugar," I'd purr into the phone, "and I'll tell you what it is."

So this young urban professional is standing behind me looking like he'd died and was meeting the Virgin Mary. I'm trying to figure out what fantasy of his we'd played out. But I'm scared. Way scared. If word got out that Stormy is a tranny, I'd lose my job for sure. I fix this guy with the same icy stare I'd learned from my mother, and he eventually slinks away to inspect the Pringles.

My mother died before she could hear the blue-haired ladies ask "Hoowahyoo" of the tall-tall woman with mascara running down her cheeks. She never heard the producer from the Ricki Lake show ask me,

"Who are you?" when I told her I wasn't a man or a woman. My mother never heard the Philadelphia society matron ask me the same question when I attempted to attend her private women-only AA group.

My mother only once asked me, "Who are you?" It was about a week before she died. "Hoowahyoo, Albert?" she asked anxiously, mixing up names and pronouns in the huge dose of morphine. "Who are you?"

I told her the truth: I was her baby, I always would be. I told her I was her little boy, and the daughter she never had. I told her I loved her.

"Ha!" she exclaimed, satisfied with my proffered selection of who's. "That's good. I didn't want to lose any of you, ever."

The *Trayf* Jew

Chav Doherty

Editor's Note

While the first modern sex reassignment surgeries (SRS) were performed in Berlin in the early part of the twentieth century (partial FTM in 1912; MTF in 1931), it wasn't until 1952 that the sensationalized transition of former U.S. Army officer Christine Jorgensen introduced the word transsexual into the American living room.[1] In the present day, the story the media tells about transsexuals has changed. Sex change operations are now relatively commonplace.[2] The struggle for civil rights, the annual ritual marking the untimely deaths of gender-variant persons, and the unprecedented decisions transgender persons make are what the contemporary media finds newsworthy.[3]

Over the past few years and across the spectrum of Jewish observance, stories that parallel those in the American mainstream have emerged. Inclusion is the order of the day. In 2003, the governing rabbinical body of the Conservative movement approved a responsum concluding that individuals who have undergone full SRS and whose sex reassignment has been recognized by civil authorities are considered to have changed their sex status according to Jewish law.[4] Also in 2003, Reuben Zellman entered Reform rabbinical school as the first "out" transgender man, and in 2008, after a sabbatical, tenured professor Jay Ladin returned to work at Yeshiva University (an Orthodox organization) as Joy Ladin.[5]

These momentous breakthroughs mask the difficulty transgender people encounter in their attempts to live a Jewish life. Chav Doherty explains what it's like to grow up Jewish and transgender, when a complicated identity is viewed (by the mainstream of Jewish life) not in the kabbalistic sense of the unification that results from the merging of opposing forces, but rather, as trayf. The word trayf is typically used to describe food that is not appropriate for an observant Jew to eat; food that is not kosher. Trayf

had become deeply rooted in the community. My bat mitzvah was an occasion of joy and pride for me—I led as much of the service as possible in Hebrew. The event was marred only by the fact that I was required to wear a dress.

In my early twenties, I asked my parents' help to seek sex reassignment surgery (SRS). My parents protested; they were convinced that, due to my small stature, I would not be perceived as convincingly male ("Oh, Chav, you'll never pass. Your hands are too small!").** Through the media, we knew of men who'd become women through surgical and hormonal intervention (I am thinking of Renée Richards and her struggle to compete as a woman on the professional tennis tour. She eventually prevailed through the justice system). But there didn't seem to be any accounts of people born female who wanted to become male. No one, that is, but me. I let go of my dream to change my sex as impossible.

I subsequently came out as a lesbian, an identity which doubly marked me as female: a woman who loves women. It didn't feel like the *right* life—it felt like the *only way* to have a life. And I am grateful for the path I took; on it, I met my future wife. Though she is not Jewish, my partner is attracted to Judaism and knows the liturgy. She is happy to keep Shabbat and observe other important Jewish holidays. She has even considered conversion herself. I was completely beguiled when, upon meeting her, she engaged me in a discussion of *tikkun olam* (the Jewish task to repair the world)—I certainly didn't expect that! Both of us were engaged in the repair and healing of our worlds, one of many shared goals that brought us together.

I was drawn to study Judaism as a graduate student because of my interest in reading and interpreting biblical texts. When I arrived at the Graduate Theological Union in Berkeley, I found a small community of scholars studying European Jewish intellectual history and Jewish

---

*I now tell people I meet that Chav is short for *Chaver,* the Hebrew word for "friend," thanks to a workshop student who assumed this derivation.

**At that early date, none of us could conceive of the powerful masculinizing effects of testosterone, which would make "small hands" a moot point.

mysticism. I was immediately drawn to the study of kabbalah; I was hungry for a representation of the feminine divine within Judaism. Though hindered by my lack of Hebrew skills—why hadn't I learned more in Hebrew school?—I threw myself at arcane texts of Jewish mysticism, from the prophets of the Bible and the rabbis of the Sepharad, through the stories of the *Ba'al Shem Tov* (the founder of Hasidism) and early Hasidism. I developed a deep appreciation of midrash, the intertextual tradition of the rabbis.

My experience at the GTU was peculiar. The program was small, with each student pursuing her or his own area of interest. I experienced little collegiality. I easily came out as a lesbian and, as my colleagues remarked upon my last name, I came out as a convert to Judaism. I was not prepared for the stereotypes and assumptions that followed the disclosure of my conversion. Instead of asking questions about my experience, my colleagues apparently assumed a past for me that included celebrations of Christmas and eating pork! I was very surprised to feel more comfortable being out as a Jewish lesbian than as a convert.

In the fall of 1994, when I was studying the hagiography of the Ba'al Shem Tov, I suddenly had a startling and elaborate vision of myself as a man. Here is a snapshot of me translating a passage from *Shivhei ha'Besht* (In Praise of *Israel [ben Eliezer] Ba'al Shem Tov*), which contains writings and stories about the founder of Hasidism. I am sitting on a futon in a cave-like room (standard issue graduate student accommodation) containing many books and all my worldly possessions. The door is closed. A full-length mirror hangs on the back of the door. I look up from my bed, amidst a pile of books and papers, and catch a passing glimpse of my reflection. Instead of a woman, I see the man I am to become. I immediately stop working and meditate on this brief apparition. I hear a man's name that I recognize as my own. Somehow, in my text study, I'd discovered an image of my true self, a reflection I'd been seeking.

Following this vision, I could no longer relegate the notion of sex change to the realm of fantasy. But given the attitudes of my peers in

Jewish studies toward conversion, I *really* wasn't sure how to handle my gender issues as they reemerged in the final year of my graduate program. A trans convert? What would my peers make of me? Would I be accepted in the Jewish community? What would the rabbis have to say?

Before embarking on transition, I thought very carefully about what I was doing, and why I needed to move forward. I knew that I was risking the loss of family, friends, and community over this decision. But I also knew that I needed the world around me to acknowledge, and reflect back to me, that sense of myself as a man. My physical transformation was a means to this end; as my voice dropped and I developed facial hair, the people in my world responded to me as a man. I engaged my community of friends and family in a negotiation over my gender; this affirmation of my masculinity was exactly what I needed. Over time, almost everyone has come around to support me in this transition. I believe that others have learned to expand their definition and understanding of what it means to be a man through this tacit negotiation with me.

I have often thought that I would not have chosen transition if I lived an isolated and self-contained life. As a younger person, I craved this kind of isolation—probably seeking respite from the stress of gender incongruity. In any case, as a social being, I've found I could not live cut off from others.

I made contact with the female to male (FTM) transgender community in the San Francisco Bay Area, delighted to find that I was not alone. Not only were there other people like me who were in the process of moving from female to male, but also, a lot of them were Jews! There seemed to be a disproportionate number of Jewish transmen in the community, and several self-identified as converts. For each of us, conversion held a different meaning. Among those of us who converted, my friend who converted during his gender transition is most comfortable with his Jewish identity. For this young man, conversion and transition were analogous and parallel processes. Each confirmed the other.

For me, however, transition further problematized my identity as a Jew. The laws of kashrut are based in separation of kinds: milk from meat, flax from wool, clean from unclean. My own uneasy relationship with halacha has been challenged by the reality of my transition and embodiment as a man. I was drawn to the study of mysticism, in no small part, for its antinomian expressions and the collapse of categories experienced in *unio mystica*.* Here was a hidden, disregarded, and marginalized way of being Jewish, one that might accommodate the contradictions I experienced in my own life. I was born Christian but have known nothing other than a Jewish life. I was born female but live as a man. I embody concepts that are commonly held to be antithetical to one another. Although I experience my Jewishness on a soul level, as deeply as I experience my maleness, I have not felt at home within the Jewish community since transition. Perhaps this is because, in my efforts to understand what kind of Jew I am, it became clear to me that, according to the mainstream of Jewish belief and practice, the mixture of categories I embody would be seen not as a basis for mystical experience (itself delegitimated by the mainstream) but rather as *trayf,* contaminated flesh.

To recognize and lament the difference between the mainstream opinion and my own view of myself, I secretly appropriated the identity of a *trayf* Jew, which captures the mixing of categories that I celebrate in my life, as well as the connotation of impurity such mixtures hold for the mainstream. So let me see: convert, transsexual, and married to a shiksa. Could one possibly be any more *trayf?* I have not been sure what to do with this identification, especially since it has reinforced my sense of alienation from Jewish community. I had, it seems, moved from a centered Jewish identity, held in a loving synagogue, to a marginalized one. I felt exiled from Jewish community. Although I knew I was irrevocably Jewish, I couldn't find my way home.

---

*Antinomianism refers to the idea that a given body of moral law is neither universal nor unalterable. *Unio mystica* is the idea of mystical union that is often expressed in Hasidic thought through the word *dveikuth. Dveikuth* means cleaving or clinging to God with every thought and action.

Inside/Outside

How did it happen that I, a stranger who found a home and a strong sense of identity (including support for my masculinity) in my Jewishness, suddenly found myself outside that home, an exile? Perhaps I embodied one difference too many? I sought the counsel of a local rabbi. I was heartened by a teaching from the Talmud, posted on the door outside his office: "Whoever saves a single life, it is as if he had saved the whole world" (Sanhedrin 4:5). At this point in my transition, I was estranged from my family and many friends, who were struggling to come to terms with the visible signs of my transition. The rabbi was welcoming; he heard my story and invited me to join his synagogue. However, he warned me against coming out as transsexual there; although the community was progressive—it welcomed lesbian and gay members, and had a female rabbi—his feeling was that his congregants would not be ready for my kind of difference. My partner, who identified as a lesbian until we got together, joined me at the synagogue's monthly gay and lesbian events. While we felt welcome, and our difference as an apparently heterosexual couple might be named there, we both felt uncomfortable and disingenuous. It was challenging to explain ourselves—"No, really. We're queer!"—and our presence there, at a time when we were both coming to terms with our separate struggles related to identity. My wife and I did not find ourselves at home there; we did not go back.

Mosaic Man

Unification and brokenness are simply a matter of perspective. In a quotation attributed to an unknown rabbi from a commentary on the Torah called Kol Demama Daka (The Small Silent Voice), "it is a Jewish custom that when someone accidentally breaks a cup or other vessel, people say, 'Mazel tov!' The root of this is as follows: When something is broken, it is a divine instruction that on the inside there has been a unification, and the thing has been transformed."

What transition has been about for me is the fracturing of identity, or the myth of identity as a self-consistent construct. I am certainly not the only Jewish person to have lived the reality of conflicting identifications. From biblical to modern times, Jewish people have lived among diverse communities and embodied conflicting identities. Examples include Moshe, who was adopted by a pharaoh, raised among wealth and privilege, and became a leader of an oppressed people seeking freedom from bondage. Jews of the Diaspora, to the extent they have lived among and mixed with other cultures, have certainly experienced the strain of multiple and conflicting roles and identifications, from the Hellenistic period through the Enlightenment in Europe. Different, yet not different, I too am a mosaic man—identity shattered and reformed, refracting multiple realities.

It has been much too easy for me to simply turn away from my Jewishness. Some of my alienation from Judaism can be attributed to grief I felt over the loss of the beloved synagogue of my childhood. (My family moved from California to the desert Southwest when I entered high school. As a family, we spent several years looking for a new community. We kids seem to have given up, but my parents find their religious and spiritual home with Chabad, a Hasidic and Orthodox movement committed to serving Jewish people in far-flung parts of the world.) It is not uncommon for young people to disaffiliate from the religion of their youth, as they break away from family to establish their own identity. The fear of being too different, disinclination toward Orthodoxy, and distress over having to prove both my maleness *and* my Jewishness factored into my decision to turn away from Jewish community. The spiritual cost, however, has been very high. I have lost sight of this important aspect of myself.

A mosaic is a very apt metaphor to describe my experience of identity. Although the term *identity* generally connotes self-consistency and coherence, the way I have lived my identity suggests a more complicated picture. I embody differences commonly regarded as distinct and contradictory: male and female, Jewish and non-Jewish, queer and straight. These differences have, at times, bent me up and torn me apart. Like a literal mosaic, my identity is composed of pieces broken and arranged to form a new whole. It includes shards of each distinct identification. The glue that holds them together is my lived experience. In addition to punning on the description of a Jewish man (*Mosaic* being the adjective used by the church to describe the laws of Moses), the idea of the mosaic man captures my understanding of identity.

While I have maintained distance from the Jewish community to spare myself the distress related to my nonnormative Jewish identity, this decision has not served me. I am aware of my need for Jewish community to support my spiritual growth, and to affirm my Jewishness. This is the last task of my transition. I am aware of organized efforts to educate Jewish communities, synagogues, and temples about the need for outreach to Jews who happen to be trans. Groups like Jewish Mosaic: The National Center for Sexual and Gender Diversity actively advocate on behalf of queer Jews within the broader community. Open and affirming congregations are welcoming queer Jewish members. I know of several transpeople who are rabbis or in the process of becoming rabbis. Trans activists are becoming visible in their communities. I can only imagine what the consequences of my own reaffiliation might be; the time is right to take that risk.

I have always loved Judaism for its commitment to social justice and the needs of the oppressed; both the Torah and the Talmud preserve teachings that speak to inclusion of the other. The Talmud, in particular, conserves the voice of the other, the minority opinion—just in case there may be use for it among later generations. I do not believe that my hope to find my way to a spiritual home, despite my complex and contradictory identity, is either unreasonable or impossible.

Change Yourself, Change the World; Heal Yourself, Heal the World.

Prior to transition, I was focused on the injustices I perceived in the world, racism and sexism chief among them. I was, in equal measure, dedicated and frustrated in my efforts to effect change; the world simply couldn't change fast enough for me. With transition, I focused all my efforts on changing myself. Strangely, I noticed that the people in my immediate world began to change as they sought to remain in relationship with me; this was completely unexpected, and very gratifying.

As a counselor and an educator, I actively encourage those around me to question their assumptions and experience as gendered people; this work has been rewarding. I am comfortable describing the experience of male privilege, and its correlate—sexism. Most of the people with whom I speak see immediately the spuriousness of such oppression: I am the same person, whether I appear female or male to you; and today, whether I appear male or female to you is up to me, thanks to modern medicine.

Similarly, I have come to believe that the work of *tikkun olam*, the healing of the world, begins with the healing of self. This is, perhaps, a moral imperative in a world that knows so much suffering over differences that are, at least initially, a matter of chance.

Transparent on High

Jhos Singer

Editor's Note
With characteristic eloquence, in the essay below Singer writes, "To, at
five years old, recognize that the right answer might also be false, and the
true answer might also be wrong, set me on a lifelong path of confusion."
As stories of holy fools do in every tradition and culture, this story tells
the reader how surface perceptions can lead one far from home, and perceptions taken through the lens of human compassion can lead one safely
home again.

Of all my parental accomplishments, I am particularly proud that I have
managed to delude at least one of my children into thinking that I am
both omniscient and clairvoyant, and that beneath my rapidly thinning
hair there lurks a never-sleeping eye always spying from the back of my
head. My youngest son believes that I see his every move and know his
deepest secrets. On countless occasions, I have anticipated his needs as
if by magic. For example, without looking up from my laptop, I will
nonchalantly hand him the book he is looking for. Feigning a yawn, I
might say, "This what'cher lookin' for?" I delight in giving one-word
answers to questions that are just about to leave his lips, leaving him
sputtering, wondering how I knew what he was about to ask. From across
the house I have heard an almost inaudible clinking, compelling me
into the kitchen just in time to find him pulling his still small hand out
of a tub of off-limits jellybeans. I stand silently behind him, my jaw set,
one eyebrow raised, forehead furrowed. He turns around, his paw loaded
with a chaotic candy rainbow: busted again.

I hear him getting dressed after a shower, and I yell up the stairs, "Put
on a clean shirt!" I know he has yanked on the same beloved but filthy
skull and crossbones T-shirt he has worn for the last two days. I creep

up the stairs as he yells, "Dad!!!! I did!!" I catch him in the hall and tell him to show me what's under his hoodie. He growls and shuffles. "Okay buddy, let's see then ..." I wait. He grumbles. I know the grimy black-and-white Davy Jones lurks just underneath his sweatshirt. "Wanna show me, bud?" I ask. He delights me by becoming simultaneously indignant and sheepish. I respond by channeling Clint Eastwood, curl my lip and point at his chest whispering the command: "Clean T-shirt, Mister ... now." He stomps back into his room, crashes around, opens his dresser, and then stomps back out of his room. I head back down the stairs. In my mind's eye I see that he is about to throw the dirty shirt on the floor. I feel like Big Brother. I yell up to him, "Sir, put it in the hamper please." He keens, "DDDAAAAAddddd! Whaddaya think I'm doing!" He rails against me, hollering accusingly as he clambers down the stairs after me, "Why do you always blame me?" I look at him with confidence, lean toward him, and softly say with an Indiana Jones grin, "Dude, I am *so* on to you." At that moment his indignation fades, and glimmer of admiration flickers in his eyes. On his face is an unspoken question: "Wow Dad, how'd you do that?" And, with love, a dash of fear, and a dollop of fascination, I can see that he thinks I'm an evil genius. Which, for the record, I am not.

What I am is a transgender person who as a child survived the 1960s in America, who came of age in the late 1970s in Los Angeles, California, and who managed to fit into the world of politically correct, come-to-consensus-OR-ELSE lesbian feminism in the San Francisco Bay Area in the 1980s. All my life I have been profoundly aware of how I do or do not fit into my social surroundings. Mostly I've lived outside the norms of femininity. I have been a tomboy, a firefighter, a butch dyke rock drummer, a deckhand, a neo-Hasidic androgyne, a Jewish lesbian spiritual leader, and finally, a married-with-children, transman rabbi-*maggid** serving a small congregation. Hardly the trajectory presented to me as a girl-child. I realized early on that if I was going to live to tell the tale, I could either totally tune in to the subtle cues of my cohort and con-

---

*A Jewish preacher.

form, or I would have to utterly ignore all social conventions and bush-whack my way through the binary gender jungle. Mostly, I've done the latter. Regardless, I had to know who I was dealing with at all times, and take a chance on finding a way to fit in, or be so outrageous that fitting in simply ceased being an option.

There is a teaching in the Talmud, *"Dah lifney mi atah omed,"** which is usually translated as "Know before whom you stand," or in contemporary parlance, "Yo dude, don't look now, but God is watchin'!" Our rabbis insist that each of us is being seen, understood, known, and considered in every moment, every act, and every feeling. *Dah lifney mi atah omed* is a reminder that even in our most private moments we are standing before God. This is the very feeling I have tried to instill in my son (and it seems I have been somewhat successful). I suspect that at this stage in his life he feels spied on, interfered with, and controlled by my intrusions into his private life. In time I trust that he will understand that my nagging and rule-setting were an expression of just how much I loved him and wanted him to be safe and well cared for. However, I know that one day he will hit a difficult crossroads. Soon enough he will realize that his seemingly all-knowing parent was simply a very imperfect placeholder for God. And that realization will signal that his spiritual journey has begun in earnest, when—like Abraham—he leaves his father's house. Oh yeah, that is when the real fun begins.

I never really had a "father's house."** As a child I was unaware of any adults who had the foggiest clue who, or what, I was.*** For better or worse, my children are well-known to their parents, and we see them

---

*From the Babylonian Talmud, Berachot 28b. The original is stated in the plural, but it is most often quoted in the singular as above.

**That is to say, a safe cultural home base.

***It is only fair to add that my mother, of blessed memory, was remarkable in her acceptance of my genderqueerness. While she did dream that her daughter would wear cute little dresses with matching handbags, she almost gave it up by the time I was in kindergarten. For my fifth birthday she gave up completely, and gave me a white button-down shirt, a tie, and a pair of navy blue chinos. I was blessed to have her as a parental role model.

in all of their complexity, with all of their paradoxes. Growing up in the San Francisco Bay Area in the twenty-first century with queer parents affords our children a rather wide berth for their expression and identity. Gender? Schmender! As parents, our primary guidelines for them are that they be true to themselves, do more good than harm, and brush at least twice a day. I, on the other hand, was born in 1959, when gender unequivocally predetermined who and what I was supposed to be in the same way that a paint-by-numbers canvas dictates its painter's brush. It was clear to me from early on that I simply could not follow the rules of being a girl. I wouldn't wear "gender appropriate" clothes and eschewed dolls, the color pink, and playing with little plastic tea sets. I was the only girl in packs of boys or I was alone. I generally just coped with the sad fact that there didn't seem to be a soul like me for miles around. Thus, my spiritual journey began young.

Humans, as a rule, seek familiar others. We expect our children to look up to adult role models. And, like all kids, I observed and sought an adult version myself, a fully formed example of who I might become. Sadly, the cupboard was bare. My quest to find my Self, in the limited adult male and female archetypes that were available at the time, proved frustrating at best, and terrifying at worst. Women were made up and sprayed up and had huge pointy breasts swathed in bright floral prints. I could not see myself ever dressing that part. It actually scared me to think of it. Men, on the other hand, were cropped and boxy, tight and buttoned down. While slightly more appealing, it still didn't quite feel like that was the direction for which I was destined. Women seemed too colorful and sexy; men seemed too dour and dull. I was some strange hybrid: part serious and stalwart, part merry and gay. I was part boy, part girl, and everyone else seemed to be ALL boy or ALL girl. By the time I was five years old I had developed a style and persona that literally stopped people on the street who, with no shame whatsoever, would ask, "Are you a boy or a girl?" I could barely answer them because I knew that there was a right answer (girl) and a true answer (no).* The more I looked around me, the less I felt there was a place for me. Instinctively, I developed my own version of *Dah lifney mi atah omed*. Rather than

"Know before whom you stand," my meditation was more like: "Know who stands in front of you (and do your best to be just like them)." And with that somewhat warped notion guiding the way, I launched my quest to find out who I was to be.

I suppose all of us develop methods of coping with our existential disappointments. The blonde, straight-haired kid who wishes to have brown curls; the goy who secretly covets dreidels, latkes, Yiddish, a God who laughs, and eight days of Chanukah; the girl who would rather be a boy. I was all of the above and was in deep need of a powerful rite that would help me transcend what seemed at the time a rather mean-spirited practical cosmic joke. That rite was a mind game I called "Who Would I Rather Be?" I played my game in line at the bank or the supermarket, at a movie theater or concert, riding the bus, sitting on the beach, anywhere and everywhere. It became my ritual, my supplication, my constancy, my meditation, my prayer.

Here's how you play: 1) Look closely at all the people in your immediate surroundings. 2) Note age, stature, body type, style, ethnicity, identifying markings, and personal habits. 3) After perusing the variety of nearby humans, you have two minutes to pick the one you'd rather be. It's like a choice you might have faced if *Let's Make a Deal* were hosted by God: would you cash out your life and identity for the good-looking, thirty-something stud muffin with ringlets standing next to Carol Merrill on the showroom floor? (For me, the more he looked like Mandy Patinkin in *Yentl,* the more likely my answer would be a resounding "YES!") The goal of the game was identity suicide.

I played "Who Would I Rather Be?" for decades. I was so uncomfortable in my own skin that nearly everyone I saw seemed an improvement over being me. I was seeking definition, recognition, and simplicity. Like most of us, I had totally bought into the two-box gender system. There were men, there were women, and you needed to be one or the other.

---

*This was a rough revelation in and of itself: to, at five years old, recognize that the right answer might also be false, and the true answer might also be wrong, set me on a lifelong path of confusion.

Deep down, I knew that I was a little of each, but if I had to choose, I was more drawn to masculinity than my native femininity. Originally, I focused on physical appearance and discovered that I was prone to covet nice packaging. Generally, my longing was based on the paradigm of binaries. One could be male or female, handsome or ugly, smart or stupid, debased or respectable. This was certainly supported by our culture, where we tend to cluster those qualities into a mythical perfect person. Thus, when I played "Who Would I Rather Be?" I assumed that a handsome fella would be smart and reputable too. Handsome outside equated handsome inside, so for a long time, the handsomest man, or occasionally a handsome woman, would be my choice when I played "Who Would I Rather Be?"

But then, inexplicably, when I was about twenty-four the game crashed. I was standing outside a club in San Francisco casing the nearby crowd. While everyone around me was cruising for someone to be with, I was cruising for someone to be. There were loads of hot, young, hip people. I caught sight of a young man who was stunning to look at, exceedingly cool, understated but brilliantly coiffed, and sharply dressed. Ordinarily, he would have been a slam-dunk candidate for my imaginary morph. Then, just as I was about to mentally cash out my frumpiness for his elegance, something about him set off a red flare, shattering my reverie. My vision of him got very focused, and all of a sudden he looked "off." I found myself looking past his beauty, his fit, smooth body and silky masculinity, to a place an inch or two below skin level. There was, in his spirit zone, an energy that did not seem smooth and beautiful, but rough and bitter. The tip-off was at surface level: I saw a brief facial spasm, a split-second sneer that warped his otherwise heavenly mouth and sent a shock through me. I looked closer at his eyes: slightly cold. Then I noticed his jaw kept flexing and relaxing, popping a cheek muscle up and down like a jack-in-the-box. His hands were busy wringing, dancing in and out of his pockets, fussing with a button, raking through his hair. Nice hands, but none too clean, and his nails were bitten-down pink. He was almost imperceptibly nervous, microscopically twitchy, and on closer inspection, just a tad grimy. On a macro level, beautiful and put together, but deeper, he was unsettled. After studying my fellow humans for two decades, I had finally developed an eye that really could see who stood before me. Twenty years of research, practice, and prayer paid off. The scales fell from my eyes, the myth of human perfection finally debunked. That night, surrounded by sinewy, well-clad hipsters, I broke the chain, and chose to be imperfect, gender-confused, and flaxen-haired. I chose me.

Alas, old habits die hard. I continued to play, scan the faces, the hair-styles, the clothes, the bodies. Observing people had become a habit, but my eye had been changed. Other people didn't seem so perfect any-more. I began to notice that lots and lots of handsome people had unpleasant habits, or were just as anxious and insecure as I was. It was getting harder and harder to find a slam-dunk persona I would have preferred being. The closer I looked, the more I saw, and the more I saw, the less I coveted. My faith in physical beauty and archetypal masculin-ity took a downturn at almost the same moment that the binary gender paradigm took a major hit. In the 1980s through the early 1990s an amazing cultural shift took place. The firm definitions of male and female were beginning to erode nicely. Annie Lennox donned a man's suit and wore a mustache at the 1984 Grammy Awards.* Boy George redefined manhood with mascara, lip liner, and a sassy hair band. In cinema, *The Crying Game* put forth a likeable, sympathetic, and brave (not to mention gorgeous) transvestite.** A nascent queer aesthetic was being born in the mainstream, of all unlikely places. A tiny sliver of gender-fluid people became visible, and they weren't being laughed at. Their albums were being bought, their music danced to, their styles copied, their movies watched, and, by God, they were hot!

Amazingly, I found myself thinking that my own flaws weren't so bad after all. A multidimensional gender reality started to take root in

---

*For more on drag and other queer aesthetics in performance, see Fabio Cleto, ed., *Camp: Queer Aesthetics and the Performing Subject* (Ann Arbor, MI: University of Michigan Press, 1999).

**Portrayed by Jaye Davidson, whose performance earned him an Academy Award nomination.

the binary gender world. More and more when I found myself playing "Who Would I Rather Be?" I passed up door number one and door number two because now there was a door number three.

Knowing who we are in relationship to the world and/or God and having a clear understanding of what is around us are flip sides of the same coin. Judaism is a profoundly relational path, and I would argue that being transgender is as well. Dah lifney mi atem omdim, knowing both before whom we stand and who stands before us, sums up a big part of our transgender journey. To make sense of this world, transgender folks have to be awake and alert, we have to study and observe, we have to reconcile how things appear and how they really are. To make sense of ourselves we have to grapple with and integrate all of the contradictions and paradoxes that we were blessed with from birth. I tried for so many years to see those in front of me as only utterly perfect or utterly flawed, black or white, which, truthfully, diminished their wholeness as well as my own. When, finally, I was able to perceive the glorious grays, a depth of knowing began to supplant my discomfort and yearning. God's complexity displaced my human desire to bifurcate. And thus, yea verily, did my complexity become evidence of my own holiness. No longer preoccupied with who stood in front of me, I began to know, rather, before whom I stood.

One day I'll tell my kid that my "psychic powers" are simply the byproduct of studying the microscopic facial twinges, vocal tics, and naughty tendencies of my fellow humans since I was half his age. I will explain to him that it's a habit that developed into a prayer of sorts. I'll let him know that my superpowers are a vestige of my youth as a tranny-in-training, and I'll share a little Talmud as I bless him: Dah lifney mi atah omed.

Lech Lecha!

Eliron Hamburger

Editor's Note

As other essays in this volume have shown, transition can be a profoundly spiritual endeavor. The process of searching within to discover the source of one's feeling of difference from one's fellows may lead the searcher down a number of blind alleys before yielding its truths. As in a computer game, though, even a blind alley can lead to a revelation and the next step in the journey. The benefit of hindsight allows the searcher to recognize that the twists and turns of the path follow a pattern that was invisible during the wearying and often frightening steps of the journey. Another word for hindsight is reflection, which is a key component of spiritual experience. This jewel of an essay reflects on the process of seeking that lead Eliron Hamburger to make the decision that felt right for his son's circumcision, and also, unexpectedly, lead to the revelation of his own authentic self-expression. Eliron's journey is told in tandem with the biblical patriarch Abraham's journey away from his father's house to an unknown destination that God would reveal to him, and the moments of sacrifice and revelation both travelers encountered as they walked on their way.

I spent the first thirty-six years of my life being a Jew and the last ten years becoming Jewish. I was taught the rules appropriate for girls. Understanding the large and unruly set of commandments of our people was not required, and reading them was the unenviable privilege of boys. I embraced duty and obligation, a secular prescription common among first-generation Americans born to survivors of Jewish genocide. It wasn't until I sought to inscribe my newborn as a Jew that I realized how little I knew about being Jewish. Naively, I opened the Torah expecting to find the recipe for Jewishness and discovered more than I bargained for: I gained courage to come out as transgender.

Somehow, though the words were written thousands of years ago, Torah revealed to me a path from daughterhood to parenthood, awakened me from an unsympathetic and disassociated sense of self, and is now guiding me as I wrestle with the meaning of gender and the need to visibly express gender authentically. As the individual braids of a challah together make one loaf, these three journeys are woven together by Torah to integrate my previously estranged body and bewildered soul into the person I have become, a consciously Jewish and gender-dexterous being.

Finding My Voice

When the biological clock I didn't know I had began to tick loudly enough for me to hear, I began to awaken. As my first task, I prepared my body for childbearing. I quit smoking and became a vegetarian; then I marshaled the resources to get pregnant as a single person. I also wanted to be a conscious parent, not only to be aware of what I was doing, but to be able to explain why I did what I did. I felt an urgency to learn about my obligations as a follower of the covenant. I started reading an introduction to Judaism text as a prerequisite to parenting.

The first commandment I would face, were I to bear a son, was the obligation to circumcise. The Brit Milah is the visible sign of the covenant made between G-d and Avraham, and I quickly understood that G-d banished any descendents for their failure to carry out this obligation.

> Any uncircumcised male, who circumciseth not the flesh of his foreskin, that soul shall be cut off from his people; he hath broken my covenant. (Gen. 17:14)

From the start, I got mad—it was as though G-d were threatening my own child if I were to fail in this duty. Judaism was proving to be headed by a commanding and unforgiving G-d. To parent consciously, I needed to reconcile this ultimatum with my own rationale about the Brit Milah.

By seeking deeper understanding of this tradition that most others accepted as fundamental to being a Jewish man, I was not only differentiating myself from my family of origin and their rules for being a Jew; I was also sowing the seeds to grow the soul of a Jewish adult, possessed of the ability to separate from the religious ideas of my childhood and to personally engage with the tradition.

My parents would tell you that given a choice, I always chose the hard way. However, I never saw myself as having independent choices. I viewed everything I did in relation to its impact on my family—and was strongly critiqued by my family for every action. Because of the obligation to transmit the Jewish faith to the next generation (usually expressed via the Hebrew phrase *l'dor va dor*), adhering to the Brit Milah was not a choice.

With the birth day fast approaching, I realized that I might not be able to complete this traditional Jewish rite of passage, either for my child's sake or for my own. While I had learned much about the Brit Milah, including reading both contemporary halachic (Jewish legal) authorities and ancient rabbinic commentary, neither the functional nor spiritual reasons for performing circumcision felt like *my* reason for carrying out this mitzvah (commandment). For the first time ever I was driven to study directly from Torah in the hopes of finding my own explanation.

Just beyond the section on circumcision, I found the Akeida, the Hebrew name of the part of the Bible in which G-d requires Avraham to sacrifice his son, Isaac. It begins when G-d calls Avraham:

> And it came to pass after these things, that G-d did tempt Avraham, and said unto him: Avraham; and he said: *Here I am.* (Gen. 22:1; emphasis mine in this and each of the next two biblical references)

Avraham complies with G-d's command, but he does not tell Isaac what he is about to do. Then on the journey to the mountain where the ritual is to take place, Isaac grows suspicious because there is no lamb for the sacrifice. Isaac calls to his father:

> And Isaac spoke unto Avraham his father, and said, "My father;"
> and he said "*Here am I, my son.*"(Gen. 22:7)

Then, in what are surely the final moments of Isaac's life, when Isaac is bound to the altar and Avraham has the knife raised in the air to slay his son, an angel calls to Avraham just in the nick of time:

> But the angel of the Lord called unto him out of heaven, and said,
> Avraham, Avraham; and he said, *"Here am I."* (Gen. 22:11)

The ritual sacrifice is prevented by the angel, and Avraham goes on to slaughter a ram caught in a nearby bush.

A literal reading of these events suggests that we should do what we are told and all will be well. I saw such faith as blind and foolhardy, so I contemplated further. I wondered about a deeper meaning associated with Avraham speaking the words "here I am" *(hineini)* three times.[1] Avraham displays amazing spiritual courage in the face of what seems like the call to murder his son. In speaking the word *hineini* repeatedly, Avraham's answer is a testament that he is present not only physically, but spiritually as well.

While I was being confronted with carrying out the Brit Milah, I discovered that Avraham used his own voice to refocus on being present rather than speculate on what the future held, and thus he had the courage to continue on the journey. As Avraham had to surrender his mental construction of the future, I too needed to surrender the presumed fait accompli that would follow if I chose not to circumcise my son. Ironically, it was my sense of Jewish obligation to the next generation that led me to delve deeper into the tradition. Now, with Avraham as a guide, I accessed a degree of mental respite from the decision about what I would *do* and instead began to feel empowered by choosing how I could *be* in the world. I drew strength from this newfound space in my psyche. This personal engagement with Torah bore a tentative voice inside me that said, "There is an ancient way to be authentic and Jewish."

At that moment, while anticipating the birth and without having found *my* reason to perform the commandment, I could remain authentic only by deciding to stay this ritual sacrifice. Through that first revelation, I emerged from daughterhood into parenthood with a tender new root of authenticity held in a nascent personal and Jewish relationship with G-d. This early Torah revelation showed me that traditional text could provide me with a spiritual entry point and help guide me in my life as events were unfolding. I was not yet aware that I also needed that revelation in order to be present to other aspects of myself that remained hidden from my conscious mind.

Disconnected

Shortly after the birth, I looked at a picture of the child emerging from my womb. The tentative voice nourishing my new sense of self was stricken silent as I witnessed my estrangement from the woman in the picture. Years later, I recognize just how terrified I was to experience this schism between my body and my soul; at the time, I simplistically considered myself as lacking maternal instincts. I panicked that I could not take care of my newborn, and I was afraid to tell anyone. I was certain that if anyone knew what was happening inside me they would take my child away to prevent harm. The shock that followed this lack of recognition of my *self* as my child's mother sent me into a tailspin, and I snapped psychologically.

My usual response in times of crisis is to *do*, and, given my inability to connect and trust myself, I *did*—everything, in this case, to secure replacement care and protection for my child if anything were to separate us. I had over many years perfected this strategy of *doing* rather than *being*, not ever recognizing that I was compensating for how disassociated I felt from my *self*. When I was younger, I was seen as gullible and amenable, though I now know that I was abandoning my own needs in favor of helping others to meet theirs. As I got older, I appeared giving and generous, and I quelled my unmet needs with drugs and alcohol. While 12-step programs and long-term sobriety have helped me to recognize my behavior as codependent, I am still far from being in remission.

I can tell you these things now because I have already lived through them. At the time all that was apparent was that I was trying to manage by making things seem more doable, compartmentalizing my duties into smaller chunks. As "mother," I breastfed for three years whether at home or at bus stops, and I never popped open a jar of baby food, but cooked every morsel from fresh organic ingredients. As "father," I took care of business with a higher-paying job with better benefits, though further away from home, and became increasingly recognized in my field. I also bought a house and life insurance and allowed my girlfriend to adopt my child. While I was repeating a pattern of neglecting my own needs in favor of the obligations of family, job, and community, I believed that this was the life of a responsible adult and parent; it was my job, according to the modeling I saw around me. Meanwhile, my health began to deteriorate.

With the help of a good therapist, I began to recognize that I had a pattern of over-providing, then getting depressed. My particular expression of gendered behavior and my self-understanding on top of a history of familial rejection as a lesbian and self-blame, neglect, and shame led my therapist to suggest during one session that I might be transsexual. Instead of her words, I heard, "You have a terminal illness." Transsexuals do not live, they die. I understood intuitively the overwhelming sense of duty and obligation that drove and consumed me—I was literally staying alive for my child, long enough to put things into place until there was nothing left for me to give, nothing more that I should or could *do*. That word, *transsexual*, reinforced my anxiety that my child was better off without me.

For most of the year that followed, I displaced my anxiety and anger. I looked to things outside of myself to feel better. I tried to reduce my confused feelings about self-image; surely this would prove to be nothing more than a midlife crisis, just like anyone might face. Eventually, I came to see that underlying all my *doings* was the desire to have things neatly ordered and everyone taken care of, either so that I would not be too much of an imposition on the world around me, or, if I worked hard enough, I might earn some favor toward getting some of my needs attended to, too.

When I reached the end of all my doings, I was exhausted to my core. I longed for the imagined relief that death could bring. I shouted to G-d, *"Hineini!"* But G-d did not swoop down to congratulate me on a job well done and take me up to have my next soul experience. In spite of everything I had accomplished, in spite of having had the spiritual awakening from rigorously working a 12-step program, in spite of giving life to a new generation, and in spite of years working for *tikkun olam*, I wasn't getting to pass out of the rest of this lifetime. I was going to have to live. I was going to have to come face-to-face with my gender.

The thought of being better off in another body was not new to me, but it was certainly a distant memory dating back to my teens. In the intervening twenty-five years, I had come to tolerate my female body and enjoyed a wide range of fe/male personification. But it wasn't the right time to step this up and choose *decidedly* to be male. I bargained that I should be able to stick with a female presentation until my child reached adulthood and my parents passed on. If I still wanted to face a gender transition I could do so without bothering anyone. My naive sense of Jewishness from youth—that sense of duty and obligation—continued to bind me as surely as Avraham had bound Isaac. When I made this connection, albeit intellectually, I went back to Torah again.

Who Am I?

I reread the Akeida. To my surprise, I found two other aspects to consider, immediately after Avraham responds to G-d's call.

> And He said: Take now thy son, thine only one, whom thou lovest, even Isaac, and get thee to the land of Moriah; and offer him there for a burnt offering upon one of the mountains which I will tell thee of. (Gen. 22:2)

This time the reading provoked different questions. After all the trials of faith and gifts bestowed on him by G-d, why is Avraham's faith challenged again? And what is the connection between his fate and that of his son's? Since I was asking G-d, why me? in the face of the impossible challenge of emerging as a different gender, I wondered why Avraham didn't ask G-d, why me? when G-d asked him to do the impossible and sacrifice his son.

One way to understand this portion of Torah is that G-d allows Isaac to survive because Avraham did what he was told. An alternative interpretation of the text is that Avraham's faith and Isaac's salvation are unrelated. It is the angel who stops Avraham's hand, suggesting that Avraham's actions may have no effect on Isaac's destiny, for good or ill. Graciously, this revelation tendered the possibility that my actions did not foretell the fate of the people I loved. My child and my parents would be okay if I changed my gender.

What Shall I Be Called?

In the middle of Avraham's story, twenty-four years after he first ventures away from his home based on G-d's promise to make him a great nation, G-d reiterates this promise and discloses that it will be fulfilled through Avram and Sarai having a child, who shall be named Isaac. To indicate their emergence as patriarch and matriarch, G-d bestows new names on Avram and Sarai.

> Neither shall thy name any more be called Avram, but thy name shall be Avraham; for the father of a multitude of nations have I made thee. (Gen. 17:5)

> And G-d said unto Avraham, As for Sarai thy wife, thou shalt not call her name Sarai, but Sarah shall her name be. (Gen. 17:15)

Avram and Sarai start their spiritual journey, but it is Avraham, with his foreskin circumcised, and Sarah, cojoined as parents to the nations that will descend from them, who complete it. I was inspired by the symbolism of their name changes. God chose to honor the physical change in Avraham, as well as Avraham and Sarah's shared destiny. While at the time I could not commit to changing my physical body in a specific way, I could change my name. I took a Hebrew name to distinguish the life

I had lived for the past forty-five years from the exploration of gender that I was compelled to undertake with Avraham as my copilot.

I chose the name Eliron, which literally means "G-d is my joy." The first letter, *alef*, invokes the divine presence. I carry my past in my new name by retaining the first syllable of my birth name my parents gave me. I also carry the future by incorporating in my new name part of my child's Hebrew name. Like Avraham, Eliron is better able to answer the call to begin the next part of life's journey.

Thus Far

At the outset I had no explanation connecting the three catalytic experiences—questioning the Brit Milah, profound disconnection from my body after giving birth, and the unyielding internal pressure to explore my gender presentation—except to say that somehow my child was on one side and my deepest desire to be a good Jew seemed to be on the opposite side. Each of my experiences along the way was held in isolation from the other; each was a separate crisis to be managed. Ten years later, prompted by a rebbe's invitation to tell my story, I decided to read Avraham's journey from beginning to end, rather than rely on various smaller pieces as I had when the events were unfolding.

I learned that the ten tests of faith of our first patriarch, Avraham, begin and end with G-d's command, *"Lech lecha!"*[2] In fact, these are the only two occasions in the Torah where this command is given. As I focused on how Avram evolved into Avraham, I found the thread to weave my own story.

The first time, *lech lecha* launches Avram's epic journey across the desert to a far away and unknown land.

> Now the Lord said unto Abram: *get thee* out of thy country, and out of thy birthplace, and from thy father's house, unto the land that I will show thee. (Gen. 12:1; emphasis mine)

In this first test, Avram and Sarai are sent away from all that they have come to know in the physical world. I can imagine that this first *lech lecha* was as daunting and unfamiliar to them as it is to me now as I step into the world every morning, unsure yet yearning to express myself more authentically. The second time, at the end of Avraham's journey, *lech lecha* commands Avraham to go to the land of Moriah, where he will bind and sacrifice Isaac (Gen. 22:2, quoted above). The destination and the objective are specifically commanded, in marked contrast to the first *lech lecha*. Similarly, I was compelled to travel to a Moriah to connect my soul with my female-born body—even while it seemed that going on this journey would threaten my parents' and child's well-being.

Avram's transition is symbolized by his thrice-repeated response to being called: *"Hineini."* Avraham's tests of faith, bookended by the command *lech lecha*, teach that there is an imperative to go forth and evolve one's self authentically, consciously, and faithfully. At the beginning of the journey, Avram sacrifices himself by leaving all that he knows. He is made vulnerable, and over time the tests of faith render him fully emptied, such that at the conclusion all Avraham has left to offer in response to G-d is "Here I am." Likewise, my responsibility as a Jew and a parent is to be present, to be empty of self, of ego, so that I can become fully conscious. This awareness is needed to be of service to the next generation, as is represented by Avraham, now uncovered by circumcision, offering the identical response, "Here I am," to his child's call. Finally, I am reminded to develop my faith in the world around me, which Torah hints is perhaps the hardest lesson, as represented by Avraham needing to be called not once but twice by the angel, to which he again responds with "Here I am."

Integrating the complete Avram/Avraham journey ten years after the birth of my child, I have now arrived at *my* reason to perform, reject, or revise the Brit Milah—the decision where my Jewish spiritual journey began. Like Avraham, whose test of faith is to first circumcise himself, I too must first remove my foreskin, at least metaphorically. Specifically, I must actively uncover the meaning of gender and gender variance, in order to authentically express myself. Through my study of Torah over time, I know now that whether or not I decided to circumcise had nothing to do with G-d accepting or banishing either me or my child from the covenant. Rather than a literal removal of foreskin, the Brit Milah is a metaphor about the dangers of complacency in the face of one's spiritual obligation to cut off, to remove, anything that can alienate one from the Divine Source. The Brit Milah is the commandment to dis(un)cover one's self, to seek to be authentic first and then model the journey for future generations; this I have committed to do for my own and my child's sake.

Lech lecha, G-d's direct and imperative command to "Go!" teaches that walking one's path, authentically, consciously, and with faith is the only assurance for *teshuvah*.[3] When I can embody the teachings of Avraham, I become present; my body and soul connect here and now. In this moment, I contain past and future, I am full, and also I am empty of everything but this moment, my soul and G-d inseparable. When I set out to mark my child as a Jew, I had no idea I would also face a parallel journey played out against the backdrop of gender. This was not an outcome I could have predicted. Jewish tradition—perhaps G-d's will—revealed certain aspects of itself to my awareness. I felt a drive as deep as the drive that set my biological clock ticking to undertake this gender odyssey, to respond to this profoundly spiritual call to go forth.

Lech lecha! May you continue to go toward yourself.

Notes

1. Our sages teach that the repetition of a word or phrase in Torah indicates more than one layer of meaning.

2. *Lech lecha* is commonly translated "go forth," but it can also be translated literally (but with an uncommon spin) as "go toward you." The ten tests of Avram/Avraham's faith are (1) to leave his home at age seventy-five, (2) to go to Canaan, only to be forced to leave because of a famine, (3) to rescue Sarai when she is kidnapped by Pharaoh, (4) to fight four kings to rescue his nephew Lot, (5) to take Hagar for a wife, (6) to circumcise himself at age ninety-nine, (7) to rescue Sarah when she is kidnapped by King Avimelech, (8) to send Hagar away, (9) to send Ishmael away, and (10) to sacrifice his son Isaac. The tests, which all involve a divine promise followed by personal action and ultimately blessing and fulfillment, have many levels of significance. Most simply, faith is something learned; it is a muscle that is exercised and strengthened over time and with the experience of mistakes and successes.

3. *Teshuvah,* which literally means "return," is translated as "repentance." Jewish mystical interpretation suggests that the commandment *lech lecha* means that a person should leave his will, his natural inclinations and traits, in order to fulfill G-d's will. Avraham's journey from his beginning as Avram to his return to the land of Moriah can be seen as a metaphor for the journey of a soul returning to G-d.

Crossing the *Mechitza*

Beth Orens

Editor's Note

Some of my transsexual friends and acquaintances balked at Balancing
on the Mechitza *as the title for this anthology. For some, there was no
desire to "balance" between the genders; for others, the "between" options
were simply not viewed as livable Jewish spaces. Beth Orens writes to give
a* frum *(Orthodox) voice to the many members of the community who
only temporarily and uncomfortably "balance" on the mechitza before
happily and permanently crossing to the other side.*

As an Orthodox Jew, balancing on the mechitza was never an option
for me. There was a time when I looked over the mechitza from the
men's section and wondered at the strangeness of a world in which I
was trapped on the wrong side. I used to wonder what it would feel like
to be on the women's side—the right side—but I don't think I ever
thought I'd find out. Now when I look over the mechitza from the
women's section, I find it hard to even imagine a time when I stood over
there, feeling so out of place. I sometimes wonder, if I were to cut my
hair and put on a suit, what it would feel like over there.

Of course, I experienced something very much like that during the
months leading up to my transition. In a matter of days I'd gone from
pining after a life I knew I could never have to feeling like a disguised
girl in the boys' locker room. I know transwomen who say they felt that
way all their lives, but I didn't. In their book, *Gender: An
Ethnomethodological Approach,* Suzanne Kessler and Wendy McKenna
invented the term *gender role identity,* as distinct from *gender role* and
gender identity, and used it for the gender role that you *think* you should
be filling. Not the gender you feel that you are and that you're supposed
to be, but the role that you're aiming to portray.

I was married with two children, living in a bedroom community of Jerusalem, and though I'd felt the dysphoria of being physically male all my life, and a good eight years before had come to terms with the fact that my gender identity would always be female, my goal in life was portraying a male to the best of my ability.

Once that switch flipped, though—once I realized that I'd been fooling myself, thinking that playing the male role was a reasonable thing to be doing with my life—I started feeling like a spy. Like a real-life Yentl, living in a man's world, with no one suspecting who I really was. It was a surreal feeling, almost dreamlike.

And although I transitioned overnight, going to the airport only hours after the divorce, taking off my *kippah* behind a large advertisement in the airport, and never once identifying myself as male after that, it was a long time before I'd find my way to the right side of the mechitza.

Transitioning while *frum* is not for the fainthearted. Not that transitioning is a walk in the park in the best of circumstances, but TWF (transitioning while *frum*) is hardly the best of circumstances. I found myself in Manhattan some twenty hours after having lost the woman I thought was the love of my life and our two children, with two containers of belongings and about $650 to live on. That, and a good friend I'd met online, who let me stay with her until she'd found me an apartment and a job. And it would be eleven months before I'd find my way into a synagogue.

The thing about being Orthodox is, the law is the law, even when it's inconvenient. I'd started electrolysis treatments, but the only way I could show my face in public without stubble or shadow being obvious was to apply what my friend called "big, thick, tranny makeup." But that sort of makeup wasn't something I could use on Shabbat. So for eleven months, I spent every Shabbat alone, in my apartment.

Had it not been for my apartment burning down one Friday night as I was eating a solitary dinner (a story for another time), I don't know when I would have mustered the courage to go out on Shabbat. I'd even spent Rosh Hashanah and Yom Kippur alone in my apartment, buying a shofar and doing my best to blow it on Rosh Hashanah all by myself.

To this day, there's a certain car alarm that snatches me back to that Yom Kippur, when I lay in my bed for hours, listening to a car on the street playing its emergency melody over and over. And over.

Once I realized that I could be with other people on Shabbat, I ventured, for the first time, into a synagogue down the street from me. I waited to see if I'd feel some sort of epiphany, standing in the women's section of the synagogue, but it just felt . . . normal. It was remarkable in its utter lack of remarkableness. One woman I spoke with there told me about a women's prayer group in the neighborhood which met once a month. I'd always loved reading Torah, and I knew I was good at it. And this was a way to continue using that skill without violating Jewish law, so I began attending that group.

Even today, twelve years later and living in another city, I belong to a women's prayer group of the same kind. Yet the one I attended in New York was special. The first time I was called up to the Torah by the new Hebrew name I'd chosen, I felt as though I'd gone through a rite of passage. But it didn't make me less of an alien in the rest of my life. I still went to the transsexual women's support group that met every other week, and after each meeting, when we all went to a nearby café to schmooze and socialize, everyone would order food. And I'd order a Coke. Even in a tiny and marginalized group, which was still scorned at the time by most of the GLB community, I sat apart.

When I went for surgery, a year after transitioning and a month and a half after my apartment burned down, I ran into issues yet again. The doctor I went to had a facility where meals were provided for us. When I asked his receptionist to see if it was possible to arrange for kosher meals, she transferred me to the man who did the cooking. The silence after I asked him my question was palpable. "I . . . uh . . . didn't know you people did this kind of thing," was what he managed to stammer out eventually. I told him that "we people" don't, but that I needed to. We were able to arrange with a kosher restaurant in the area to supply kosher airline-type meals, but sitting in the dining room while everyone else ate the fresh cooked food was one more experience of separateness.

I've had people ask me, in contexts completely separate from Judaism, why I would want to be female and have to put up with being a second-class citizen in so many ways. Once I was working for a company where everyone was Jewish, and most of them were religious, and they hired a man in my department. He was supposed to do the same things that I was doing, but he did them poorly, and only had to come in four days a week. And he got paid more than I did, under the philosophy that men have families to support. I was aware of the double standard before I transitioned, even if I hadn't experienced it personally. And no, I don't like it. But whoever said I *chose* to be female?

When it comes to religious issues, however, I'm not as bothered by the discrimination. Judaism is based on "discriminate." It's one of the most basic things about Judaism. We discriminate between light and darkness, between Shabbat and weekdays, between Jews and non-Jews, between *Kohenim* and non-*Kohenim*. And yes, between male and female. Judaism is not bound by *Brown v. Board of Education*. As Orthodox Jews, we don't see separate or different as inherently unequal. Women are neither superior nor inferior to men in Judaism. Just different.

Do I miss reading Torah? Sure I do. But I'm fine with not being able to do so in a regular synagogue. Do I miss learning Gemara with a *hevruta* (study partner)? I do. But people who are both on a comparable level of learning and share my basic religious premises are generally male, and it's not all that appropriate for us to learn together.

I think the most difficult thing for me, as a *frum* post-op transwoman, is accepting the fact that those who view me as no more than a mutilated male, based on rulings from some of those few rabbis who have addressed the issue, are entitled to think that. In the absence of a central authority, Judaism recognizes the possibility of multiple valid views.

In the first and second centuries CE, the students of Hillel and the students of Shammai disagreed on who was a *mamzer* (illegitimate according to Jewish law). Since a *mamzer* isn't allowed to marry another Jew (except for another *mamzer* or a convert, but even then, their children are *mamzerim* as well), it was important to know the answer to that question. Had a dispute like that happened today, we know what would probably happen. There would be invective flying from both sides, and each side would protest that those they viewed as non-*mamzerim* shouldn't be stigmatized. But do you know what the students of Hillel and Shammai did? They made a point of letting each other know who among them was a *mamzer* according to the other school of thought. Even though they disagreed. Because they recognized that you can disagree with another position and still recognize that those who conclude otherwise aren't necessarily fools or knaves.

I know who I am. I know that I'm a woman. But I can't require everyone in the Orthodox community to agree with me, much as I wish I could. What I *can* do is insist that they respect my right to disagree with them. And that's the way I've chosen to live.

Queering the Jew and Jewing the Queer
Ri J. Turner

Editor's Note

> *Interlaced with personal narrative, Ri Turner's essay contributes to an ongoing discussion within Jewish gender studies concerning the relationship between Jewishness and queerness and factors the term genderqueer into both sides of the equation.*

Taking the broad political meaning of the word *queer,* it is inherently queer to be a Jew in U.S. diaspora. It is queer to be different from the American Protestant majority; marginality is queer. It is queer to be proud and strong in that marginality. It is also *genderqueer* to be a Jew in U.S. diaspora—genderqueer in that a "Jewish woman" (or, as James Michener is fond of writing in *The Source,* a "Jewess") is not the same gender as the unmarked American "woman" (meaning a white, middle-class, able-bodied, heterosexual, Protestant, non-elderly citizen). Similarly, a "Jewish man" (or perhaps the gender-unmarked, and thus male, "Jew") is not the same gender as the unmarked American "man"; "Jewish boy" and "Jewish girl" are not the same genders as unmarked "boy" and "girl."[1]

This is easy to see. Picture in your mind a woman. What image do you see? What about a Jewish woman? The image you see is different, isn't it? What happens when you imagine a man? How about a Jewish man? When I do this thought experiment, extensive experience deconstructing "woman" notwithstanding, I imagine a "woman" to be white, filled-out-but-not-fat, a maternal type, able-bodied, American, probably Protestant, most likely a biological mother—even though when I speak the word "woman," I intend simply to refer to a person's gender self-identification. In my head, a "Jewish woman," on the other hand, is fatter, dark-haired (although still white-skinned), loud, sarcastic, and humorous. (Not incidentally, a "Jewess" is even darker-haired and -eyed, younger, laughing but mournful and poignant, wearing a long skirt, probably barefoot. Certainly not American.) A "man," to me, is white, balding, maybe a little potbellied, likely to wear a suit and tie, almost certainly brown-haired. His voice is deep and authoritative. A "Jewish man," on the other hand, is a little self-deprecating, laughing, witty, more bent over, jumpier, curly-dark-haired. That's just a subset of my own internalized stereotypes, stereotypes that vary depending on the day and my mood.

When we talk about queering gender, it is important to understand, first of all, that gender is a normalizing system, one that assigns roles and traits in a very specific binary way, and one that punishes those who don't or can't follow those prescriptions. Not incidentally, that system pretends that it is describing maleness and femaleness *only,* while in fact it is describing gender—well-genderedness, to be specific—in terms of many other factors, some of which I listed above: body size, ability, citizenship, race, age, religion, and many more. Under this system, in other words, an unfeminine black woman might get punished not only for not being feminine enough, but also for being black—because being black in itself means that she is not feminine enough—because to be well-gendered as a female, one must be white.[2]

Similarly, to be Jewish inherently queers one's gender, because if you are Jewish, you cannot possibly be "quite" female, no matter how stereotypically feminine you are, or "quite" male, no matter how stereotypically masculine you are—because to be "properly" female or male, in the U.S. context (and increasingly elsewhere, as U.S. hegemony spreads across the globe) means to be Christian (culturally at least), and more specifically, Protestant. Also, if you are recognizably Ashkenazic, you are for racial reasons never going to be "quite" female or male. (Add to that that if you are Jewish but not recognizably Ashkenazic, and/or if you are Sephardic, and/or if you are non-white, and/or if you are working-class, you are not only "not quite" female or male, you are probably also "not quite" Jewish.)

Not only is it queer and genderqueer to be Jews in U.S. diaspora—it is, I would argue, also transgender. By *genderqueer* I mean queering gender by failing to or choosing not to follow the prescriptions that define well-genderedness. By *transgender*, I mean transgressing gender in a way that specifically (and sometimes even explicitly) engages the gender *binary* against the grain—in other words, queering gender in a way that resists or transforms the gender binary specifically. As described above, even Ashkenazi Jews who identify as cisgendered (here I am using this term to mean non-transgendered *and* non-genderqueer) tend to fail to be well-gendered—but not only do they fail to be well-gendered, they fail to be well-gendered by being too effeminate if they present as men and too masculine if they present as women.

Imagine the stereotypes again—or even the cultural trends as you've experienced them. Jewish men and boys are (or are thought to be) scholarly, shrewd, short, small-penised, and hopelessly awkward on the playing field—not athletic, not macho. Jewish women and girls, on the other hand, are (or are thought to be) assertive, argumentative, intelligent, highly or even excessively rational, and dominating (perhaps even emasculating toward their husbands and sons) in the family realm. Thus, because, as many feminists have described, masculinity is often characterized by presence and femininity by absence, Jewish men and boys are feminized by virtue of their lack of necessary masculine attributes, while Jewish women and girls are masculinized by virtue of their possession of traits supposed to be the province of men. Thus, stereotypically, not only are Jewish women "not quite" women (that is, genderqueer)—they are in fact "almost men" (transgender). And, in parallel, not only are Jewish men "not quite" men—they are in fact "almost women."

I was a frilly little girl. I remember twirling around at my sister's wedding in the blue dress I loved, the poofy dress with the petticoats. I felt like a grand colonial lady (yes, specifically colonial). I read girly books— *Little Women, A Girl of the Limberlost, Betsy-Tacy, Ballet Shoes, The Blue Fairy Book*—and on the Jewish side of things, Sydney Taylor's All-of-a-Kind Family series. I loved reading about fancy balls and parties, imagining myself transported there like Cinderella, my beauty blossoming unexpectedly, surprising no one more than myself.

I never idolized blonde princesses. Give me a black-haired one any day, with long wavy tresses and olive skin. Likewise, I never idolized soprano voices—as early as third grade I wanted to be an alto. (No such luck—although it took me another decade and some very sore vocal chords to acknowledge my actual range.) I was incipiently aware that my preference for the stockier, darker, lower-voiced, stronger heroines reflected some contrariness (what I now label "resistance"). Indeed, it is probably fortunate that I didn't grow up hoping to be blonde and delicate. However, it is unclear how much healthier my actual dark-and-beautiful-future-Ri fantasies were—they mostly involved supple, skirted, "exotic" Jewesses or lithe, silent indigenous women (like my namesake, Rima the bird girl of W. H. Hudson's *Green Mansions*).

My girly books and my fairy-tale fantasies ultimately betrayed me. In a particularly superstitious phase of my life (most likely around second or third grade), I read a story in one of Andrew Lang's Fairy Books. The villain in the story was an old miserly Jew. Caught in a child's obsessive-compulsive dilemma, I promised God fifteen times in rapid succession that I would never touch Lang's books again—and at the same time I couldn't shake the guilt of wanting to lose myself in those pages again, to accept that the old man *was* an evil miser because he was a Jew, to slip back into that world in which maybe I could hope to be pretty someday and in which I would never have to fight to be whole.

As I grew older and admitted to myself that I would never look like a princess (or barefooted village Jewess or innocently seductive Indian girl), the women I wanted to be gently became the women I wanted to love. I came out as bisexual, then queer, then lesbian, then bisexual, then queer, redefining the labels and letting them redefine me with each iteration. I began to recognize rapidly that even in the LGBT world, I seemed to have ended up in the wrong story. How could I be a lesbian if I wasn't a tomboy as a kid? (And, not incidentally, how could I be a "real queer" if I was "only" bisexual?) I cut my hair and wore boy pants and stopped shaving my legs and felt like I looked even stupider than before. I watched an Oprah show on transgender youth, asked myself whether my "inner gender" was boy to my body's girl, and came up with a surprising answer—that my "inner gender" felt like girl to the boy I was forcing on myself out of my desperate desire to "fit" into "dyke."

So, I grew my hair out and started shaving my legs again and spent three years letting myself be "girl" and trying to find a way to be "girl," to dress and wear my hair in a way that I could "respect" (that is, a look that helped me feel some kind of congruence between inner and outer realities, and also a look that was well-gendered enough not to cause me internalized transphobic/anti-Semitic shame). I got to a point at which I felt pretty decent about how I looked when I was "all dressed up." I also tried to find a way to look well-gendered and still retain recognizable markers of queerness—partly to combat the fact that my queerness felt invisible when I dressed femme, partly because intentional androgyny felt more comfortable than the eternally unreachable "pretty"—and partly because sometimes I simply experienced a visceral compulsion to strip off the skintight clothes and put on baggy pants and huge long-sleeved T-shirts. But when I looked at photographs of myself, more often than not I still felt ashamed and disgusted.

I was starting to realize that I felt genderqueer—"not quite" female. Even with my long hair, I would meet other women my age (in the ladies' restroom at college, for example), and feel like an impostor—unworthy of membership in their select ranks and completely dependent on their goodwill. My hair was never right, makeup was still a mystery, other girls seemed to know the most arcane fashion "rules" as if they were common sense. I mean, who knew that ankle-length pants and high-waisted underpants were fashion errors despicable enough to have earned their own derisive names—highwaters and granny pants? Where do people *learn* stuff like that? What part of Girl 101 did I miss, and where was I when everyone else was learning it? My figure was too curvy and my hips too wide; I had acne, and glasses, and a monobrow (although I got it waxed once during my extremely dedicated femme year). Try as I might I couldn't get myself to wear any bra but a sports bra (and strapless was out of the question). I still wore pads instead of tampons (until I got my hippie DivaCup). I hated pastels, I wore stud earrings because I was too lazy to change them, I was too cheap to get the right clothing brands or even specific styles. I didn't wash my face often enough to wear mascara regularly (and besides, it made me think of this science video I watched years ago about mascara-eating eyelash mites). I was too short, I was too dirty, I was too informal, I shared too much information, I was too sexual, I was never grossed out by anything. I wasn't discreet enough, I was too honest, I was too embodied, I was too smart, too rational, too analytical, too good at math, too confident, too confrontational, too insistent upon advocating for my own well-being and defending my ideas ("too pushy"), too competent, too aware of my own competence. And my nose was ugly.

I just didn't make a good girl. Now, as then, I continue to demand to know why I must look butch in order for my queerness to be visible. However, at that time I swung to the other pole and became extremely focused on "accomplishing" successful femininity. This was a rubric that I did not score well on, a test I would never pass. And I was allowing that reality to make me feel terrible.

One day, without warning, I needed to be bald. I got my head shaved to an eighth of an inch by a surly flaming hairdresser who seemed to take my fashion decision personally. After that, I suddenly and completely ditched all my femmy clothes. I felt completely and inexplicably comfortable in my new gender. I began to find it useful, when intimidated by folks who could "do woman" well, to explain to myself that I was a different gender, not a failure at "woman" gender. A lot of the fear, shame, and intimidation began to peel away.

And I was starting to realize that my genderqueerness at least partly stemmed from the fact that I was a Jew, and a racially recognizable Ashkenazi Jew. I am a fairly aware person—but it still took twenty years of life to dawn on me that when my mom told me, "If I hadn't gotten that nose job, my nose would have been awful," by "awful" she meant recognizably Ashkenazi. Suddenly, I realized that my fixation about my "ugly" nose might not be just about beauty or even just about gender. What else about my badly-genderedness wasn't "just" about gender, but also about my Jewness? When I felt like I made a bad "girl" because of my love of language, my joy in precision, was the shame I was experiencing as purely gendered shame actually partly ethnic and cultural shame?

I am the child of multiple exiles, many iterations of diaspora. I grew up in New Mexico, born to transplanted New Yorkers. My mother talked about New York City as a kind of mythical homeland—the Cloisters, "her" bridge (the George Washington Bridge), even the subway system made up the infrastructure of "home" in my childhood imagination. In my head, as a result of listening to my parents talk and watching movies like *Crossing Delancey*, that "home" was peopled by elderly Jews who cared about good grammar and knew the difference between a half-sour and a full-sour pickle—and who said "boo-all" and "doo-ag" like my parents and grandparents instead of "bahl" and "dahg" like my brother and me. Most of them, I imagined, were relatives—and when I finally came to the East for college, it took me a year before I could hear a Brooklyn accent and not look up expecting to see some cousin or great-aunt.

New York was my parents' legendary homeland—and yet their parents must have grown up hearing about the shtetls of Eastern Europe. For what lost patch of earth did my great-great-grandparents harbor nostalgia?

I hated the fact that my parents couldn't just come to rest and be where they were, instead of harking back to a land that I was beginning to realize had never quite existed. I hated that "if only we were in New York" became an excuse not to grapple productively with the reality of where we in fact were. And yet I too loved the East Coast. And I moved there the first chance I got.

My parents coped with exile by resisting assimilation—and by attempting to prevent their children's assimilation—in some strange ways. What I remember most was their effort to set our family apart from other families over the most obscure and (apparently) random issues. *Other* families let their kids learn to bike using training wheels— our kids didn't need that "crutch." *Other* families ate ham—not because they were non-Jews (we ate pork chops and even bacon) but because they weren't "health-conscious." *Other* men wore boxers, but our men wore briefs (preferably in burgundy or turquoise). *Other* children liked pop music, but we didn't listen to "that trash." *Other* families had birthday parties and sleepovers, but we celebrated special events "within the family." *Other* families gave allowance, but our kids weren't "obsessed with money." *Other* children had chores, but in our family, the mother "did her job" and took care of the house. *Other* children played with Barbies, but we didn't "need every new toy the second it came out." *Other* families dropped the *g* when pronouncing *-ing* words, said vee-HICK-le instead of VEE-hicle, pronounced *route* "rowt" instead of "root," called their parents Mom and Dad instead of Mommy and Daddy, called the evening meal "dinner" instead of "supper," said "panties" instead of "underpants," said "who" when it should be "whom," and split infinitives—but WE DIDN'T.

And it was never just "we don't"—it was always also, "They do—how ridiculous, how unthinkable, how contaminating."

In some ways I now believe that this process of "self-othering" (because there was no illusion about the fact that "other families'" ways, not our "superior" ones, were the mainstream) was about preserving specific Jewish cultural and immigrant values. In some ways it was about preserving and passing down an East Coast linguistic identity in a western regional context. In some ways it was about retreating into and defending class privilege. In some ways it was about attempting to absolve the guilt of upward mobility—or perhaps, to put a more positive spin on it, it was about attempting to maintain touch with working-class values and a working-class immigrant past despite recently acquired class privilege. In some ways it was, I think, merely a miscalculated response to the pain and terror of generation after generation of exile—an attempt to create the illusion of safety through the illusion of stasis and controlled "inner family space." However understandable the impulse, one result was stagnation, as well as enforced social and emotional isolation.

In any event, this setting of boundaries became yet another source of my genderqueerness. First of all, my limited access to mass media, the means of consumption (money and independence), and a peer social milieu effectively meant that I received no Girl 101. In seventh grade, despite my still-long hair, I was branded "gay" for the first time because of my peach jeans and tie-dyed shirt. A girl in my seventh-grade physical education class told me that I looked like an ape because I didn't shave my legs, and another girl in the locker room told me with the best of intentions that my print fleece was too bright.

In some ways, I think gender was just one other arbitrary site upon which my parents acted out the pain of exile, merely more of the same attempt to defend against change and outside influence through social isolation. In other ways, though, the refusal of socially established gender roles was quite specific. I received a sort of generationally transmitted training in genderqueerness. "Other families" let their girls shave their legs in middle school; "other families" let their boys have war toys. But "other families" also expected their girls to be pretty and popular and successful with boys, and "other families" taunted and punched their sons into athletic prowess. "Other parents" didn't let their boys wear bright printed shirts or learn to knit; "other parents" didn't encourage their girls to excel in math and in verbal repartee. "Other parents" didn't have the experience of living in badly gendered bodies—"other parents" didn't understand how damaging gender-specific pressure was.

This was never articulated in terms of oppression, sexism, or global capitalism—merely in terms of that same nonverbal disgust for "other people's ways," that click of the tongue or dismissive eye-roll that meant the topic was closed. But in this particular silence lay a fairly well-developed antisexist practice. My parents knew from their culturally Jewish gendered experience how much of a struggle it was to exist against the gendered grain. Also, their particular relationship to money led them to refuse not only the rigid norms of the gender binary, but also the cultural mandate that gendered legibility be achieved through participation in "superfluous" (by their definition) consumption. My parents refused, and trained me to refuse, to locate self-worth in participation in a culture of well-gendered-legibility-through-purchase.[3]

It frustrated me, of course. As a young girl I blamed my badly-genderedness on my parents' behavior, instead of blaming the system that determined my worth based on my distance from the prescribed norm. I was glad my mother understood what it meant never to get asked to a dance, but at the same time I wanted her to stop assuming that I never would, to stop ridiculing my attempts to try (especially since her ridicule seemed designed at least partly to preserve my social isolation, to deny me access to peer connection, and to refuse recognition of my developing maturity, sexuality, and independence).

So my mother and I struggled, and I blamed her when I felt ugly. It took me another decade to recognize the relationship between my mother's refusal to help me cultivate my femininity and her own experience of being badly gendered as a Jew—and her particular way of responding to that kind of diasporic and exile-based pain by defining a black-and-white boundary between acceptable and unacceptable choices for herself, for others, and especially for her children.

In the meantime, given that I've now gone to the other gendered extreme, my mother, formerly dismissive of my interest in makeup and exasperated with my attempts to perform the role of "American girl," now would like me to wear more dresses and sighs each time I come home with my head newly shaved.

These days I dress almost completely in men's clothing, and I keep my hair cropped very short. I don't attempt to pass as male, nor do I usually desire to (although it tickles me when I am read as male upon occasion). It would be too simplistic to say that I finally "discovered" my stable, intrinsic internal gender, and that now that I have learned to express it, everything is peachy. First of all, everything is not peachy—I continue to feel shame and discomfort about my body and gender (even when I can talk myself out of that shame on a theoretical level). Not only is everything not peachy with my gender, my gender is certainly not "finished"—I have not reached some point of permanence. (Most recently, I've been possessed by the urge to experiment with becoming a drag queen.) Rather than something that I "finally discovered," then, my gender is something that is constantly evolving. It's something that is influenced by my biology and my identities—and not least my raced, classed, and sexualized experience as a white, upper-middle-class, same-sex-loving Ashkenazi Jew in U.S. diaspora. My gender is also influenced—or constituted by—the decisions I have made about how best to cope with my experience and my identity in a sexist, heterosexist, and anti-Semitic context. (As I told a professor once during my last semester of college, "I never know whether I became proudly queer because I was too Jewish to be straight, or became proudly Jewish because I was too queer to be white.")

In so many ways, my Jewness—specifically my diasporic Ashkenazi Jewness—has helped to create me as a genderqueer subject. In turn, the tension I felt and feel as a genderqueer (and female-bodied) subject in a violently restrictive and misogynist gender binary has helped me discover and develop a lens for recognizing structural oppression and the need to become part of collective and intersectional resistance. Again in turn, my understanding of gendered structural oppression has led me to an understanding of other forms of structural oppression, which has gradually led me to a discovery of my own experience with the historical and present trauma of anti-Semitism. In turn once again, my developing understanding of collective resistance has led me to begin to develop a (very queer form of) Jewish cultural, religious, and ethnic pride.

I have learned that my Jewness, my queerness, and my queerJewness are not to blame for the pain and danger—but rather are rich sources of strength, wisdom, and community for healing from that pain and danger. Like Jacob, who had to recognize that he was wounded before he could become able to heal, I had to learn the language of my brokenness before I could even envision what it might be like to be whole. My Jewness and my queerness/genderqueerness together brought me to that awareness of brokenness, and I am engaged now in a lifelong process of healing. In my brokenness and in my process of healing myself, I am discovering the strength, nurturing power, and knowledge that allows me to extend my personal project of healing to the project of *tikkun olam*—healing the world and its peoples of both systemic and individual destruction and shame. I am whole in my brokenness and powerful in my vulnerability, and I give thanks to the miracle of existence as

I step into my adult life as a multilayered, committed, powerful, and amazed survivor.

Notes

1. Thanks to Marla Brettschneider for her thought-provoking session "Your Fabulously Gendered Jewish Self on the Move," presented at the 2008 National Union of Jewish LGBTQQI Students (NUJLS) conference at Columbia University, February 9, 2008.

2. I learned the term *well-genderedness* from Gabriel Ely.

3. This actually was not as purely anti-oppressive as it seems at first glance. This refusal to take part in consumption-based gender dichotomization took place in the context of a generally insufficient understanding of class. First of all, the refusal of consumption (which in itself might have been motivated by the desire to maintain working-class, immigrant values and a working-class understanding of the destructive power of capitalist consumption) took the form of the disavowal (read: concealment) of class privilege through a surreptitiously downwardly mobile lifestyle. This denial, like most forms of denial of privilege, resulted in various forms of complicity with class oppression. In addition, the refusal of consumption combined with the understanding that the enforced gender binary is oppressive, in the context of my family's general tendency to dismiss anything different from its own choices as somehow tainted, set the stage for a disgust for individual and cultural gendered performances different from our own gentle tendency toward androgyny. The idea that it might be possible to embrace femininity, in particular, in a subversive way was missing from my family's gendered consciousness, and thus those who did choose to perform a high femininity were considered, essentially, victims of a naive false consciousness (although most emphatically not in those terms). In a further twist, because a subversive understanding and performance of high femininity and a more stereotypically macho (physically strong) performance of masculinity are more common in the working-class world, this disgust for and fear of (apparent) cisgendered performance ended up being taken out in particular on people with fewer economic resources than we had. Most ironic of all, the fact that my family identified this kind of cisgenderedness with consumption allowed the blame for consumption culture to be scapegoated onto working-class people and working-class genders, while my more affluent family tried to claim the "moral high ground" for "doing away with all those frilly extras." This elided cisgendered performance, particularly working-class cisgendered performance, with consumption, and with oppressive gender binarism, and ignored the ways in which cisgendered performance can be essential to economic and cultural survival. Ultimately, this gender-judgmentalism became yet another way for a middle-class family to look at working-class expenditures and give a quintessentially classist response: "Look how they waste their money. Why are we paying for that?"

Spiritual Lessons I Have Learned from Transsexuals

Margaret Moers Wenig

With immeasurable thanks to Reuben Zellman

Editor's Note

This essay is an exception to the "first person narratives in the first chapter" rule. It's appropriate that a book about gender variance should transgress its own boundaries. This essay is simultaneously a love song to the Hebrew language and to boundary crossers.

Modern Hebrew is a binary-gendered language; nothing can be spoken without first attaching either masculinity or femininity to one's words. How does Hebrew bridge the conceptual gap in translating the word "transsexual"? Can a gendered language come to terms with a word that both surpasses and embraces a gender binary? How does Hebrew deal with reconstructing the concepts Americans understand as embodied in the process of transitioning? In this essay, Rabbi Wenig employs translations, transliterations, and other conceptual constructions to translate the word "transsexual" into Modern Hebrew—and in the process familiarizes her audience with the concepts transition embodies.

How do you say "transsexual" in Modern Hebrew? What word does Hebrew use to describe a person who is raised as a girl, but from a very early age knows himself to be a boy and eventually chooses to live exclusively as a man? There are two ways a foreign word makes its way into Hebrew. Either it is transliterated or it is translated.[1] "Transsexual" first made its way into Modern Hebrew through transliteration rather than through translation. "Transsexual" became *transexuali* in Modern Hebrew; *transexualim* in the plural.

Consider for a moment what the Modern Hebrew word for "transsexual" should be were it translated into Hebrew rather than merely transliterated. Which Hebrew root could be used—which Hebrew root *should* be used—to form the basis of a new Hebrew word to convey the meaning of "transsexual"? I think there are four possible roots that might capture the meaning of transitioning from male to female (MTF) or from female to male (FTM). Exploring these roots, considering their appropriateness and inappropriateness, provides some insight into the experience of transitioning and the spiritual lessons we might learn from that experience.

The first possible Hebrew root I ask you to consider is בּין (*beyn,* from the Hebrew letters *bet, yod, nun),* which means "between," as in the Hebrew phrase *beyn adam l'chavero,* "between one person and another." Leslie Feinberg says about herself [hirself]: "It's not my female sex that defines me. It's not my masculine gender expression. It's that my gender expression appears to be at odds with my sex. It's the social contradiction *between* the two that defines me."[2] Or as one FTM has put it: "Now I feel I'm neither man nor woman (though the limitations of English force me to choose sides if only so I may have terminology with which to define myself.) So, I'm a guy. Much more comfortable with male pronouns than female, but not really feeling like a man. I'm living *la vida media*—life in the middle. I have not crossed the bridge from 'female' on one side over an immeasurable chasm to become 'male' on the other side. Rather, I have *become* the bridge."[3]

The root בּין *(beyn)* captures that betweenness, and a transsexual could be called, in Modern Hebrew, a *beyn min,* or *beyn mini* (sexually in-between). Some transsexuals might feel comfortable with this appellation, but for others, using the root בּין *(beyn)* might pose a problem. For *beyn* is a status. It fails to convey any sense of process. For that we need a Hebrew root that expresses some movement. One such Hebrew root is הפך *(hafach,* from the Hebrew letters *hay, pey, chaf).* That's the root Rabbi Eliezer Waldenberg used in his *teshuvah,* in which he suggested that an MTF recite שהפכני לאשה *(shehafchani l'isha),* "Blessed are you, Eternal our God, Sovereign of the Universe, *who has changed me into a woman.*"[4] It is remarkable that Rabbi Waldenberg honors the experience of the MTF with a liturgical change such as this! Remarkable that Rabbi Waldenberg can imagine that God played a role in the transition and therefore deserves thanks for its results.

But with all due respect (and gratitude) to Rabbi Waldenberg, I believe that his choice of the Hebrew root הפך (hafach) shows a misunderstanding of the process the MTF or FTM has undergone. For הפך (hafach) implies radical change or reversal from something to its opposite, as in the bitui (expression) הפך לעורו (hafach l'oro), which means "being a turncoat" or "changing one's mind"; literally "changing one's skin." An MTF would not say she has become her opposite. She would say she has become herself. She would not say she has reversed her gender. She would say she is now free to live it. Her figurative or literal change of "skin" does not reflect a change of mind. L'hefech (on the contrary), an MTF has always felt herself to be an F.

So if הפך (hafach) is not the best root, then which Hebrew root would better express the experience of a transsexual? A third possibility is the root תרגם (targum, from the letters tav, resh, gimmel, mem). This is the root used to express what we call in English "translation." Targum is in the title of the famous translations of the Bible into Aramaic, Targum Yonathan and Targum Onkelos. The root תרגם (tirgum) is a possible root because some transsexuals say of themselves, "I am the same person, but I've found new language that lets me really be who I am without restraints." So Modern Hebrew might call a transsexual a תרגמי (tirgumi), "a translated person."

The problems with this root, however, are twofold. First, it presumes that what it means to be human can be translated into language; yet, as Walt Whitman insists, "I am untranslatable." The second problem with this root is that translation is an intellectual process, something you can do sitting at your desk or in the library, or with a cup of coffee and a dictionary, or at a meeting of people who do not share a common language. Translation can be hard but not as hard as the process of transitioning undertaken by a transsexual. For that process is more active, more scary, more dangerous. That process is more like giving birth; giving birth to the self, to the curled up fetus within. That process is more like crossing the Sea of Reeds from slavery into freedom with enemies close behind. That process is more like crossing the River Jordan from wilderness into homeland. Such a crossing doesn't solve everything. Far from it, for many dangers still lie ahead. But it's an enormous step, a crucial step in a long, long journey.

A fetus is an עבר *(ubar,* from the letters *ayin, bet, resh).* To cross the sea, to ford a river is לעבר *(laavor),* from the same root. This root is used in Modern Hebrew for many things for which we use "trans" in English: "Transatlantic" is *ever Atlanti.* "Trans-Jordan" is *ever Yardeyn.* The root עבר *(avar)* is promising because the process of transitioning is like crossing a sacred boundary, a line that society says should not be crossed but that the transsexual knows *must* be crossed. That's what rabbinic Hebrew would call an עברה *(averah),* "a transgression," and view with disapproval. But when a person crosses the sacred boundary from M to F or F to M, that crossing should not be viewed as a transgression but as an experience of transcendence, for such a person has transcended the limitations placed on us by society. Or transition should be viewed as a subversive and righteous transgression that contains the potential to change or remove the very boundary it violates.

To translate "transsexual" into Modern Hebrew, then, I would use the root עבר *(avar)* and say *eyver sexuali* or *ever mini*—"a gender crosser." And for the nickname "tranny," which some insiders use for themselves and for each other, they'd simply say עברי *(ivri).* Yes, *ivri.* I don't believe it is a coincidence that the Modern Hebrew word for transsexual could be *ivri.*[5] I could stop right here and spin out what it might mean that the Hebrew words for "transsexual" and "Jew" could be one and the same. But I believe that this root has even more to teach us than we can learn from the name *ivri.*

The meanings of Hebrew verbs change significantly when you change the preposition that follows them, so *chazar b*... means "to regret," but *chazar al*... means "to review" or "to repeat." The root *avar,* the best Hebrew root for "transsexual," means not only "to cross over," but also "to pass." But if you follow the verb *avar* with the preposition לפני *(lifney)* or על פני *(al p'ney),* then *avar l*... means "to appear," "to show up," "to take one's place." As in *avar lifney hateva,* the expression used in rabbinic literature for serving as *sh'liach tzibur,* the messenger of the congregation who "takes his place before the ark" to lead a community in prayer. The process of transitioning is something like *avar lifney hateva,* taking one's rightful place, finally appearing, being seen, being acknowledged as a member of the community and even as one of its leaders.[6]

But *avar lifney* sometimes means even more than "to appear." *Vayaavor Adonai al panav,* "God *revealed* something of himself" to Moses. Moses asked to see God's face. God warned him: "No one can see my face and live." So when God placed Moses in the crag of the rock atop Mount Sinai, God didn't show Moses something you can see with your eyes. God revealed to Moses something that cannot be seen, only known in the depths of one's soul. When people transition from M to F or F to M they *reveal* to us something that cannot be seen. It's not the body, it's a belief; it's a truth or a set of truths.

Four truths have been revealed to me by the transsexuals I have known in person or through books:

The first truth is that *not everything about our bodies is necessarily a given.* When a person who appeared at birth to be a girl and was raised as a girl, but always knew inside that he was a boy, begins to live his life as a man, he reveals to us the truth that although our bodies may feel to us like a curse; like a given, not a gift; like a punishment, not a source of pleasure; like an immutable sentence of solitary confinement; and although it feels as though *vtachtoch kitzvah l'chol briyah,* "God has set the boundaries of our lives," *v'tichtov et gzar dinam,* "and inscribed our destinies";[7] God has also, paradoxically, given us the power and perhaps even the obligation to *change* these givens for the better. We are, on some level, like God. Like God we are potters, too, and our bodies are a pile of clay. We are partners with God in the work of creation, including the creation of ourselves. Life has no meaning—said Joseph Campbell. We bring meaning to life. So, too, our bodies have no inherent meaning. We give our bodies meaning. "Meaning is something we build into our own lives. We build it out of our own past, out of our affections and loyalties, out of the experience of humankind as it is passed on to us, out of our own talents and understandings, out of the things we believe in, out of the things and people we love, out of the values for which we are willing to sacrifice something."[8] We decide how to express, how to present ourselves. We are like sculptors and our bodies clay. We are like painters and our bodies canvases. We are like architects and decorators and our bodies a room for the soul!

But, and now for the second truth transsexuals have revealed to me, *there is more to us than flesh and blood.* When a person who appeared at birth to be a boy, who was raised as a boy but always knew herself to be a girl, chooses to live as a girl, she reveals to us a truth that ultimately we are more than just our bodies. We have an essence, a personality or an identity that transcends our biological sex, that transcends our physical appearance, that transcends our anatomy, our genitals, our shape, our size, our hair ... something that is deeper, truer, and more enduring than anything we can see. We have a beauty that transcends our outward appearance. We have a soul that knows much more than our bodies can possibly express. We have a heart that feels pain even when nothing physical hurts. We have a spirit that can exult even when every bone aches. Go ahead, look at a person's body and know that it tells a story. But also know that we may or we may not be able to read it. We shouldn't assume that we can. When we look at our own bodies, know, on the one hand, that biology is not destiny and birth is not the last word. It is our right to inscribe the stories we have to tell on our own corporeal canvas. It is perhaps even an obligation—a mitzvah—to inscribe the Torah we have to teach on our own skin. On the other hand, when you look at a person's body or look at your own, know that ultimately we are more than what we can see, just as the Torah is more than the words inscribed on the parchment, and God is more than any image could possibly convey.

This leads to the third truth transsexuals reveal: *our bodies do not tell our entire stories; in fact, nothing does.* We can be known only *partially* by outward attributes. Our titles—rabbi, doctor, professor—tell only a fraction about us. Our labels—GLBTQ or straight—tell only a fraction about us. Our roles—father, mother, daughter, son, partner, girlfriend, boyfriend—reveal only a fraction about us. Even our names—Margaret, Maggie, Mags—express only a fraction of who we are. Mr., Mrs., Ms. Not one of these accurately expresses even a fraction of what it means to be transsexual. A transsexual is *mystateir,* "a mystery," as God is *el mystateir.* As we are all—on some level—*mystateir:* mysterious, untranslatable, ineffable, hidden, sometimes by our own design, sometimes by the blinders our culture wears, but mostly by our own human inability to fully express who we know ourselves to be and by our own inability to fathom the depths of another human being. The full story we have to tell, the full Torah we have to teach, cannot be seen. No one can ever fully know us. No one but God. Perhaps we cannot ever fully know ourselves. And we cannot ever fully know another human being—not even those closest to us, not even our parents or our children, our partners or our best friends. (A transsexual has, most likely, known this truth since childhood. I, for one, am only now beginning to learn it.)

Pieces of Torah, bits of truth transsexuals reveal: We impart meaning to our bodies. But we are ultimately more than our bodies. No one can ever fully know us, and we cannot ever fully know another; but—and here comes truth number four—we can *avar lifney, avar al p'ney,* reveal to others what we *do* know and *can* express even if it is only glimpses of the truths we carry inside. God promised Moses, *"Ani e-evor kol tuvi al panecha,"* "I will reveal all my goodness to you." "Seek the good in everyone [including yourself]," teaches Rabbi Nachman. "Reveal it, bring it forth." True: we can never be fully known by others, but we can and we should reveal our goodness to them.

Notes

1. Thus, through transliteration, "AIDS" became איידס (aids) and "opera" became אופרה (opera), while through translation, the word for "airplane" became מטוס (matos), derived from the root "to fly."

2. Leslie Feinberg, Transgender Warriors: Making History from Joan of Arc to RuPaul (Boston: Beacon Press, 1996), 101. Attentive readers will note that the pronoun herself refers to Leslie's own use of that pronoun in the book cited; hirself is added in square brackets here to indicate Leslie's present-day (2009) preference for the gender-neutral pronouns ze and hir.

3. Reid Vanderburgh, "Living la Vida Media," www.transtherapist.com/vidamedia.html.

4. A teshuvah is a response by an authority in Jewish law to a question posed to him. The question posed to Rabbi Waldenberg was: Is a heterosexual marriage automatically dissolved if the M (the husband) transitions to F? Or is a divorce decree required to dissolve such a marriage? Rabbi Waldenberg, in a minority position among Orthodox legal authorities, answered that since such a radical transformation has taken place it is as if the husband no longer exists; thus, a divorce decree is not required. He goes on to suggest that the MTF is like a new person; she is a woman, yes, but unlike other women the MTF should not say in the daily morning blessings: "Blessed are you ... who has made me according to your will," but rather "Blessed are you ... who has changed me into a woman."

5. Ivri means "a Hebrew" or "a Jew."

6. In 2003 Hebrew Union College – Jewish Institute of Religion admitted to its rabbinical school its first openly transsexual applicant.

7. From Unetane Tokef, part of the liturgy for Rosh Hashanah and Yom Kippur in Ashkenazi synagogues.

8. John W. Gardner, "Self Renewal," Futurist (November/December 1996), quoted in Virginia Ramey Mollenkott and Vanessa Sheridan, Transgender Journeys (Cleveland: Pilgrim Press, 2003), 17. Here the pronouns have been changed from second-person singular to first-person plural.

The God Thing

Joy Ladin

Editor's Note

This essay gives birth to transgender Jewish theology, which, among other characteristics, views ambiguity as a divine power and opposing binaries as generative forces. In "The God Thing," Joy Ladin says of God's silence, "Our craving for presence contains in embryo the presence that we crave." The Möbius strip such a sentiment represents can be frustrating as a theological position, but the statement expresses a position that is eminently transgender. As transgender persons, we spend most of our lives longing to be recognized by the gender of our souls rather than the gender of our bodies, until we slowly and painstakingly convert those molecules of longing into nascent being. If we are created in God's image, then God is in transition, too.

Ladin's phrase is reminiscent of the Hasidic idea of d'veikut—to cleave or cling to God with every thought and action, even when the Deity appears hopelessly distant. The act of clinging becomes proof of God's existence. Just as reading about God's footsteps in the biblical account of Gan Eden (the Garden of Eden) indicates that God has a foot, d'veikut implicates the existence of that which is clung to. The action of Ladin's story follows the midlife reminiscences of a transgender woman in a reflective conversation with God and Jewish tradition, as she recalls the spirituality of her youth, the journey of transition, and the ramifications of a profound human transformation to family life and to one's relationship with Deity.

God comes after the worst nightmare I've ever had.

I'm at the family house, at the end of a visit. My wife and children are leaving, on their way to do something that involves boots and down vests. I'm curious. I'm always curious about their lives these days.

My dream-self, dressed, like my waking self when I'm with my family, in a loose shirt that conceals the breasts my son insists I don't have, asks my wife what they are going to do. "Oh, a lot of things," she says vaguely. "But what?" I ask. My voice has a note of pleading that I censor when I'm awake.

My plea hangs in suddenly emptied air. My wife and children are gone. I hear them outside on the deck, laughing, murmuring about their plans.

In waking life, I've learned that leaving them doesn't mean the end of life. I don't even cry anymore. My dream-self, though, hasn't learned to survive. It starts to sob. Not the stifled, make-sure-the-children-don't-hear sniffles my wife and I perfected while I still lived in the house, but full-blown, lung-emptying screams. In the dream I want my children to hear me cry. I want my screams to dissolve the wall that separates my pain from their happiness. Deeply asleep, choking on my own anguish, I'm still trying to manipulate and punish them into love.

Then I realize what's going on. Light is leaking through the branches, nudging me awake, and now that my eyes have started to open, I start talking to God. You see how I feel, I say belligerently. You expect me to live through this?

God, as usual, responds with silence. God's silence comes in many flavors. There's the testy "No comment" with which God responds to Holocaust theologians, and the heavy Scandinavian muteness, like a blanket of icy snow, beloved of Ingmar Bergman. But God also bespeaks more intimate silences, like the moonlit silence that used to bathe my sleeping son when he was an infant. We had no curtains, so when the moon was full there was nothing to stop the light pouring toward him from the heavens. I'm here, God seemed to say through that silence. Or rather, God seemed to be that silence, gazing with me at the rise and fall of my son's chest, magnifying, as though his face were still at my shoulder, my son's breath.

Then there's the silence that constitutes God's contribution to our post-nightmare tête-à-tête.

"You see how I feel," I say to God, holding up my nightmare for inspection.

God, of course, responds with silence. It sounds to me like assent.

"You expect me to live through this?"

Silence that sounds like a shrug. God, who doesn't live in time, is unable to expect. You are alive, the silence says. Life is this. Expectation is irrelevant. You live what is.

"I can't—I won't."

Another silence. It's slightly quizzical, this silence; there is even a hint of amusement. You've been here before, the silence says. How is this time different? And what exactly do you mean: you can't, or you won't? If you can't live through this, you would cease to exist. You can live through this; you are; you have. Won't is a different story—and here the silence clearly, infuriatingly, smiles, offering a glimpse of God's teeth, the pointed, inhuman acceptance of all that is.

A being who doesn't exist in time has no business smiling like that.

"You have no idea how it feels to have your children reject you."

The silence broadens into something like laughter.

"All right, you *do* know how it feels. Your children reject you all the time. I reject you all the time. Stop changing the subject. The question is . . ." I pause, realizing that the silence has managed to turn my assertions into a question, and that asking a question has already moved me imperceptibly beyond the need to scream. "The question is, when your children reject you, how do *you* live through it?"

Silence. There's no answer, because there's no question. To love is to live.

God wins the argument again.

I know what my father would say. He loved to recount a cynical little experiment conducted at the dawn of the age of computers. Subjects were told that they were communicating with a therapist through a computer keyboard and screen. The therapist would ask them questions, and they were to respond. In fact, there was no therapist, only a computer program. "How are you feeling?" the computer would ask, and if the subject answered, "Sad," the computer would say, "Why are you feeling sad?" building questions and affect-affirming "responses" around the parts of speech in which the programmers expected the "clients" to communicate their feelings. There was no artificial intelligence involved, simply patterns of ones and zeroes cued by other patterns of ones and zeroes. Yet according to my father, even those involved in the experiment, who knew what was going on, would sneak in after hours to "talk" to the program about their problems. To be counseled, comforted, cured.

For my father, this experiment demonstrated the absurdity of not only therapy but communication. The sense of being understood, of attaining clarity through self-unburdening, was a purely mechanical response to purely mechanical statements. No training, no understanding, no consciousness, was required; all people needed was the illusion of a sympathetic presence to produce therapeutic effects.

God's silence, my father would say, is my version of the computer program, a fantasy of response that produces a fantasy of insight or, at best, enables me to recognize what I already know. No God required.

But to me my father's anecdote suggests the opposite: that our craving for presence contains in embryo the presence that we crave.

––––––

According to the Torah, God has a deep aversion to the transgendered: "A woman must not put on man's apparel, nor shall a man wear women's clothing; for whoever does these things is abhorrent to the Lord your God" (Deut. 22:5). It's easy to contextualize the teeth out of this blunt expression of divine disgust. There is evidence that the law is aimed not at the transgendered but at Canaanite religious practices that involved cross-dressing. Jewish law, even in its most Orthodox forms, is evolving, not static; it takes account of post–Bronze Age advances in medicine and psychology. Non-Orthodox Jewish movements have already moved toward acceptance of transsexuals, and individual rabbis have begun adapting Jewish life-cycle rituals to transsexual transition.

But though I've never followed more than a fraction of traditional Jewish law, I have been unable to rationalize, modernize, or ignore this sentence since I first read it as a child. Perhaps it's because this is the only time the Torah explicitly acknowledges the existence of people like me. Perhaps it is because I too long for the ontological stability that the yin and yang of the gender binary seems to promise. If everyone is simply male or simply female, then perhaps every act is simply good or simply evil; every answer simply yes or simply no; every religion simply true or simply false; every life simply full or simply empty. A binary world, a world in which I couldn't exist, would be infinitely clearer. As long as men and women stayed on their own sides of their closets, God would not abhor us.

But as hard as I've tried not to, I do exist, and so does the verse in Deuteronomy, and so neither the world nor my relationship with God can be as clear or simple as I long for them to be. Despite the law, both God and I have known since I was a child that I would sometimes wear women's clothes. My child-self tried escaping this spiritual—or is it moral?—dilemma hermeneutically. I was a child, not a man; perhaps the law didn't apply to children. But codes of masculinity and femininity were as strictly enforced in my life as in Moses's Bronze Age wilderness. My sister's wardrobe and mine had nothing in common. God's abhorrence was not a factor in our almost entirely secular lives, but abhorrence of gender transgression was all around me, in the people I loved, in the air I breathed—in myself. I didn't *want* to transgress gender boundaries; I wanted to be good, I wanted to make sense. I didn't want to be a boy wearing girls' clothing; I wanted to be a girl.

Perhaps that was how I could convince God not to abhor me. I wasn't a man or a woman, a male or a female; I was a transsexual. Either I had no gender to transgress, because my female self and male body canceled each other out, or the law was inoperative because I had no way not to transgress it. Whether I wore male clothing or female clothing, I was always in some way cross-dressed.

That sounded right to me, but what were the chances that a God revolted by cross-dressing would bother to go through the tedious and inconclusive exercise of sorting out my gender? God would abhor first and ask questions later. After all, that's what I did, when I saw myself not through the lens of my longings but simply in terms of my behavior.

Obviously, I shouldn't wear girls' clothing; it was wrong, it was stupid, and no matter how much I wanted it to, it would never transform me into a girl. It would only make me abhorrent.

And yet there I was, again and again, cross-dressing. I couldn't stop. That, perhaps, was the loophole I was looking for. Starving Jews are allowed to eat nonkosher food. I was starving to be a girl, and the nonkosher food of female clothing was the only way I knew to feed my malnourished self. Perhaps the law really meant "God will abhor you for cross-dressing, unless you are dying to do it." After all, God had made me a boy who was dying to be a girl. How could God abhor me for being what I was made to be?

Unfortunately, neither God nor I were comfortable with the claim that my desire to be female constituted a revelation of God's will that superseded the Torah. If my desperation to be a good child had taught me anything, it was that I sometimes—often—wanted to do things that were just plain wrong. I knew that desire, even overwhelming desire, to do an abhorrent thing didn't make the thing permissible. But though I stifled many impulses in the name of morals, I continued to cross-dress. Perhaps I wasn't a basically good child doing an abhorrent thing; perhaps I myself was abhorrent.

That was it. It didn't matter if I cross-dressed or not. What was at stake here was not behavior but essence. I was a transsexual, someone created to put on the clothes of the opposite gender. The law in Deuteronomy wasn't cutting me off from God; it was showing me that God and I had something in common. We could abhor me together.

———

Until recently, I had no idea what the word *faith* meant. Even now, I'm a little shaky on the definition. Faith—I'm guessing here—is a sense that enables people to detect presence in absence. That's a sense I've never had, which is probably why it's so hard for me to believe in my own existence.

When my wife and I were freshmen, arguing our way toward half a lifetime of love, a lot of what we argued about was God. An ex-Catholic who had seen through nun-drummed dogma when she was eight years old, my wife, who would later convert to Judaism, was what you might call an "IQ" atheist; according to her, belief in God was incompatible with intelligence. Though everything I said about God proved I was an idiot, every now and then, I said something that suggested I was someone smart enough to be worth arguing with, which meant too smart to believe in God. "I don't *believe* in God," I would tell her, with a spiritual smugness life had not yet beaten out of me. "I don't believe in air either. I just breathe."

It wasn't quite that simple—I was smarter than I sounded—but almost. God was something I had always felt shaping my life. In fact, God seemed a lot more real to me than I did. God was always there. I was something between a wish and prayer, and rarely seemed to be anywhere.

The contrast between the palpability of God's existence and the tenuousness of my own became clear to me when I was seven. Our family was on a summer camping trip. One day, we got up early and walked up a winding trail to the top of a small mountain. It was a perfect summer day, the sun warm, the mountain air still cool. The peak was flat and fertile, a dense maze of trails lined with blueberry bushes. My parents had given me a pail and let me wander off. There were berries everywhere. Wherever I stretched my hand, dusty blue globes tumbled forward to fill it. Bees buzzed around me, drawn by the same sweetness. I wasn't afraid. I knew they wouldn't hurt me. They were gathering; I was gathering. What they wanted, what I wanted, was right there, all around us. That was the way the world was, the way God intended us to see it. There was enough for each of us. Wherever I stretched my hands, the world leaned forward to fill them. The perfect generosity of the world unfolded before me, a blossoming, buzzing backdrop for the vast stupidity of humanity, of wars, of starvation, of fear. There was nothing to fear, no need that couldn't be met. The world was a maze of bushes bursting with blueberries, and God was there for the taking, a thudding abundance in a bottomless pail, a tart blue stain on my lips. It was all so clear, but no one seemed to know it. It was a secret, and it was my job to tell it.

My parents called me. It was time to descend, time for me to tell them the truth about the world we were living in and the God we were living with. They were up ahead, chatting with other grown-ups. I'll wait till they're finished talking, I thought. I'll wait till we're walking down the mountain. We walked down the mountain and they kept talking. There were little silences, pauses for breath or laughter, and I kept opening my mouth and shutting it again. The words that had been on the tip of my tongue vanished. They were grown-ups; I was a child. Whatever I said would sound as stupid to them as it had started to sound to me. We were almost at the end of the trail. I knew that if I didn't tell them on the mountain, I never would. It was my job, my first responsibility in the world, and step by step, silence by silence, I was failing. The mountain was behind us now, we were heading toward the car, I was bickering with my sister. The vision of that perfect, abundant world had soured within me. It was the same vision, the same world, but now it would always be stained with my failure to reveal it.

It was hard to imagine God as other than disgusted. I had seen so clearly that there was nothing to fear, and yet I was afraid. What was I so afraid of? Why was it so hard for me to tell the truth? The truth about God and the truth about me—I would never tell either to anyone. Entrusted with the great simple secret of life, and the small complicated secret of myself, I failed, failed daily, to deliver them.

God was there, beyond a doubt. But I—I was missing in action.

———

Of course, I was much less concerned with delivering world-saving prophecies than with becoming a girl. Despite God's Deuteronomic disgust, it wasn't hard to convince myself at night, as I stuffed my genitalia back into my body, that God was very close to granting my prayer—or was it a wish? Where, exactly, was the line between wish and prayer, and what, exactly, was the difference?

I didn't care. I just wanted to wake up different. Like many transkids, I spent nights bargaining with God. In exchange for becoming myself, I offered—terrible things. I don't care, I whispered to the silence, I don't mind, whatever you want I'll give you, please—just let me wake up different. And sometimes I would sink into sleep with a tingling spiderweb sensation goosefleshing my arms and legs, and something red stirring in my stomach, where I didn't yet know my womb should be, and I would go to sleep smiling, because I knew that I was finally going to change.

If God keeps old prayers, there must be a special section for those of transsexual children. Strange prayers. Prayers that precede overdoses of pills and crudely knotted nooses, prayers ravishing in their loneliness: *You made me what I am; you, at least, must understand.*

How, I wondered, could such prayers fail to evoke a response from God? It didn't seem like I was asking that much. I would get out of bed in the morning, and standing would be different—my feet would feel the floor, and my hair would be longer, a tickling tumble over my shoulders, and I would stand up straighter, and I would open my door and pad in my new but not so different flesh across the hall to show my parents what had happened—what I had become—what I had always been ...

And then my life would begin.

Except that it never did. I know now that it was a wish, not a prayer. A wish can only be answered by action. Prayer can be answered by silence.

The silence was there, but I didn't realize that it was speaking to me. I only knew that I was trapped, and that God, like a righteous or sadistic jailer, could, but wouldn't, set me free.

———

A few weeks after my father died, I went back to the city where I was born. I'd left home when I was sixteen. I had never seen the house my mother now lived in. I hadn't been present in my parents' lives for a quarter of a century, and the art on the walls and the pictures on the refrigerator were entirely unfamiliar. I had always been focused on how little my parents knew me; now I realized how little I knew them. Of course, my indifference was a form of anger. This was the life that had refused to see me. Now here we were, eyeing each other with barely controlled hostility.

My mother put me in my father's room. His desk, his computer, his papers, a closet so full of his clothes that I barely had room to hang the few things I had brought. "I suppose you don't want any of these," my mother said, a little mournfully. She gave me my father's watch to pass on to my son, then surprised me by giving me a watch of her own. It was a smaller version of a man's style, androgynous in a way that I would never have chosen; but even though I wasn't at home with it, it was at home on me.

My mother and I didn't talk about what was going on. We didn't mention that this was the first time I'd been welcome in her house, or how I felt about being in my father's room, or how she felt about having her son return as a woman. I didn't intend to tell my mother more about me than she wanted to know, and other than whether I intended to have sex reassignment surgery, she wasn't asking any questions. There was nothing to say, and no language in which to say it. I was a member of the family again.

My father's decision to refuse dialysis had led my parents to a local hospice organization. In addition to nursing and other support, they provided my mother with a social worker, and she had asked to meet the children—my sister and me—whom she had heard so much about. I had no agenda other than smiling, looking as close to pretty as I could manage, and shaking hands. Since my mother said that she had nothing that she wanted to talk about, it promised to be a short visit.

And so it would have been, if the social worker hadn't fallen in love with my family. "I really romanticize your family," she confessed. "You care so much about each other."

I looked around to see if I had wandered into the wrong counseling session. No—there was my mother, smiling proudly at her social worker. For a moment, I panicked. If this was the right room, then I had the wrong memories, had somehow grown up in the wrong family.

"I don't romanticize my family," I said coldly. The social worker smiled at me acceptingly. She was here to get to know me, not to project her feelings onto my life.

But I couldn't answer questions about my family without telling her about my family—not now, not after forty-six years of lying and hiding. I answered honestly, carefully, then not so carefully; then I was no longer answering, I wasn't waiting for questions, I was pouring out my long-hoarded history of self-hatred and suicidal crises, living out some long-deferred dream of telling my mother how much I had suffered. Someone had finally joined me in the nightmare that had been my family; someone could finally see the agony I had endured without anyone noticing.

Transsexuality was the least of it, though I threw some of that in too.

So there I was, spilling my guts to a smiling, empathetic woman I'd never met before and a stunned, stony mother. It wasn't until the session was winding down that I realized that I was in danger of entering the Guinness Book of World Records for shortest relationship with a mother. Telling her I was transsexual had started it, and telling her about my childhood had probably ended it.

"Don't worry," the social worker assured me with a smile. "I've listened to your mother talk about you week after week. She really cares about you."

My mother had already started out the hospice doors. I caught up with her and we walked together toward the car. I stayed a respectful step behind her, staring at her shoulders for some clue as to how much damage my bout of truthfulness had done. She opened the door for me and moved slowly to the driver's seat of the old gold Camry. The silence as she pulled on her belt felt distinctly devoid of God.

"Do you feel like going home?" I asked solicitously. "Or—we could go somewhere to talk . . ." I was surprised, after my bitterness and anger, to hear a note of tenderness in my voice. This *was* a miracle—I was worried not only about how what I had said would affect my fledgling life, but how it had affected my mother. "No," she said shortly, putting the key in the ignition. "I'm fine." She paused before turning the engine on.

"It's just that—" her voice started to break. "It's just what?" I asked, dreading the answer. "It's just that it was all a lie," she said, referring to the happy, caring family she had lived in until a few moments before.

I looked at her closely. She was staring fixedly out the windshield. "It wasn't all a lie," I said gently, not sure if I was betraying or telling the truth. "Some of it was a lie, some of it was true, and all of it was a long time ago."

She turned on the engine. That was her answer—to move to the next item on our list of activities. How like me she is, I thought. No matter what happened, no matter how we felt, we were going to *do*. But my mother was still driving me, still talking to me, still going through our planned list of activities. She hadn't cut me off. She wasn't my father.

Our next stop, appropriately enough, was the scene of what I had just been characterizing as a crime: my childhood streets, the house I'd grown up in. There was the park that had stood for freedom during my truncated adolescence. It was little more than a forested hill with some playing fields and a pond, but when I was thirteen, it was the beginning of the rest of the world. It was there, by the pond, that I had fallen in love for the first time, with a boy with huge brown eyes and pale olive skin. It was a pure love, as thirteen-year-old loves go, for I had no body to express it. He couldn't even see me there, couldn't see the girl who was loving him. He thought we were two boys, best friends, learning tai chi and trying to impress each other with pseudo-intellectual arguments. The pond was a blaze of gold behind his black-tressed head; there were geese crying and veeing above it. I was cold, and as a girl I wanted him to notice and as a boy I didn't want to admit my weakness.

Then the park was behind us, and we were turning down streets whose names I knew. "Does it look different?" my mother asked, as I gawked at porches and trees like a tourist from another world. "Yes and no," I murmured. The houses had been painted different colors, and there was a sense of vacancy, of meaninglessness. No one I knew lived in these houses; they weren't my lost past. They were ghosts, or I was a ghost—no, I wasn't a ghost, I was the future. I looked down at my skirt, my mother's watch on my wrist, the slight, bra-enhanced curve of my breasts. I had been a ghost when I haunted these streets with my adolescent yearnings. I was middle-aged now, but somehow time had run backward. Then I felt that my existence was almost over; now it had barely begun.

My block wasn't long, but we drove it slowly, my mother updating me on who now lived where. I was only half listening. There I was, eight years old, walking home alone from a friend's house in a pitch-black downpour, thunder booming as I let my pants drop to my ankles so that I could pretend my yellow raincoat was a dress. "Please," I had prayed, knowing that in a few feet I would have to pull my pants up and surrender to boyhood again. "Please change me!" It had felt so right, the plasticized fabric brushing my bare, wet legs like a hem. "Please," I repeated, inching my trousers upward. There was still time for God to turn me into a girl, there were still a few steps left. . . .

But there weren't. There it was, the house I had grown up in. There was the place I had lain down in the snow—no snow now, in this preternaturally warm autumn—determined not to get up again. There was the scraggly little tree—it had been protected by a fence, my mother reminded me, because it was so small and delicate—that I had stared at through my window. Now it was unfenced, massive. There, above the porch, was my window, the one I had spent hours gazing through.

There *he* was. My God, he was still there.

"Do you mind if I get out?" I asked. My mother kept the motor running as I stood on the sidewalk, gazing up toward the boy I had been. I could feel him there, behind the window, hurting himself over and over. All these years, he had been there, hurting, waiting for me.

"Please," I whispered, praying not to God but to the child I had been. "You can stop now," I whispered. "I told you I would come back to you, and I have."

I could feel the boy unclench his fists, I felt his hazel, time-blinded eyes turn in my direction, I heard the silence, the silence of God, smiling with satisfaction. God was smiling, laughing silently at our astonishment that both of us, the past and the future, the tortured boy and the woman he thought he would never be, could be answered by a single moment.

"You prayed for a miracle," the silence said. "Let's see what you make of it."

CHAPTER TWO
Avodah (Service)

Introduction

Pirkei Avot (Wisdom of the Fathers) lists the second pillar of Judaism as *avodah* (service). The documents in this chapter are artifacts of some aspects of transgender Jewish service to God. I have made no attempt to be inclusive of all possible life-cycle events or all aspects of Jewish service.[1] I chose to include two transition rituals, representing sex changes in both directions, crafted by Joy Ladin and Catherine Madsen and Aaron Devor. I include them because unlike weddings and funerals, sex and gender changes are the unique ritual contributions of trans-people to the Jewish life cycle, and both of these examples are adequately contextualized within their traditions. The rite marking passage from infancy to Jewish boyhood is transformed by Tobaron Waxman into a transition ritual. Waxman also uses text study as a religious practice to provide the foundation for an exploration of the simple meaning *(pshat)* of a complicated transgender body. The honor of being called up in synagogue to read the blessings before and after the reading of a Torah scroll during services (a process called taking an *aliyah*) provides an opportunity for Ari Lev Fornari to reflect on the simple but daunting barriers to transgender participation in synagogue life, and also presents the difficulty of changing the norms that enable those barriers to remain standing. The ritual washing of the deceased, called *taharah,* becomes for Catherine Madsen and Joy Ladin the setting for a ritual commemorating the death and consequent rebirth of a transitioning woman. Ritual washing in the *mikveh* (ritual bath) becomes an opportunity for Tucker Lieberman to reflect on the meaning of performing rituals that might not apply to a transformed body. The *hatafat dam brit* (ritual circumcision of the already circumcised male prior to religious conversion) becomes an opportunity for Martin Rawlings-Fein to reflect on sex reassignment surgery as a conversion ritual. I include Max K. Strassfeld's essay on the relationship of transfeminist masculinity to feminist thought in this chapter as a call for compassionate cooperation between all Jewish feminists. Finally, the essay jointly authored by Rabbi Elliot Kukla and Judith Plaskow is a present-day example of the traditional *chevra,* two students wrestling together with a text. While traditionally this is performed in the *beit midrash* (house of study), Elliot and Judith undertake this activity via e-mail.

Note

1. This chapter does not represent even the various types of rituals and blessings that are currently available to assist transgender Jews. For example, Rabbi Elliot Kukla wrote a blessing for injecting oneself with testosterone, which can also be used to commemorate self-identified milestones in transition. See Elliot Kukla, "A Blessing for Transitioning Genders," *TransTorah,* www.transtorah.org/PDFs/blessing_for_transitioning_genders.pdf. This anthology is not a catalog of transgender ritual forms. When I have included ritual, it is to demonstrate how transgender Jews engage with tradition. For example, with respect to "marryin' and buryin'," the staples of pastoral care, I have chosen to include no wedding ceremonies in which one or both members is transgender even though quite a few examples of such rituals exist. (Two good sources are TransTorah, www.transtorah.org, and Jewish Mosaic's LGBT Resource Library, www.jewishmosaic.org/resources.) I was able to solicit only one crucial and timely essay about care of transgender bodies at the end of life. I made these choices in part because wedding rituals have been published elsewhere, but also because to be of benefit in an anthology like this, such wedding rituals should be accompanied by an analysis of the theology they bring into existence, and no such analytical work is yet extant. In contrast, the essay by Lynn Greenhough on transgender funeral practices is included here because it lays a broad and stable foundation (alongside traditional *minhag* [custom]) upon which future work with the transgender body may comfortably rest.

Ritual for Gender Transition (Male to Female)

Catherine Madsen and Joy Ladin

Editor's Note

Transgender laypersons and clergy are beginning to create transition rituals that mark gender transition as a rite of passage in the Jewish life cycle. Much innovative and new Jewish ritual avoids pain and loss.[1] A bar mitzvah, for example, is a celebration, absolutely. But it is also a time of change, and change always involves loss and the death of some formerly held illusion. Catherine Madsen and Joy Ladin created a ritual to mark Joy's transition from male to female that doesn't omit negative emotional states. While the challenging emotional states brought about by a close family member's transition made it impossible to conduct this ritual when it was written, capturing those harrowing emotions with appropriate biblical language certainly proved cathartic to the ritual's creators.

The ritual provides a good model of transition as a rite of passage into a new body and its concomitant renewed spiritual life. The ritual employs traditional language, and, while it is ultimately a celebration, it does not flinch from fear, despair, or loss. Instead, it marks the unique dread of transition with text from the Book of Job that can now resonate in a new way: "For the thing which I greatly feared is come upon me, and that which I dreaded is come to me" (Job 3:25). The ritual marks with text from the Book of Psalms the inexpressible pain of being labeled "an abomination" by God while at the same time seeking relief from the same source: "You have put away my friends from me; you have made me an abomination to them; I am imprisoned and cannot come forth. / My eye mourns from affliction; I have called you, Adonai, every day, I have stretched out my hands to you. / Will you work wonders for the dead? Shall the dead arise and praise you?" (Psalm 88; the emphasis on you is mine). As Catherine Madsen pointed out to me, based on her reading of David Blumenthal's Facing the Abusing God, *you can leave a family member who abuses you, but you don't have that option with God.[2]*

Joy's poem (toward the end of the ritual) is drawn entirely from words occurring in the Bible (often recombined). Catherine comments, "I was interested in the way traditional Hebrew b'rachot *(blessings) and statements could be turned on their heads—the much-maligned 'who has not made me a woman' used not in a triumphalist but in a tragic sense, to 'bless God for the evil'; and 'who has made me according to your will' used with a combination of relief and defiance; 'who has made me in your image' used for an identity that's been blocked and is just coming into being; the entanglement of death and resistance to death implied in (among other things) the family saying Kaddish while the person in transition gives the responses."*

The ritual offers a necessary catharsis and marks the subject's headlong plunge from despair into death and through a transformative mikveh *(ritual bath) and out into a new—and joy-filled—life.*

Notes

1. Not to say that the tradition ignores sorrow and grieving. As Rebecca Alpert has pointed out: "Holidays like Yom Kippur, Yom HaShoah, rituals that point to the pain of the Egyptians during the Seder, funerals where people are supposed to cry and show emotion, not to mention the work of contemporary *hevrey kedisha* in dealing with the reality of dead bodies, using the breaking of the glass at weddings to focus on the problems inherent in marriage and the sadness/tragedy in the world (examples just off the top of my head) make me question that argument." Personal correspondence, May 23, 2009. Used with permission.

2. An atheist or other proponent of Jewish secularization will surely disagree with Madsen's statement.

Preparing for the Ritual

The person undergoing transition and a few carefully chosen witnesses are present, including the family members most closely affected, so far as they are willing. There is a covered mirror in the room, three buckets of water, and a vessel large enough for a person to lie in (or the ritual can be done in a room with a tub or a drain in the floor). The person in transition is wearing a *kittel* and has washed meticulously as for immersion in a *mikveh.** All are seated on the floor.

The Ritual

PERSON TRANSITIONING
> Have mercy on me, LORD, for I am wretched.
> Heal me, for my limbs are stricken.
> And my life is hard stricken.
> —and you, O LORD, how long? (Ps. 6:3–4, Alter)
> For the thing which I greatly feared is come upon me,
> and that which I dreaded is come to me. (Job 3:25)

WITNESS *(A neutral witness, not part of the family)*
> Man is bound to bless the evil as he blesses the good:
> as it is said, And you shall love the Lord your God
> with all your heart, and with all your soul,
> and with all your might. (Mishnah Berakhot 9:5)

PERSON TRANSITIONING
> *Barukh atah Adonai eloheinu melekh ha-olam, shelo asani ishah.*
> (Blessed are you, Adonai our God, ruler of the universe, who has
> not made me a woman.)
> Adonai, God of my deliverance,
> I have cried day and night before you:
> let my prayer come before you;
> incline your ear to my cry.
> For my soul is full of troubles,
> and my life draws near to the grave.
> I am counted with those who go down to the pit;

---

*A *kittel* is a white robe used as a burial shroud; also may be worn on Yom Kippur and other solemn occasions. A *mikveh* is a ritual bath.

I am like a man with no strength;
free among the dead,
like the slain that lie in the grave,
whom you remember no more,
and who are cut off from your hand.
You have laid me in the lowest pit,
in darkness, in the deeps.
Upon me your wrath lies hard,
and with all your waves you have afflicted me.
You have put away my friends from me;
you have made me an abomination to them;
I am imprisoned and cannot come forth.
My eye mourns from affliction;
I have called you, Adonai, every day,
I have stretched out my hands to you.
Will you work wonders for the dead?
Shall the dead arise and praise you?
Shall your lovingkindness be declared in the grave,
your faithfulness in destruction?
Shall your wonders be known in the dark,
and your righteousness in the land of forgetting?
But I, Adonai, I cry to you,
and in the morning my prayer will outrun you.
Why, Adonai, do you cast off my soul?
Why do you hide your face from me?
I am afflicted and ready to die from my youth up;
while I suffer your terrors I am distracted.
Your fierce wrath goes over me;
your terrors have cut me off.
They came about me daily like water;
they compassed me about together.
Lover and friend you have put far from me,
and my acquaintance into darkness. (Ps. 88)

He tears his clothes.

Let the day perish wherein I was born, and the night when it was said, a man is conceived. Let that day be darkness; let God not regard it from above, nor let light shine on it. Let darkness and the shadow of death stain it; let a cloud cover it; let the blackness of the day appall it. And that night, let darkness seize upon it; let it not be joined to the days of the year, let it not come into the number of the months. Let that night be desolate; let no sound of joy be heard in it; let them curse it that curse the day, and them that lead the mourners. Let the stars of its twilight be dark; let it crave light but have none; neither let it see the glow of dawn: because it did not shut the doors of my mother's womb, to hide misery from my eyes.

Why did I not die from the womb, perish as I came from the belly? Why did the knees receive me, or why were there breasts for me to suck? For now I should have lain still and been quiet, I should have slept. (Job 3:3–13)

He lies down. The family members tear their clothes and recite the Mourner's Kaddish. The person in transition gives the responses.

WITNESS
> And God created man in his own image:
> in the image of God created he him;
> male and female created he them.

Or singing in trope:
> *Vayivra elohim et-ha-adam b'tzalmo,*
> *b'tzelem elohim bara oto,*
> *zakhar un'keivah bara otam.* (Gen. 1:27)

PERSON TRANSITIONING
> *Barukh atah Adonai eloheinu melekh ha-olam, she'asani b'tzalmo.*
> (Blessed are you, Adonai our God, ruler of the universe, who has made me in your image.)

WITNESS
We are made in the image of someone who has no image; whose image we seek perpetually and do not find. Our minds search the universe for a body that is not there.

PERSON TRANSITIONING
O God, you are my God, early will I seek you; my soul thirsts for you, my flesh yearns for you, in a dry and thirsty land where there is no water. (Ps. 63:2) My soul waits for the Lord more than watchers for the morning. (Ps. 130:6)

The witnesses pour three buckets of water over him, as for a taharah.*

PERSON TRANSITIONING
Barukh atah Adonai eloheinu melekh ha-olam, asher kid'shanu b'mitzvotav v'tzivanu al-hatvilah.
(Blessed are you, Adonai our God, ruler of the universe, who has made us holy by your commandments and commanded us concerning immersion.)

She rises, leaves the room, and dresses in new clothes, then reenters and uncovers the mirror.
Barukh atah Adonai eloheinu melekh ha-olam, she'asani kir'tzono.
(Blessed are you, Adonai our God, ruler of the universe, who has made me according to your will.)

ALL
Barukh atah Adonai eloheinu melekh ha-olam, mechayei hametim.
(Blessed are you, Adonai our God, ruler of the universe, who revives the dead.)

---

*Taharah is a ritual cleansing for a body after death.

At this point the person undergoing transition takes a new name, either through a simple announcement or through a more complex statement such as the following:

PERSON TRANSITIONING

Are you the city that was called the perfection of joy?

No one treads you with joy.

Although you shout, they are not shouts of joy.

Your heart knows its bitterness, and no one shares its joy.

Do not grieve for joy.

Many weep when they see this temple, while many others shout for joy.

No one can distinguish weeping from shouts of joy

When God has filled you with joy.

Days fly away without a glimpse of joy.

You remember how you used to go, leading the procession with shouts of joy.

Though you have seen deceit in the heart of joy,

You still have this consolation—in unrelenting pain, your joy.

Do not grieve for joy.

All these things have you sacrificed for joy.

The trees of the forest weep with joy,

Anointing God with the oil of joy.

God will yet fill your mouth with laughter and your lips with joy.

Turning and returning you to joy,

God will be your joy

When you have no glimpse of joy.

Do not grieve for joy.

The morning stars, that sing for joy,

Will remove your sackcloth and clothe you with joy.

The ache will perish in joy.

Announce this with shouts of joy:

There is joy even where there is no joy.

Hearts throbbing and swollen with joy,

Ruins burst into songs of joy.

Do not grieve for joy.

Even sorrow shouts for joy.

When morning dawns, when evening fades, you shall have nothing but joy.

Those who go out weeping seed

Return with sheaves of joy. (JL)

ALL

Give us joy for as many days as you have afflicted us, and for the years we have seen evil. (Ps. 90:15)

PERSON TRANSITIONING *to family*

Hamakom y'nacheim etkhem b'tokh she'ar aveilei tsion virushalayim.

(May the Omnipresent comfort you among the mourners of Zion and Jerusalem.)

FAMILY *in response*

Brukha ha-ba'a.

(Welcome [feminine form].)

ALL

Barukh atah Adonai eloheinu melekh ha-olam, shehecheyanu v'kiyemanu v'higianu laz'man hazeh.

(Blessed are you, Adonai our God, ruler of the universe, who has kept us alive and sustained us and brought us to this time.)

Narrow Bridge
Aaron Devor

Editor's Note

Aaron Devor is in the first generation of scholars who are transgender themselves and who study and write scholarly works about transgender concerns. This short essay tells the story of how he ritually marked his own gender transition. The story outlines the value that this ritual had not only to Aaron and his wife, but also to members of their community as they learned to adapt to his new identity.

כל-העולם כלו גשר צר מאד
והעקר לא לפחד כלל

Kol ha-olam kulo gesher tzar m'od
V'ha-ikar lo l'facheid k'lal

The entire world is a narrow bridge
But the main thing to recall is not to be afraid at all.

      −KOL HA'OLAM KULO, HEBREW SONG. WORDS BY RAV NACHMAN
          OF BRATSLAV.

I didn't think it was a good idea at first. After all, I had spent pretty much my entire life up until then trying not to be such a spectacle. People had been staring at me and wondering about my gender since I was in my early teens. In the early days, other kids, intending to humiliate what they took to be a long-haired hippie boy, would call out, "Is it a boy or a girl?" Later, people on the streets just gawked and wondered. Women in public washrooms would get scared and either leave or screw up their courage and tell me that I was in the wrong place. Going out in public was rarely ever casual.

Over the years I learned how to be graceful about it. I knew how to put people at their ease when I could, and how to avoid those situations where I could not. I built a very successful and polished professional life for myself in which people learned to overlook my "difference." Still, it took a lot out of me every day, steeling myself for the effort. I used a lot of psychic energy every day just calming the waters as my passage through social spaces created whirls and eddies of befuddlement and unease. It wearied me, and I became emotionally exhausted and brittle inside from the effort of making it possible for everyone around me to remain undisturbed by my presence among them. Of course, no one knew any of this other than my wife and a very few of my closest friends. For my efforts to succeed, my surface had to remain smooth and unperturbed. It had to look effortless or the effect would be lost.

When I finally decided to make my life easier and to start living full-time as a man, I knew that a great many people would have to make their own transitions along with me. They would need to learn to think about me in a new way, to see me differently, to speak about me differently. For most of them this would also mean that they would need to examine and adjust some of their deeply held beliefs about the nature of sex and gender, about the meaning of identity, and about the limits of meaningful personal change.

Out of respect for the processes of the people around me I took it upon myself to have personal conversations with upward of one hundred people to tell them directly that I was soon going to be living full-time as a man. I wanted them to have a chance to ask me their questions and to have some time to digest the news and prepare themselves before participating in and supporting my transition. Since I had worked so hard for so many years to put people at their ease, no one reacted poorly and few were surprised. Mostly they just wanted to know why I felt the need. It seemed to them that I was so entirely comfortable with myself that they couldn't see why I would bother.

One of the many people with whom I had one of these conversations was the rabbi at my synagogue. He's young, and cares a lot about being socially progressive. His first words were: "That's so cool. Let's have a ceremony!" "No, no, I don't think I'd like that," was my reply. The thought of ritualizing it, of making it a public thing, was the last thing on my mind just then. I was, instead, preoccupied with concerns about how much I had at stake in making this move. I had a highly paid, highly responsible job in the public eye. I had a professional reputation that stretched around the globe. I knew that those closest to me would go with me but I didn't know what the rest of my world would do with this news. I wanted to go slowly and cautiously. A ceremony just seemed too public. I didn't want to shine a spotlight on what I was doing. What I really wanted was to magically fast-forward to a time when it was all so far in the past that no one even gave it a thought.

The weeks went by as I went through my list of people to tell. One by one they wished me well and I became more confident that it was going to be okay. When I told my brother, he said, "Just make sure you do it healthy." When I told the president and vice president at work (my immediate superiors) their first response was "What can we do to help?" Because my job required me to interact with thousands of people I had decided to choose a date (my actual birthday) to make an all-at-once public announcement at work. The president and vice president suggested that we issue a joint statement on the president's letterhead. As that day drew near some new feelings bubbled to the surface.

About two weeks before the big day I had a dream. The dream told me that I needed to say good-bye to my old self before I could truly move into my new life. That morning when we were in our pajamas in the kitchen before breakfast I told my wife, Lynn, about my dream. I said to her, "I think that I need a ceremony after all." A bit exasperated that I had left it to the last minute to figure it out, and a bit relieved that I had finally figured it out, she got to work. She called on her best girl-friend and the rabbi, and they made it happen. One week later we had a beautiful ceremony.

It was early evening on a calm and mild fall day. I didn't know what to expect as we gathered in an expansive, lush, and picturesque public park. The location they had chosen was an old stone bridge over a duck pond on which wisps of mist were rising among the languid mallards and Canada geese. People came from all parts of my life: family, friends, my workplace, the synagogue, queer people, transgender people, people from all stages of my life and in every stage of their lives from babes in arms to octogenarians. The women stood at one end of the bridge as the men waited for me at the other end. Seven women had been asked to write and recite their own seven blessings (reminiscent of the *sheva brachot* spoken at weddings) to guide and protect me on my journey. The eldest, a woman in her eighties who had known my mother before she died, gave me a double blessing by invoking my mother's name along with her blessings that day.

After many hugs and loving tears from the women, my wife accompanied me partway up to the apex of the bridge. The women sang sweetly in Hebrew and in English. My wife then returned to the tears and arms of her women friends as I continued alone to the top of the bridge where the rabbi waited.

We stood together as he blew the shofar, the ritual ram's horn, and boomed out a proclamation, first in Hebrew and then in English, renaming me and welcoming me to my new life among men. The rabbi then walked me down to the other side of the bridge, where the men waited. They immediately surrounded me and began to sing as we danced, our arms on one another's shoulders, to the traditional Hebrew song *Hinei Ma Tov* (How Good It Is for Brothers to Be Together.) After much back-slapping and handshaking and many mazel tovs a few of us repaired to a local coffee shop for refreshment and conversation.

At the time, my wife and I thought that the ceremony was just for our benefit. Everyone else was there to help us along our path. It never occurred to us that it would mean anything for anyone who had not been there. In the weeks and months that followed we learned many things about the value of that ritual honoring the traditions of our people and our revision of those rituals for a new future. We learned that invoking ritual proved to be surprisingly helpful in easing the transformation for all of us.

An entire community of people needed to make that transition along with me. The ritual assisted each of them in their process of learning to think and act differently with me and about me. It supported each of them to examine their own beliefs and values about the meaning of gender in their own lives as well. Enacting a communal ritual gave everyone there, and everyone who later heard about it, a way to connect to and to participate in marking their/my transition. It marked their own experience of transition for all who were there, or who knew about it. And in so doing, it allowed everyone around me a way to process it among themselves. Because I had chosen to make such a public event of it, everyone knew, at the same time, when they should start to adjust their thinking. The public nature of it also gave people permission to speak freely among themselves about what was happening. This made it easier for them to talk to me as they needed to sort things out and to help each other to move through their own mental/emotional transitions.

Somewhat remarkably to us, the ceremony also gave a surprising number of people the courage to share and heal some of their own private wounded places. Somehow, they felt that if I could have the courage to do what I was doing then they could be brave too. If I could share with them something so deeply personal and so profoundly life changing then they, too, felt emboldened to move out of some of their own long-hidden hurts. People shared with us, and with the rabbi, that our bridge ceremony had enabled them to uncover their own stories of past pains and deeply buried shames. They too began to shed patterns that had imprisoned them.

In the end, an entire community of people benefitted from a ritual collectively enacted. In Judaism, we celebrate our life passages communally. I did not walk across that bridge alone. My community witnessed and supported me every step of the way. As they did so they opened their hearts, not just to me, but to themselves, to each other, and to those who will come after. I think that we all learned that on the narrow bridge that is life, the main thing is not to be afraid.

Ya'amdu*

Ari Lev Fornari

Editor's Note

The biblical story of Joseph wrestling with the angel provides the appropriate textual counterpoint to this essay. Fornari makes visible for readers the complicated thought process of a transgender person deciding where to go to shul. He shows how the strong desire to participate in Jewish life can be derailed by something as apparently "simple" as a pronoun. I love this essay because it shines a light on "real life" in shul. One's eyes are not cast exclusively upward in supplication toward remote Divinity, but across the aisle and up two rows where someone cute just looked over, or over there in the corner, where the gabbai is looking around for people to stand up to read the blessings before and after the Torah reading.

It was Simchat Torah 5767—mid-October 2006. Having spent the previous summer in Palestine unlearning zionism and having recently come out as transgender, I did not have a synagogue I called home. The queer synagogue in my community says a prayer for the state of israel, the liberal synagogue has gender-segregated call and response, and the Orthodox minyan has a mechitza, gender-segregated seating. So I opted to go to the almost-egalitarian Modern Orthodox minyan, where most everything is in Hebrew, and the hetero-patriarchy is masked by a halachically inspired effort to be egalitarian. I knew at the very least there would not be any overt zionism, and I would hardly know any of the people or the words. I was banking on spiritual anonymity.

I was sitting in the back right corner trying to daven, but mostly day-

---

*Ya'amod is Hebrew (masculine) for "stand up!" Ta'amod is the feminine form. Ya'amdu is a third-person plural form.

dreaming about my complicated sex life and deconstructing the group's gender dynamics. After completing the traditional seven *hakafot* in which the men danced around the room carrying the Torah while the women danced around each other in the corner, they announced the section of Torah we would be reading aloud. Someone also announced that anyone who wanted an *aliyah* (to be called up for a Torah reading) would have the opportunity, and that men interested in an *aliyah* should stand on the right, and women on the left. I zoned out, half wanting an *aliyah* but totally unwilling to flip the gender coin. About two-thirds of the way through, the *gabbai* approached me and asked if I wanted an *aliyah.* "Yes, but I am not willing to stand on the men's or the women's side." "That's fine, you can stand wherever you want." Although this didn't really solve the issue at hand, it avoided it sufficiently for me to tell him my name. "Ari ben Victor," I said. And he walked away.

Ari ben Victor. Not only had I never said that name before, but I would never have even articulated my name like that. My nervousness attenuated "Ari Lev" to Ari, and caused me to revert to an English rendition of my father's name, Victor, rather than his Hebrew name, Mazliah. I altogether forgot my feminist inclinations to place my mother's Hebrew name first, Hana v'Mazliah. Not to mention *ben,* "son of," instead of the gender-neutral rereading, *m'bet,* meaning "from the house of," that my dear friend Max designed for just this moment.

Ari *ben* Victor, not Hadassah, the Hebrew name my parents gave me, which is Esther's Hebrew name, and always felt fitting because of her metaphoric "coming out" moments. Not Hadas, meaning "willow," an earthy male rendition of Hadassah. Not Asher, my chosen Hebrew name, one of the twelve tribes of Jacob, and also quoted in Exodus 3:13 as one of the names of god: *Ehyeh Asher Ehyeh,* translated as "I am that I am," "I am who I am," "I will be what I will be." Not Afo, my soul-searching wandering Jew alter ego, which means "where" in Hebrew and is also a contraction of my first initial and last name.

Ari son of Victor, not child, not genderqueer in-between transperson, not mentioning my mother or grandmother. Ari son of Victor it was.

"Ya'amod, Ari ben Victor," chanted the *gabbai.*

Barachu et adonai hamevorach

My hands trembling on the wooden scrolls.

Baruch adonai hamevorah leolam vaed

The sea of gender-normative twenty- and thirty-somethings chanted back.

> *Baruch atah adonai, eloheinu ruach haolam, asher bachar banu im*
> *kol ha amim v natan lanu et torato. Baruch ata adonai noten hatorah.*
> And Jacob awakened from his sleep, and he said, "Indeed, the
> Divine is in this place, and I did not know [it]." (Gen. 28:16)

This week in Parashat Vayishlach we read the story of Jacob as he wrestles with an angel. Throughout the story, Jacob begs the angel to reveal its name, but the angel is unwilling. Whether the struggle is metaphorical or lived, whether the angel is inside Jacob's soul or a character unto itself, up there on the bimah, celebrating the completion of another Torah cycle, I saw myself like Jacob. I was wrestling with god, wrestling with gender, wrestling with israel.

Having spent a summer in Palestine, it was hard to imagine celebrating many of the words of the Torah: words I did not agree with, words that told us stories about destroying sacred land, conquering neighboring countries, and occupying the Jordan Valley. Stories that do not reflect my deepest values, stories that do not include my genderqueer ancestors, stories that barely let women speak. And yet, standing up on the bimah, I was awoken from my zoned-out place, and I could hear god bouncing off the parchment.

> And an angel of God said to me in a dream, "Jacob!" And I said,
> "Here I am." (Gen. 31:11)

Here I am secretly shaking as I listen to the words of Torah; here I am trying to find myself in Jewish spaces, Jewish history, Jewish stories. Here

I am, coming back to Torah week after week, even when I disagree with Your words.

> Then the man said, "Your name will no longer be Jacob, but Israel, because you have struggled with beings divine and human and have overcome." (Gen. 32:28)

In Jewish law, to change one's name, a person need only be called to the Torah by a new name. You don't have to pay $335 to the government or wait in line at the courthouse with a doctor's note and a pay stub. You don't even have to go to psychotherapy. But perhaps, as this parashah describes, it might involve a bit of wrestling.

Many transpeople must transform what we have been *told* is true about us into what we know to be our own truth. We must name ourselves, and say, Here I am—this new person, who is also the same person. We must call ourselves into being.

The story of Vayishlach is the story of one's wrestling, and the potential to be reborn, to be renamed, to be renewed through that struggle. Just when I was counting on spiritual anonymity, I found myself being named publicly. Just when I was starting to lose faith, I asked for a blessing. And renamed me.

In the year since, I continue to unpack that blessing. I continue to be called to Torah and to realize that embedded in my naming is a commitment to stay in conversation with Torah. Perhaps this is what Jacob has taught me. That in fact, the blessing is not the naming itself, which we read in the first lines of this parashah; but rather, the continual struggle to stay present, and whole, and in conversation with the divine. For me, the blessing of being named gave me the courage to be called upon, to be called to Torah, to be called to make more space in this world for gender-nonconforming people and Jews who support Palestinian self-determination.

May we all continue to wrestle with Torah and with our relationship to that which is holy in each of us. And may we all be blessed by an angel when we need it most.

Hearing beneath the Surface: Crossing Gender Boundaries at the Ari Mikveh

Tucker Lieberman

Editor's Note

> *This essay illustrates one of the greatest spiritual lessons I can imagine an "othered" person learning: wherever you go, presume welcome. Lieberman confronts the right of a Jew to enter Jewish gendered space without apology, explanation, or approval. The essay recognizes how that right may be supported or confounded by communal minhag (custom). Implicit in the discussion as well is the role of expectation in human perception. While Tucker describes his torso as "ambiguous," because of the expectation established by the banner "No women allowed beyond this point" and the minhag of this holy site, the other men who immerse with Tucker see a man's body. Finally, the author considers the meaning of a ritual stripped of its traditional gendered purposes (the ritual cleansing of women after menstruation and men after emissions), which do not apply to a person whose body performs neither of those functions.*

An Unorthodox Body

My body is not an abomination, but it is unorthodox.

Like many Jews, at the age of twenty-four I joined the Birthright tour for a free trip to Israel, and as part of the itinerary found myself in Tzfat, once home to Rabbi Isaac Luria, the "Ari" (an honorific acronym that also means "lion"). When several of the men from my tour group decided to immerse themselves into the Mikveh of the Holy Ari, I decided to join them although the prospect terrified me. What neither my tour group nor our host city's residents knew was that I am a female-to-male transsexual. Beneath my masculine appearance is a torso that is ambiguously sexed. Undoubtedly, it would be unwelcome in an all-male *mikveh*.

I deliberately left my wallet in my room, taking only a shekel for a donation. I remember exactly what I wore: a white silk shirt, blue dress slacks, a red string bracelet given to me in Jerusalem, sandals without socks. The chill of resignation spread through me, and I heard my own thoughts rattling in my skull with an unusual detachment as if I were observing myself from the outside.

For me, the short walk to the *mikveh* was a long grappling with fear, a Jacob's angel wrestling match on the banks of the river that flows through and divides me. One side of my brain tried to calm myself, assuring that I was merely a tourist and that this scenario existed merely for my amusement. The other side raced with fear. As my sandaled feet progressed ever closer to my destination, I felt like a kid confronted with an impending encounter with the sacred, mysterium tremendum, the terrifying unknown.

The *mikveh* was enclosed in an unassuming building on the crest of a hill overlooking a field, marked with the banner reading "No women allowed beyond this point."

"Male Privilege" in Tzfat

Rabbi Isaac Luria was a sixteenth-century mystic and poet. Known for, among many other things, his conceptualization of *zimzum*, the notion that G-d "contracted" or "shrunk himself" to leave a void in which to create the world, he was believed to have spoken with several deceased teachers before him, as well as Elijah, the prophet.

Tzfat, home not only to Luria but to several schools of kabbalists and, today, sects of Hasidim, enchanted me with the way religion infused every moment of life and, indeed, the city's very structure. One of the ways this was most apparent was in the distinction between men and women. I saw both genders dressed modestly, men in black coats and top hats, women in multicolored clothing with pants under their skirts. Not every resident of the city fit this profile, but in the heavily religious Old City, gender roles appeared far more crisply defined than they are in the United States.

Men's access to space denied to women is called "male privilege" by feminists. Though some female-to-male transsexual Jews feel guilty about having access to men's-only religious spaces, I personally do not. I remember all too well how it felt to be classed as a woman without feeling like one, to grieve every waking hour that I could not reconcile my conviction that I was male with the way the world treated me as a female. Now, I am simply glad to be free. I sympathize with feminist frustrations, but I cannot speak for women because my outrage as a transsexual comes from a different slant. I don't perform women's spirituality, except as an ally, because I am not a woman.

Anatomical *Zimzum*

The "face of the waters" existed before G-d said, "Let there be light" (Gen. 1:2–3) and before G-d proclaimed creation to be good. Later, when humanity ceased to be good, G-d told Noah, "I am going to bring floodwaters on the earth to destroy all life . . ." (Gen. 6:17). The flood was sent to wipe out evil, yet the water itself was amoral, washing away everything in its path: human, animal, plant, and mineral, good and bad. Later in the Torah, water honed its moral discretion: the Jews walked through the parted Sea of Reeds, and then the water drowned their pursuers. Water, therefore, has a face, as it did even before the creation of the world, but its features continue to be imprinted over time. Is it reflecting our faces? Is it reflecting G-d's?

Though the *mikveh,* or ritual bath, echoes the primordial waters of birth and creation, it, like the Red Sea, must be discriminating. Within a traditional *mikveh,* water cannot be dirty, plague-ridden, or stagnant; it must be *mayyim chayyim,* "living waters" (Lev. 15:13), which has been interpreted as water with a natural current running through it. Jewish law instructs that before immersing in a *mikveh,* we are to strip off every thread and jewel, every smudge of makeup, even to clip our nails and slough off the thick skin on our feet, so that there is no barrier between our bodies and the water. Intimate encounters with our own bodies are powerful for most people. For me, meeting my own body is tinted by the effects of transsexual body dysphoria, the sense that one's body is "wrong" or not one's own. The *mikveh* rule of removing barriers to my body reminds me of how I hated myself as a teenager, how body dysphoria translated into a feeling of uncleanness, and how I wished I could take off what I saw as the excess fat on my chest—if not for a year, if not for a day, then just for a minute in the shower, so water could run down the "real" flat chest I believed was underneath. I was fortunate to get reconstructive chest surgery. Except for the scars left behind, it was like erasing part of my history, starting off clean.

The Mikveh of the Holy Ari is located inside a small, unpresumptuous building. The inside of the building looks like the inside of a stone eggshell, and contains a changing area, a bathroom, and the *mikveh* itself, fed by a spring and surrounded by stone. The immersion itself was simpler than I had feared. The pool accommodated one man at a time, so we waited in half darkness, single file (I discreetly wrapped in my towel). When it was my turn, I dropped the towel and climbed down the ladder. Facing the blank stone wall, I had a kind of privacy. The icy water sealed over the top of my scalp.

The Israeli staff at my program had told us that this *mikveh* grants wishes and answers questions. I was unable to articulate a wish on such short notice, but nevertheless went in searching for results. I tried wishing that a sore joint would heal. It didn't work. What I emerged with, however, was a sense of overall bodily integrity, the ability to remove the "Under construction" sign from my body, the belief in my authority to direct my footsteps to places where my body needs to be.

Turning toward the rest of the waiting men, I hoisted myself out of the pool and grabbed my towel in what I hoped was a single quick motion. After dressing, I emerged from the cave and walked into the waning afternoon sunlight, across the boundary marked "No women," alive and whole.

In that moment, one person, the youngest of our entire tour group, ribbed me about my apparent genital "shrinkage" in the frigid water.

Zimzum. My body appeared to shrink from what my companion believed was its natural extension. I remained quiet and concealed myself in the open air.

Hearing the Name of G-d

Accounts of the *mikveh* usually address fertility cycles and rules for heterosexual marriages. These do not present an ethic I can even attempt to live by, nor do they make sense out of my intuitions and experiences with the *mikveh*. Traditionally, the most common frequenters of the *mikveh* are women, who must ritually bathe after their menstruation and childbirth before they can be sexually available to their husbands again. Men are also supposed to bathe if they have had an emission (Lev. 15:16). For someone who is gay and sterile—my body produces neither eggs nor semen—the *mikveh* is bereft of its traditional framework. Nevertheless, I did immerse, so what did my immersion mean?

Most *mikvehs* are women's spaces. The Mikveh of the Holy Ari, however, is restricted to men, and before Shabbat, a day sacred for marital lovemaking, men in Tzfat line up to dip in these purifying waters. The concept of immersion is not inherently gendered. Anyone can do it. There is something profoundly humanizing about being welcomed into a font of renewal as if your nude body and your bare life were something very precious.

Water, too, has unique properties that blur edges literally and figuratively. Water in the *mikveh* is used as a tool to separate clean from unclean, workweek from Shabbat, men from women. Yet water itself is amorphous, concealing our bodies in refracted light and shadow and a rush of sound, making it difficult to distinguish male from female. Where we seek clarity and definition, we find boundaries beginning to soften and join us together.

For me, the answer is connected with hearing and with what often goes unheard. What we often think of as our humanity peels off like a brief, youthful fad, revealed as nothing more mysterious than clothes, makeup, body parts. Underneath all that noise, we are old and wise, at one with the history of the earth and the source of our own creation, a current that runs through everything. Across the street from my home, a pond overflows into a waterfall and runs under a bridge. The rush of water is loud when one stands on the bridge and overlooks it. Yet, just a few feet away, the sound evaporates. Due to this cloak of auditory invisibility, it took me a month to discover the waterfall, and sometimes I still forget it is there.

On the other side of the world, in the holy city of Tzfat, water trickles through a stone building and feeds a small pool about the size of a man. Just below the surface, the sound is deafening. It is the sound of hundreds of caravans pulled over the sand, of vegetables scratched from the dust, of fish multiplying, of plagues, of beautification, of sighs. It is the sound of water, the stuff of life, the skin of the earth, a shared resource that binds us together. Somewhere in that cacophony is the name of G-d.

Each morning, when I lift a glass to my lips and swallow, the pressure in my ear canal is altered. It is the sound of hearing. If I stay clean and open, the next thing I hear might be G-d in the falls.

Hatafat Dam Brit (Extracting a Drop of Blood)

Martin Rawlings-Fein

Editor's Note

*Martin Rawlings-Fein is a member of Congregation Sha'ar Zahav, a les-
bian, gay, bisexual, transgender (LGBT) and straight-allies synagogue
in the San Francisco Bay Area. In this essay he writes about participating as a transgender man in a ritual that is closed to women, and as a
Jew-by-choice participating in another person's conversion to Judaism.
Certainly there are similarities between conversion and transition. A
rabbi told me that over the course of the year of study prior to conversion, every drop of blood becomes Jewish, in a kind of divine alchemy.
It's easy to imagine a similar transformation occurs during the long process
of transition. Martin reflects on the similarities between one rite of passage that marks a man's entry into the Jewish people and sex reassignment surgery (SRS), which can mark, for some transmen, entry into the
tribe of men.*

A friend came to me during our synagogue's annual retreat, and asked
me to witness his *hatafat dam brit* (extracting a drop of blood), the token
drop that serves in lieu of a circumcision for an already circumcised
man who is converting to Judaism. My ears pricked up. It's an honor to
be asked to share in this exclusively male rite of passage, and it feels like
an even greater honor to serve as witness for a respected friend. I was
happy I could be part of his journey to the *mikveh*, the ritual immersion through which the act of conversion is achieved. I immediately said
yes, hugged him, and went about the retreat activities of my day—text
study, hiking, and avoiding poison ivy—with greater joy.

That afternoon my stomach started to churn. The feeling was one
that I knew well. Sometimes I forget that I am a transsexual, and that
not everyone knows that my formation took place in a female body. I

started wondering if I had disclosed the fact to my friend. As havdalah approached, I wondered aloud, and my wife reminded me that when I marched in the San Francisco Trans March the year before, both my friend and his child had been in the window of our shul, and had seen me wearing my Transsexual Menace shirt. My wife reminded me of the conversation he and I had after the march, where my friend laughed as though the way I came to manhood was nothing to get upset about.

Remembering, I realized why I loved this guy. His easy demeanor, his cracking wit, and his forgiving nature had made him a fast friend. The fact that I had forgotten our conversation after the march was also telling: the incident left no discomfort in my mind. My transness had been a nonissue with him on all counts. That day I met him in a cozy fireside room of the retreat center to share and dispel the discomfort I was feeling about his awareness of my status. I shared my apprehension. This is a ritual for men. I wanted to make sure that he was mindful of the way I had gotten to manhood, that my presence would be, in this Reform Jewish ritual, kosher. He laughed, and admitted that my background had not even been in the periphery of his mind when he had thought about whom to ask to serve as witnesses. Again, transness was a nonissue to this remarkable man. He said that when the rabbi had asked him which two men he wanted to witness the ceremony, only two names had popped into his head, and both of us had said yes, without missing a beat.

The *hatafat dam brit* was held during the retreat in his semiprivate cabin with his male partner sitting in as mohel (traditionally, the official who makes the incision, but in this case the incision would be nontraditional, taking the form of a piercing). As witnesses, we arrived a little early, along with our rabbi and another staff member from our shul who attended in an official capacity. This event was unlike any other *simcha* (joyous occasion) I have witnessed. For one, the queer nature of this ancient event was so poignant. Not only was the ritual bloodletting transformed into the acquisition of a special piercing, but also, one of the witnesses (me) was a bisexual female-to-male transsexual and the other was a local author known for his irreverent takes on Jewish text and spiritual thought. The rabbi and the other staff member were both feminist lesbians and visionaries; all but one person present were also queers who had consciously decided to parent children.

We stood together in a circle, and the rabbi and the cantor, both women, blessed this man who was about to mark his flesh with the sign of the ancient covenant. Then the two women entered the hallway, leaving us alone in the company of brothers.

We men laughed nervously and looked around at one another, jokingly covering our genitals. Nervousness covered itself up in the trappings of tradition, and connectedness—as Jews and as queers—was paramount in the ritual.

Naked, the convert sat, eyes closed, teeth clenched, and muscles braced, waiting for the piercing needle that would mark this penultimate step on the road to conversion. The women were waiting outside to chant the final blessings, but time stood still for the men in that moment of wonder, that moment of pain, and that moment of transformation. "Praised are you, Adonai our God, who rules the universe, whose mitzvot add holiness to our lives and who gave us the mitzvah to circumcise converts."

With those few little words it was over, and the trance was broken. The women entered the room again, and everyone hugged. When I reflected on the ritual later that day, I thought of a transperson's genital surgery, and the heady halachic (Jewish legal) debates that surround this issue. Yet, almost the same thing happened in the genital modification represented by the *hatafat dam brit*. With the blood from his foreskin, my friend was transformed into someone who was only a step away from his new people. He was still the same person, but now he was transformed by this blood ritual confirming his commitment to becoming Jewish. Similarly, a transman who undergoes the ritual of sex reassignment surgery has marked his commitment to becoming a man. As transmen are patently aware, a simple phallus does not create one's manhood; rather, becoming a man is a rite of passage marking entry into a sacred precinct that is maintained through one's behavior over a lifetime. This letting of blood and genital surgery are such similar passages. For the convert or the transperson these are milestones, events that will change one's life forever, change the way that one relates to life, the way that one is perceived by family of origin and chosen family, and the way that one is welcomed into ritual and synagogue life. Witnessing this rite of passage as a man among other men, as a queer among queers, brought a profound feeling of centeredness into my life. I remain entranced by the connectedness I felt as a Jewish man welcoming another Jewish man into the tribe. I continue to be amazed at how the process of conversion mimics the process of transition, and vice versa.

As a convert myself, I experienced new depths of connection to my own Jewishness through witnessing the entry of another man into the covenant. I underwent both of these life-changing transitions at the same time—from female to male and from non-Jew to Jew. At times it felt like walking on a balance beam. But one journey reinforced the other: my solid queer identity assisted me as I came out to my mother again as a convert to Judaism, a mother who was very much invested in both my heterosexuality and my immortal soul. As a man in the midst of transition, I passed as male. As a non-Jew in the midst of conversion, I passed as a Jew. In both instances, passing caused me to wonder if I needed to ritually conclude either process to feel complete. If I already passed, did I need hormones and surgery? If I already passed, did I need to dunk three times in the *mikveh* (ritual bath marking the conclusion of the conversion process)? However, the rituals of surgery and hormones woke the masculine energy in my body that had lain dormant, and the *mikveh* ritually purified my soul and brought me into a new Jewish life through immersion in living waters. For me these rites of passage occurred in tandem, balancing and reinforcing one another, becoming the sacred core of my life. As a participant in the ritual of *hatafat dam brit,* my understanding of what it means to be transsexually Jewish and Jewishly transsexual came full circle.

Becoming a Good Boy: A Transmasculine Meditation on Gendered Ritual Objects and the Challenges of Transfeminism

Max K. Strassfeld

Editor's Note

> *In a classically feminist manner, this essay shows that the personal (a decision to purchase a yeled tov kippah) is political. The discussion below invites thinkers to stretch the boundaries of classical feminist discourse. Transfeminist Max K. Strassfeld, a doctoral student at Stanford, considers the social and political ramifications of wearing traditionally male ritual garb as a transmasculine genderqueer. What action by a masculine transgender person supports both transgender embodiment and feminist ideology? What role, if any, may masculine privilege play in such support? Do the aims of feminism and transfeminism diverge?*

I was pawing through a bin at my local Judaica shop, trying to find a *kippah* (a man's head covering; in Yiddish, *yarmulke*) to match my partner's new striped shirt. My dedication to the task was derailed by a kippah that read *yeled tov*, which in Hebrew means "good boy." I was immediately drawn to it: I often joked that we transfolk need to wear buttons to advertise our preferred pronouns (because *he* is not automatically applied to my body that looks substantively female). In my *yeled tov kippah* I'd found the Jewish equivalent of a political billboard—*pirsum ha nes* in Hebrew, which comes from the commandment to "advertise the miracle" (of the oil lasting eight days) at Chanukah. This kippah would "advertise the miracle" of my identity: a Jewishly involved genderqueer, who is "read" (incorrectly identified) as "female" most of the time.

So I bought the *yeled tov kippah*, even though I noticed at the time that the bin did not have one that read *yaldah tovah* (good girl). I stood in front of the bin wondering if the girl version would have rainbow crayons too, as I admired the boy version's gender-neutral (and gay-friendly) imagery. I envisioned what a *yaldah tovah kippah* might look like instead, and a plethora of feminist reinterpretations of masculine ritual wear sprang to mind, images that typify only one ultrafeminine role for Jewish women: lace, frills, pink, lavender. Then I envisioned a nonfeminist parody of Jewish femininity—a kippah decorated with a pile of rubies, perhaps, or an apron and some frying latkes.

In the end, if women as consumers of ritual objects are acknowledged at all, then they are still forced to choose between pink *kippot* and blue *kippot*. I remember idly wondering which *kippot* my butch sisters would choose.

This small moment at a Judaica store highlights the dilemma of transmasculine feminists. What is the cost of my transmasculine visibility? My *yeled tov kippah* feels fraught: I want to believe that I am successfully (gender)queering the kippah by subversively co-opting a marker of traditional Jewish masculinity to instead mark transmasculinity. But I am concerned that my attempt at *pirsum ha nes* fails to mark the miracle of my genderqueerness. Perhaps instead it simply reinscribes a Jewish hierarchy of masculine over feminine, similar, in the end, to the feminist woman's dilemma of the pink or blue kippah. Perhaps all I do in choosing "masculine" ritual objects to trumpet a transmasculine identity is reinforce the limited (binary) options, aligning myself with blue.

Purchasing my kippah would have felt less loaded with symbolism if I had worn a kippah regularly when I (tentatively) identified as a woman. I wear it now because I relate to the object differently now. Like all good rituals and ritual objects, this kippah has meaning for me; it calls to me as a way to declare my genderqueerness. In effect, *yeled tov* is the reason that I fulfill this particular mitzvah (commandment).

Certainly, I am not the first writer to meld (or create conflict between) trans and feminist frameworks. Other, more sophisticated theorists have attempted to negotiate these ideological tensions. Some of the conflict seems to be rooted in the question of privilege. The argument that most readily comes to mind about transfolk and privilege is Janice Raymond's famous diatribe about male-to-female (MTF) women, "The Transsexual Empire," in which she claims that "transsexually constructed lesbian-feminists show yet another face of patriarchy."[1] Raymond's positing of a male privilege retained by transwomen, and even (or particularly) those who are claiming a lesbian feminist politics, is easy to critique; nevertheless, she succinctly articulates a challenge within feminist thinking. How do feminists formulate masculine privilege (or for that matter, how do we articulate the target of sexist oppression) in the face of shifting sex and gender identities?

This question of masculine privilege is often employed to split the trans and feminist communities, as in the example of the exclusionary "only womyn born womyn on the land" policy of the Michigan Womyn's Music Festival. In this annual gathering of music-loving women on private land, the utopian notion of taking a break from patriarchy collides with the problem of which physical bodies constitute that patriarchy and detract from a "safe space for womyn." Transpeople have been protesting their exclusion (and educating attendees) at Camp Trans across from the annual feminist gathering since 1992.[2]

The dynamic of pitting transpeople against the ideals of feminism can often be more subtle than Michigan, however. I have heard feminist studies scholars impugn MTF colleagues for their male privilege while insisting that I (a female-bodied masculine transgender person) am the "good feminist genderqueer." Creating "good" and "bad" transfolk based on how neatly our self-definitions align with the current feminist formulations of sex and gender is one of the ways in which feminism picks up on an already existing tension within the community and widens the gap between feminists and transfolk. Certainly, there are plenty of sexist transfolk—I have been witness to some very unfortunate drag performances, one of which employed, for example, violence against women (the nonconsensual kind) for a laugh, imitating the sexism of the song being performed, completely without irony. But the good guys–bad guys tactic is a dynamic that exceeds the problem of sexism in the trans community, which, after all, is a community that reflects the prejudices and limitations of the larger society.

The dynamic of the "good feminist trannies" versus "bad feminist trannies" might also form some of the tension between MTF and FTM communities. Which portion of the community constitutes the "good guys" depends on people's perceptions: MTFs are good when they join the oppressed group and relinquish ties to male privilege, and bad when they are seen to intrude into women's spaces. FTMs, on the other hand, are perceived as being more naturally feminist because many of us come out of feminist dyke communities. Alternatively, we are viewed as the "bad guys" since we betrayed the sisterhood and joined the patriarchy. Each of these seems to me a lose-lose proposition. I am thinking of Gayle Rubin's brilliant response to lesbian feminist rejections of FTMs in her article "Of Catamites and Kings," where she argues that we should "strive to maintain a community that understands diversity as a gift, sees anomalies as precious."[3] She is making the case for revising our notion of identity, even though it continues to be a useful category for political organizing, to include the notion of the anomalous, the diverse, the subjects that test the boundaries of a category.

Rubin's argument is a lovely attempt to weld the communities back together, but it does not directly answer the question of privilege. Embedded in the notion of FTM "betrayal" is the question of whether FTMs have male privilege post-transition, a question that is hotly debated both within the trans community and without. Certainly, for those of us who don't pass, it is hard to conceive of how we are granted substantive male privilege, although I think it is always worthwhile to consider such questions. But, as I've tried to demonstrate with my examination of Jewish traditionally male ritual wear, even for us genderqueers, the problem of male privilege is imbricated in how we reach for visibility, or carve a space for ourselves in the world.

Transfolk, in turn, have created a concept parallel to the feminist construction of male privilege: cisgender privilege, which can refer to the privilege awarded to the gender-normative or specifically to those who have never experienced the pain of being "unintelligibly" gendered.[4] In a sense, the feminist concept of male privilege uneasily balances beside the trans concept of cisgender privilege, and activist discourse has walked a tightrope trying to envision how to discuss privilege while marrying these concepts that appear to be in conflict.

———

After I made the decision to purchase the kippah, I began to think about what would need to change in order for me to feel unambiguously good about being a "good boy." From the perspective of parity, the existence of a *yaldah tovah kippah,* with the same silly rainbow crayons, would certainly have made me feel a little better. But somehow the phrase *good girl* feels more loaded and less playful to me than *good boy,* which probably has everything to do with personal baggage from my feminine childhood.

Good girl rings, in my ears, as approbation for fulfilling stereotypical femininity. When I was a girl I hated the phrase *good girl,* not simply because it would deny to me some of my complicated reality, but also because I associated *good girl* with the girls in my class who were able to wear a denim skirt and look normal, who seemed to effortlessly adhere to gender norms like chatting and trading stickers with the other girls, who played the right games and talked the right talk. Curses were one of my earliest pleasures in language, the epitome of un–good-girl behavior. I associated *good girl* with a particular set of characteristics—cisgenderedness, whiteness, non-Jewishness, assimilatedness, and classness—that neither I nor my mother imitated well.

But perhaps that no longer needs to be true today, when I can rethink the construction of good-girlness. I can think of Joan Nestle and all the feminist queers who have worked to reclaim both the feminine and the femme from where it was shuttered away by angry feminists. Maybe then *yaldah tovah* would not feel like a curse flung at our young girls (and boys-who-would-be-girls). Maybe then a *yaldah tovah kippah* could be as good a thing as a *yeled tov kippah.* Maybe then I would not have to apologize for my appropriation of masculine Jewish symbols. Maybe it would help to equalize my privilege: the privilege inherent in my ability to buy a kippah that reflects me.

But in a world of parity where the kippah ceases to be the purview of masculinity, as my inner angry feminist wants, will it still call to me personally as a ritual object? In other words, once *yaldah tovah* has been reclaimed, does my *yeled tov* become less compelling? My attraction stems both from its function as an announcement of my preferred pronouns and from the fact that it remains rooted as a traditional symbol of Jewish masculinity. Subverting the original meaning of the symbol is part of the attraction I find in appropriation. Once anyone can wear a kippah, and it ceases to have any association with Jewish masculinity per se, the gesture of revolt is lost. Its attraction, for me, as well as its problematic nature, lies precisely in its troubling of traditional masculinity.

What does it mean for transmen to be men? This is a frequent topic of conversation among my friends who have transitioned. Part of the "second adolescence" that occurs as a result of changing gender roles during transition is the process of relearning social norms and expectations, in order to (only) break them on purpose. From men who used to identify as butch women, for example, I have heard the frequent lament that flirtatious behavior is perceived as sex-positive and sexy when it comes from butch dykes, but the same behavior can be viewed as sexist and obnoxious from the same people who are now perceived as straight men.

Even without passing, I experience a similar dilemma in interacting with the cisgender world: the same action before someone knows me as trans is read as feminist, while after I disclose my trans identity is read as masculine. For example, when I insist to my coworkers that I can help move the heavy table, it is perceived as feminist before they understand me as a genderqueer; after I come out to them it is seen as an expression of masculinity. As a result, so often those who are attempting to be respectful about my gender identity choose to acknowledge it in sexist ways. Sometimes, this is in order to cover a moment of awkwardness, when they've unthinkingly labeled me as female and want to affirm my masculinity by calling attention to my traditionally masculine traits. That I am physically strong (particularly for a nebbishy Talmud *bocher*) is not something I associate with my masculinity. I am faced with the unappetizing choice of allowing well-meaning cisgender people to affirm my identity through sexist remarks, or correcting their fumbling attempts to make me feel more at home.

Recently I saw a very fine play by emerging playwright Ricardo Bracho, entitled *The Sweetest Hangover*. Among many interesting moments in this strong play is a scene between two black women, one of whom has recently come out as MTF and has decided to transition, and is told by her friend that she will have to give up her male privilege now. In this scene the transwoman agrees with her friend. It took me a long time to realize what did not ring true about that scene—until I realized that throughout the entire play we never see the transwoman trying to pass as male. She is costumed in female clothes throughout—as an audience, in order to feel her loss of male privilege, we would have to see her exert it. The scene clarified for me the issue of privilege and MTFs: despite Janice Raymond, when the world perceives a man in a dress, they are not lining up to afford that person masculine privileges.

This is reminiscent of an argument frequently used to discriminate against bisexuals. Since a bisexual has the opportunity to pass as straight, they are granted straight privilege that lesbians and gay men who can't pass as straight don't have. The argument is flawed by an equally limited understanding of the cruel choices offered to those individuals: attempt to pass, monitoring yourself at every moment for the slip that will betray you, or live as you see fit and accept the (sometimes brutal) consequences of not fitting in entirely with either straight or queer communities.

As a transperson who walks in masculine ways through the gender-segregated world of Palo Alto, I have lately been feeling the weight of my responsibility to consider these issues. Judaism is a fiercely gendered legal system, and working through what a modern genderqueer and trans-friendly Judaism looks like in ritual, spiritual, and legal ways is a process that has only recently begun. As transmen, even as we fight against the allegation of residual male privilege leveled at transwomen, it is time for us, among ourselves and our allies, to think about (and exert in new and perhaps more sensitive ways) any gender privileges we may have acquired during the process of transition.

Julia Serano makes this point cogently in her book *Whipping Girl,* which, for all its faults, asks an important question: why are transwomen the public face of transsexuality despite the fact that MTF and FTM people are now transitioning at roughly equal rates? Her answer is that this world has a fascination with "men" who no longer wish to "be men" … but a "woman" who wants to be a "man"? By the skewed logic of the cisgender world we inhabit, moving from female to male makes some amount of sense, since transgender masculinity ostensibly buys male privilege, and who in their right mind would want to choose an unprivileged position? If we accept Serano's argument, then we masculine-spectrum transpersons do carry a certain amount of gender privilege, even if it is only the meager amount that we hold over our trans sisters. It is time to give serious consideration to how we, as genderqueers, recognize and employ that privilege in the fight for Jewish gender justice.

Notes

1. Janice G. Raymond, "Sappho by Surgery: The Transsexually Constructed Lesbian-Feminist," in *The Transgender Studies Reader,* ed. Susan Stryker and Stephen Whittle (New York: Routledge, 2006), 132.

2. See "Michigan/Trans Controversy Archive," http://eminism.org/michigan/faq-protest.html for a nice historical summary of the tension.

3. Gayle Rubin, "Of Catamites and Kings: Reflections on Butch, Gender, and Boundaries," in Stryker and Whittle, *Transgender Studies Reader,* 479.

4. In using the notion of "intelligibility" I am following Judith Butler's controversial lead in her essay "Doing Justice to Someone: Sex Reassignment and Allegories of Transsexuality," in Stryker and Whittle, *Transgender Studies Reader,* 183–93. *Cisgender* is an adjective that refers to a type of gender identity formed by a match between an individual's biological sex and the behavior or social role considered normative for one's sex (according to the mainstream). In contrast, *transgender* refers to a mismatch between biological sex and social role.

Opshernish and self-portrait as *pshat*

Tobaron Waxman

Editor's Note

I found Tobaron Waxman's work online the first time I searched Google using the terms "transgender" and "Jewish." He's a Canadian artist living in New York who works with the embodiment of gender and time; often his work overtly employs Jewish themes. His striking image of a Chagall-esque crucifixion scene with a transgender man hanging on the cross and a leather-man in the role of Roman-centurion-with-javelin, illuminated for me everything it was possible to feel about embodiment as a gay transgender Jew.

His series on the Amidah (Standing) prayer that is central to Jewish liturgy depicts men clothed as Hasidim in the act of davening (praying), while a figure of indeterminate gender davens naked, the stranger in their midst. Even clothed and "passing" for the gender of choice, the transgender Jew is naked. Some part of her-him-hir-zir is always hidden under Jewish obligations that pertain solely to men or solely to women. The hidden part, the elephant in the middle of the synagogue, fluctuates (sometimes male, sometimes female, sometimes a combination of the two or neither of them), and has the mass and gravitational force of a black hole bending the wavelengths of light. Passing is never the end of it. Stealth is never without consequence. Despite the best intentions and the best surgery, genders flicker across transgender faces like firelight. Suffer it. Bask in it.

Waxman has a unique (and perhaps uniquely transgender) ability to capture and sanctify transgression. My favorite of his works is titled Reverence, and it takes place in that most favorite of transgender trouble spots, the public restroom. What public facility is made for people like us? Tobaron claims this closeted-in-public gay sex scene as the Holy of Holies: Yedid Nefesh is chanted in the background, the familiar trope accentuating the scene's age-play and homoerotic themes.

Beloved of the soul, Compassionate Father,

draw Your servant to Your Will;
then Your servant will hurry like a hart
to bow before Your majesty
to him Your friendship will be sweeter
than the dripping of the honeycomb and any taste.
　　　　　　　　　　　　　　　—YEDID NEFESH *(BELOVED OF THE SOUL), TRADITIONAL*

　　Opshernish and self-portrait as pshat are the two works included below. Opshernish is a transgender refiguring of an Orthodox ritual, a way to come of age as a transgender man in Jewish community. Self-portrait as pshat asks and answers the question, Is it possible to articulate a transgendered portrait without representing a body?

Opshernish

　　Opshernish was first performed at Gallery 2 in Chicago in 2001. The installation and documentation footage were curated by Daniel Belasco for the Jewish Museum of New York in September 2009 as part of the group exhibition Reinventing Ritual: Contemporary Art and Design for Jewish Life. The exhibition traveled to the Contemporary Jewish Museum in San Francisco in April 2010.

My installation began untitled with a two-day endurance-based tableau. I sat on a high stool, diagonally opposite the entrance. My waist-length hair was separated into locks and connected to the ceiling with metal clamps and airplane cable. The performance consisted of three phases. If a visitor could come around to make eye contact with me, I would hand them the cutting implement. Visitors cut suspended locks of my hair with scissors, then shaved my head with clippers and finally with a razor, until I was bald. Once all the locks were severed, an attendant replaced my scissors with electric clippers for the second phase, and for the final phase wiped my head with a hot towel and applied shaving cream from a large chrome bowl with a brush, and relieving me of the clippers, finally placed in my hand a razor.

The epilogue, called *Opshernish* after the Orthodox Jewish ritual, occurred two months later at the closing of the installation. It revisited the second and third phases of shaving with clippers, wiping of my head with a hot towel, application of shaving cream, and shaving my scalp with razors. The performance was five hours in duration at the opening, and three hours at the epilogue.

The *opshernish* is an Orthodox boy's first haircut, which takes place on his third birthday. The community comes to the family home, and everyone participates by cutting a piece of his hair, until what remains is what will become his *payot*.* He then recites a short text in Hebrew to commence his life of learning. The community collectively confirms the role of male child, collectively acknowledges its expectations of him, by cutting his infant hair, the hair he has grown since birth, and shaping it to mark his public appearance as a male citizen. My *opshernish* had to do with moving out of certain infancy of self-awareness and self-conception and releasing myself altogether from the magnetism of kinship-based models of identity formation. For me, this is not a linear progression.

The completed installation consisted of the stool, the chrome bowls, the white hand towels and cutting implements in a row on the floor by the wall, the cuttings where they landed, and an inverted forest of roughly twenty-five locks that hung from the ceiling. Combined with the shorn remains, this constituted a site of gendered expectation excised.

Payot are the unclipped curls on the side of a Hasid's head.

Over the course of the performance, the suspended locks when cut would swing slightly away from me and toward the entrance, as they had been connected to the ceiling at a slight angle. This gave a subtle effect of constant movement, both forward and vertical, a dynamic tension between the suspended locks of hair, the clippings that fell to the floor, and the live body anchoring it all on the stool. Curator Daniel Belasco of the Jewish Museum of New York has compared the image of the dark hair and black-clad body against the white space as akin to writing. Both *Opshernish* and *self-portrait as* pshat were assessed by philosopher and cultural theorist Dr. Sue "johnny de philo" Golding as an act of inscription.

The surfaces of the white cube installation space became a taboo circumstance. Rather than wander in, people entered gingerly, only after making a concerted decision to come in. Once inside the space, people whispered, if they spoke at all, some sitting on the floor, or reaching thru the locks to caress and even smell them. Otherwise a crowd watched at the threshold of the space, pressed up against the edge of the white painted floor as if against glass, like at airport arrivals.

Each cut was a uniquely different experience of human interaction. Some people were utterly brutal and treated me like I was not a person. One girl pulled the scissors from my hands without even looking at my face, to her boyfriend's embarrassment. One man ordered the clippers like a side order of fries, as he stood next to me to have his wife shoot a souvenir photo with a disposable camera.

A curator, razor in hand, demanded that I speak and tell her exactly how the piece would end: "What if no one comes? What if no one comes to shave you? How long can you sit here? Will you shave it yourself?" Another woman, the artist Kim Stringfellow, stood in front of me for some time, and finally said: "I don't think I can do this." I smiled at her, silently pressing the scissors into her open hand. As the scissors closed around her chosen lock, she closed her eyes.

self-portrait as *pshat*[1] (2001)

Process art,[2] in collaboration with Rabbi Justin Jaron Lewis. Equipment requirements: CD player, overhead projector. Dimensions variable. Completed with assistance from Mari Rice as well as Sara Varon, Ronit Bezalel, Stacy Goldate, Camilla Ha, Antonia Randolph, Andrea, Shauna and Gallery 2 staff who volunteered their time. Thanks also to Tony Wight, Barbara de Genevieve, Rabbi Elyse Goldstein for their encouragement. Photos by Thea Miklowski.

Hypothesis: It is written in 1 Samuel 25:25 *"kish'mo kein hu"*[3] (like one's name, so he/she is); that is to say, one's name both mirrors and shapes a person.[4] In the Zohar[5] it is explained that the individual is not named by one's parents, and that the parents are only a conduit for this predestined information. What, then, are the implications of a bi-gendered name?[6] Given that gender is not necessarily located in the physical body, is it possible to articulate a transgendered portrait without representing a body?

Process: The Torah study for this project was ongoing under the tutelage of Rabbi Justin Jaron Lewis. In discussions over the telephone and by e-mail with Rabbi Lewis, and with the help of a Tanakh concordance, we created a text consisting of 251 verses of Torah. Included are 47 occurrences of *Tova* (תובה) as a feminine adjective, 27 as a noun; 175 direct references to *Aharon* (אהארון) (without an article). The collection of verses is projected onto the walls and windows of the gallery. The projected text is then traced onto the walls in pencil, and in Conté crayons onto the windows. This will take many hours, and constitutes the performance element of the installation. An overhead projector casts the text both on my body and on the wall, and the text is reiterated on the wall by my body. Recordings of the chanted text play continuously in the space, alternately phasing in and out of synchronicity. I focused on Torah as a source for the text, but wanted to do it in a literate way for the integrity of the work, and so I was guided by someone who uses this material professionally on a regular basis and who also empathized with my queer identity.

Results: The effect of this edit is comparable to that of a concrete poem, and access to the text varies in degrees depending on the literacies and empathies of the spectator. These are all separate verses of Torah that have been reassembled in the order that they appear in the original text. This means that the expected flow of chant and of narrative is interrupted at various times. There are elements of interruption and surprise. (For example, there are ten instances in a row of "and Aharon said.") Such elements of interruption and surprise included alongside elements of the norm might be said to characterize a transgender poetics as well as transgender embodiment.

I cannot offer my name, though it is a queer locution, as a proof text for transgender. I respect that the only proof text for Torah is Torah. *Self-portrait as* pshat is one step in my endeavor to create a body of work that is informed and supported by an ongoing study of Torah. With this project, I created a balance in my life, albeit a temporary one—staying vital in a contemporary art context in which one rarely has interaction with Torah-literate people. The piece began as a way to have a relevant study of Torah within my art practice, as opposed to two separate activities. This is an act of resistance against the life-split that is otherwise encouraged by the dominant culture. *Self-portrait as* pshat was a significant step in realizing a transgender body of work, within my art practice, as well as a way to come out to my father, who named me after his parents.

Afterword: Spectators could read the poem (or not) depending on their level of Hebrew literacy. *Self-portrait as* pshat was the first time I used explicitly Jewish content without incorporating some method of subtitling in the composition (that is, some manner of asking for permission from the dominant culture to use content specific to my own culture). Hebrew and Judaism are visual code systems typically not encountered in a contemporary art setting, which had the effect of incorporating into the performance the spectators' attempts to make meaning out of the project in the face of cultural unintelligibility. This was met with some frustration by some white gentiles, who mentioned feeling excluded from something secret, and asked, "If it's not in Japanese or Spanish, why *isn't* it in English?" I am not aware of any transperson visiting the show or encountering this piece. I have no community in the normative sense, so I managed to sew together various pieces of information and cull together tutelage without mentors—this might read as a pun when considered alongside other conditions of transsexual embodiment.

During the entire process of projection and tracing of the text onto the walls and windows, recordings of the chanted text were played continuously in the space, alternately phasing in and out of synchronicity. The source for the audio was bar mitzvah training tapes for boys. The voices are not of vocalists per se, but of American male rabbis with a distinctly *yeshivish* accent. Many trans allies assisted me in tracing the letters, including filmmaker Stacy Goldate, who at one point joined me in the performance dressed as an Orthodox boy (figure 1), reflecting a doppelganger of my body, as a parallel to the multiple audio tracks playing simultaneously in the space.

The font we traced onto the walls and windows was not solid, but rather an outline of the letters, as a gesture of humility and gratitude to the original *sofrut* and primary text. But for the sound of the two asynchronous voices chanting Torah verses, the space at first glance appeared empty during the day. The installation is visible during daylight hours only if one enters the space and closely examines its perimeter. In this case "perimeter" alludes to *pshat,* not only as a reflection of the physical exterior of the body being the first site of meaning, but also as an invitation to the viewer to experience meaning from a place of internality. The work is observable at night from the street, via the text inscribed on the window; however, the text is seen in reverse, and spectators from the street cannot hear the cantillation. In other words, while *pshat* is discernable from outside, entering and stepping into the *pshat* offers an immersive four-dimensional diversity of experiences of limitless relationship.

Postscript: In November 2001, the Centre for Gender and Religions Research (GRR) Centre at the School of Oriental and African Studies, University of London, held its first conference in gender and religions research on the theme "Damaged Bodies: Gendered Identity in Religious Discourse," at which I was the invited artist. I presented a body of work

Figure 1. self-portrait as *pshat* (2001). Performance installation, detail.
Gallery 2, Chicago.

that included photo documentation of *self-portrait as* pshat. Respondents to my presentation were Dr. Mira Amiras, Rabbi Sarra Lev, and Dr. Cosimo Zene, as well as Rabbi David Brodsky.

> *Pshat,* in entering text, is the most literal, non-interpretive reading. The first level before you begin the transformation of consciousness. You move up to *pardes* in a model of paradise. As you rise levels, you enter into different levels of consciousness. *Pshat* is the beginning portion, before the transformation.
>
> This image is evocative of the *yad* (figure 2). The hand outstretched, the body on the ladder is forming a *yad* . . . you never touch the Torah with the hand, but with a phallic extension of the hand, the male authority/gaze into the text. The image is inside the *yad,* inside the act of Torah reading, all these layers make it [the image] already on the road past *pshat.*
>
> –DR. MIRA AMIRAS

Figure 2. self-portrait as *pshat* (2001). Performance installation. View through lobby vitrine, inscribed, with overhead projector in foreground. Gallery 2, Chicago.

Figure 3. self-portrait as *pshat* (2001). Performance installation. Street level window, detail. Gallery 2, Chicago.

In the Zohar there is a discussion of ultimately, what is the literal meaning of a Torah text? What is *pshat?* The *pshat* is ultimately the interpretation ... If you think that *Animal Farm* is about a bunch of animals living on a farm, you are missing the whole point.

—RABBI DAVID BRODSKY

You are creating yourself, on a midrash level, on a text. It parallels the creation story in the biblical story—G-d creates the primordial creature Adam (from *Adama*, which is not embodied, it's earth), creating a self-portrait that is not embodied. Then it says "and G-d created him" ("him" being both the generic and androcentric "him"), followed by Genesis 2, "male and female created he them." All of that is in the piece. The rabbis talk about the explanation of Genesis 2, that G-d creates Adam as an *androgynos*. And that G-d created the original creature as male and female is embodied in the piece.

—RABBI SARRA LEV

Figure 4. self-portrait as *pshat* (2001). Performance installation. Street level view through window. Gallery 2, Chicago.

Figure 5. self-portrait as *pshat* (2001). Performance installation, detail. Gallery 2, Chicago.

Quite interestingly and revealingly, text was going through you, and through you going on the wall, which meant a lot to me. Basically you're the text here, to be decoded [in the Derridian sense], … in fact renouncing womanhood—it takes a lot. I doubt that a man would have persisted five hours there doing that. Perhaps that was your final gesture as a woman … I certainly thank you for presenting yourself as a text, to be read.

–DR. COSIMO ZENE

Notes

1. The following notes are added as a convenience for persons interested in replicating the text study described in this essay. Reuben Alcaly, *The Complete English-Hebrew Dictionary* (New York: P. Shalom Publications, 1996) defines *pshat* as "plain meaning, literally, literalness," with a cross-reference to *pardes*, which is defined as "plain, symbolic, homiletic and esoteric (four methods of biblical interpretation)." For the Aramaic equivalent, *pshata*, Marcus Jastrow, *A Dictionary of the Targumim, the Talmud Babli and Yerushalmi, and the Midrashic Literature* (Peabody, MA: Hendrickson Publishers, 2006) has:

   PSHATA, m. (preced.) [i.e., from the preceding verb–see below] 1) plain wording; plain sense. [Examples]: Talmud *Ketuboth* 111b, *pshateh dikra bemai ketiv,* "what does the plain text (not homiletically charged) refer to?"; Talmud *Eruvin* 23b, *pshateh dikra,* etc., "what is the plain sense (not homiletically forced) of the text?"; Talmud Yerushalmi *Sanhedrin* 18a, *pshuteh dikraya,* "the plain sense of the text"; Yerushalmi *Bava Bathra* 16a, *ba'ei meitar pshateh,* etc., "wanted to give meaning (of the verse) and could not find it." 2) extension, natural course (of a river). [As in] Talmud *Gittin* 60b, *Hullin* 18b, 57a.

   "Preced." is the verb *PASHEIT, PSHAT.* The meanings Jastrow lists are: "1) to stretch, stretch forth; to straighten; 2) to strip, tear, flay; 3) to be stretched forth, reach out; 4) to explain, teach; to deduce." Jastrow begins the definition of the Aramaic verb by noting it is the same as the corresponding Hebrew verb, which is *PASHAT.* The meanings he lists for *PASHAT* are:

   [*Kal* conjugation: 1) to stretch, straighten; 2) to strip: to undress; 3) to make plain, to explain; 4) to spread, be published.] [*Pi'el* conjugation: 1) to stretch, straighten out; 2) to strip, take off] [*Nif'al* conjugation: 1) to be straightened out, be unfolded, become flat; 2) to be stripped.] [*Hif'il* conjugation: 1) to strip, flay; 2) to shed the skin.] [*Hof'al* conjugation: to be stripped.] [*Hithpa'el* or *Nithpa'el* conjugations: to be straightened, become even; to flatten.]

Chaim M. Weiser, *Frumspeak: The First Dictionary of Yeshivish* (Lanham, MD: Jason Aronson Publishers, 1995) gives the following definition relating not to Torah but to Gemara study:

> *pshat* n. 1. A manner fitting an explanation into the words of a difficult text: RENDERING. "His convoluted P. in the *sugya* makes you wonder if he's learning the same *daf* as everyone else." 2. An explanation of the logic behind or the source of a passage, event, work, etc: METHOD, INTERPRETATION. "I once had a *shiduch* in an art museum, and I made up P. in all the paintings to try to make an impression." 3. That which explains the rationale for something: JUSTIFICATION, REASON. "I thought they're friends, what's the P. they're fighting?" [< Heb. *peh shin tet* (straight).] Cf. what's *pshat.*]

Alexander Harkavy, *The Yiddish-English-Hebrew Dictionary,* 2nd. ed. (1928; repr., New Haven, CT: Yale University Press, 2005) has "*PSHAT* s. (pl. *PSHA-TIM*) meaning, sense, signification; commentary; interpretation of a text according to the plain meanings of the words."

2. "Process art emphasizes the process of making art (rather than any predetermined composition or plan) and the concepts of change and transience … In a groundbreaking essay and exhibition in 1968, Morris posited the notion of anti-form as a basis for making art works in terms of process and time rather than as static and enduring icons, which he associated with object-type art." Excerpted from the glossary of the Guggenheim Collection Web site, www.guggenheim-collection.org/site/glossary_process_art.html.

3. This phrase from a specific context is used in a completely different context by Nahmanides in his commentary on Lev. 13:29, suggesting that it may be applied as a general principle in the interpretation of Scripture.

4. A more direct source for this idea is the Talmud, Berakhot 7b, *"minah lan d'shma garim."* How do we know that the name causes/determines/affects a person's life or actions?

5. I have not been able to track this down in the Zohar. The teaching is in circulation on the internet in the name of everybody from the Talmud to the kabbalists to the Maharal, but without source references. The attribution to the Maharal seems most likely.

6. My birth name was created by my parents, a combination of my father's parents names, Toba and Aron (Yiddish).

Remapping the Road from Sinai

Judith Plaskow and Elliot Kukla

Editor's Note

This essay consists of a series of e-mail communications between Judith Plaskow, professor of religious studies at Manhattan College and a Jewish feminist theologian, and Rabbi Elliot Kukla, a staff rabbi at the Bay Area Jewish Healing Center in San Francisco and a transgender activist, writer, and educator. Together, paired in an electronic chevra (study partnership—a classic form of Jewish avodah), the two explore the potential and limits of a shared transgender and feminist movement.

Dear Judith,

When I was a teenager exploring Judaism, I read your book *Standing Again at Sinai.* What struck me most vividly was your insight that deep within Jewish thought a hierarchical rejection of difference exists that goes far beyond the marginalization of women. Inviting women to shape the future of Judaism, then, leads to fundamental theological shifts within the tradition, as it questions all the binary distinctions of Jewish life and law.

In the seventeen years since you wrote that book, quite a lot has happened in the Jewish world. Women's mounting participation in Judaism has continued to reshape its essence. At the same time transgender liberation movements have increasingly questioned gender itself and asked whether the categories male and female can (or should) be the basic way we divide up humanity.

Sometimes the goals of feminist and transgender thought appear to be at odds with each other. And yet I believe that to raise the voice of women and transpeople within Judaism, we must begin with similar agendas and goals: recognition of marginalization, rejection of hierarchical binary thinking, and an attempt to create more space within the covenant for a variety of identities and embodiments.

How might women and transpeople support each other in this proj-ect of renewing the tradition? How can we deconstruct the binary divide between men and women while working to lift the subjugated voice of women within Judaism?

You asked nearly two decades ago how the central categories of Jewish thought would be altered by women shaping Torah. What does Sinai look like to you now? How will the tradition be transformed as we begin to find ways for women, transgender people, intersex people, and every-one else to also stand again at Sinai?

—Elliot Kukla

Dear Elliot,

When I reflect on *Standing Again at Sinai* and the work I have done since, I see the most fundamental theological question I raise as that of authority: Who has the authority to define the ongoing meaning of Judaism? Who has been included and who has been excluded from the conversations through which Jewish life takes on meaning? How do hitherto marginalized groups mobilize the authority of tradition and authorize ourselves to enter into the process of shaping the Jewish future?

I'm excited by the ways in which the entry of transgender and inter-sex persons into Jewish debates about gender and sexuality both high-lights dimensions of the tradition that have long been ignored and expands on some central feminist insights. Feminists first drew a sharp distinction between sex and gender in order to make the point that nei-ther the psychological and emotional characteristics of men and women nor their social roles are biologically or divinely ordained. Transgender activists argue that the sex/gender distinction is itself problematic and that the very notion of only two sexes is produced by the same set of social processes and power relations that create gender hierarchy.

The challenge as I see it is to formulate feminist and transgender issues in ways that draw connections between our struggles. I say this because I worry that the Jewish community has a short attention span! Despite women having reshaped Judaism in profound ways in the last decades, an enormous amount of work remains to be done. It is much more interesting and fun to put programming time and energy—and even funding—into the latest hot issue than to look yet again at the more intransigent aspects of sexism.

How then do you talk about transgender issues in ways that don't "change the subject" from that of the continued subordination of women? And from my side, how do I talk about the continued subordination of women in ways that challenge the gender binary?

—*Judith Plaskow*

Dear Judith,

You ask how we can talk about transgender issues in ways that don't "change the subject" from the continued subordination of women. For me, transgender issues are not a new "subject" at all but rather a continuation of the conversation about how gender-based oppression impacts the lives of all people, whether we identify as women, transgender, intersex, genderqueer, sissy boys, or something else.

Sexism affects transpeople in multiple ways. Male-to-female transgender women are held to impossible and damaging misogynist ideals of beauty in order to be seen as "real" women. Female-to-male transgender men are often regarded as not "male enough," unable to be seen for who they are or to wield male social power. Furthermore, binary hierarchical gender norms make the lives of people who live between male and female genders invisible.

Likewise, transphobia (the fear of gender variation in society) circumscribes women's lives. Women continue to be oppressed not only because femininity is devalued but also because of the narrow boundaries that define "acceptable" female appearance and behavior.

I respect your desire to not get caught up in the latest hot issue, but it is important to be clear about what is at stake for my community in this conversation: transgender people face unemployment rates that hover around eighty percent; they experience significant obstacles when accessing health care, education, protection from violence, and other basic services. Mostly, this treatment stems from the belief that there are only two ways of being created in the image of God—male or female.

I'm curious about how the growing awareness of genders beyond male and female impacts your own theology. My generation is indebted to you for advancing feminist thinking. What tools can we use to continue to shift gender boundaries to include the liberation of people of all genders?

—*Elliot*

Dear Elliot,

Moving beyond the notion that there are only two genders will mean asking new questions of tradition and expanding the categories of Jewish thought in a way that builds on the feminist transformation of Judaism. For example, while contemporary Jews have trouble thinking beyond the gender binary, the rabbis of the past were quite aware of the existence of persons who did not fit into a dichotomized gender system. The *tumtum* and *androgynos* (hermaphrodite), whom today we would label "intersexed" persons, are categories that appear many times in rabbinic literature. The rabbis defined the *tumtum* as an individual who is actually a man or a woman, but who appears to have no genital organs because his or her genital area is covered over at birth. They defined the *androgynos* as someone who has the genitals of both sexes, so that it is impossible to determine whether s/he is male or female. Although the fundamental approach of rabbinic texts is to use these categories as thought experiments that serve to clarify and bolster a rigid gender grid, contemporary Jews could seize the opening they provide to extend or undermine a binary understanding of gender and to question our own gender dimorphism.

The concept of transgender may also be a much more fruitful way to think about God than simply adding female images to the overwhelmingly male language of tradition. Using male and female imagery for God, as do some new prayer books and feminist liturgies, tends to reify and reinforce stereotypically masculine and feminine qualities. Imagining a transgender God builds on the feminist project of recovering the female aspects of God but highlights the shifting nature of the divine gender and the ultimately problematic nature of gender categories. It incorporates the idea of multiplicity and fluidity as well as insistence on the inadequacy of male metaphors.

Both the category of androgynous and the notion of a transgender God raise a major question. Should the goal of these changes, on both the theological and the communal levels, be the dissolution of gender or the multiplication of genders? I am not willing to surrender the category of woman while people called women continue to be discriminated against—but I would like to hold that category more lightly.

—*Judith*

Dear Judith,

It seems that only the multiplication of genders and not the dissolution of gender can serve the goals of both feminism and transgender activism.

A post-binary gender identity is only liberating for those of us who truly see ourselves as post-binary and feel trapped and invisible when held within the categories of male or female. Some transgender people identify wholly with their preferred gender. For example, a person might have been assigned male gender at birth and raised as a boy but now see herself as completely female. For that person the category of woman is the most liberating gender there is, as it reflects her inner sense of self.

Gender liberation is multifaceted. On the one hand, we must fight to create space within genders for more complex and diverse ways of being male or female. At the same time, we need to allow room between genders for post-binary identities that encompass more ways of being human.

I agree that we can draw upon classical Jewish texts—the *tumtum* and *androgynos*—as a resource in these goals. Although I concur that the rabbis' primary approach to these gender-variant figures was to use them to bolster a rigid gender grid, other voices emerge from our tradition that offer different perspectives.

In the Mishnah, Rabbi Yossi says that the *androgynos* is neither essentially male nor female but a "created being of its own." This phrase is a classical legal term for exceptionality; it is an acknowledgment that not all of creation can be understood within binary systems. In my reading, it is also a theological statement. It is a proclamation that God creates diversity that is far too complex for humans to understand or ever fully categorize. There are parts of each of us that are uncontainable. All of us—whether we see ourselves within or between male and female genders—are uniquely "created beings of our own." This idea allows for infinite gender identities that are all created in the image of God.

I continue to be inspired and encouraged by your ideas. How do you answer your own question? Do you seek to multiply or dissolve gender? I am captivated and deeply moved by your image of God as transgender. What sources from within Judaism might we draw upon to bring this image into our liturgy and theology?

—Elliot

Dear Elliot,

I agree entirely that, in the world in which we live, the multiplication of genders best serves feminist and transgender objectives. So long as social, political, economic, and religious power and resources continue to be distributed along gendered lines, I cannot imagine surrendering gender categories. Moreover, I don't see how there can be real change in gendered power relations unless the multiple perspectives and insights that emerge out of women's and transgender experiences are recognized and valued. Still, I understand gender—including the sense that it reflects one's inner self—to be partly a creation of social institutions and practices. Therefore, to my mind, your goals of creating space within and between genders—goals I affirm—press toward the dissolution of gender. I want to see a society in which gender is simply one of numerous facets of identity and is far less salient than it is in ours. So for me, there is a fruitful tension between the ideas of multiplying and dissolving genders.

The image of God as transgender is an attempt to capture this tension. The sources within Judaism that might be used to develop this image are largely the sources that feminists have been talking about for the last forty years: the existence of female images, such as Shekhinah, that have been overlooked and left out of the liturgy; the natural images that suggest that God is beyond gender; the gender-crossing imagery in which a "male" God has the so-called feminine qualities of feeding and nurturance as well as the feminine divine that represents justice; and the new female and natural images that are part of many feminist liturgies. I also want to include the metaphoric shifts in the way the people of Israel are imagined in Jewish texts—most often as a male community but sometimes as a feminized community (to maintain a heterosexual position in relation to the deity).

The entry of women and of transgender people into Jewish leadership roles multiplies the metaphoric potentialities for envisioning the relationship between God and Israel and thus the nature of God. There's an analogy between undermining the gender binary by multiplying social genders and exploding the notion of a male God by multiplying metaphors for God and our relationship with God. We can think of God as masculine, feminine, female, male, both, neither, in various combinations, and in terms that have nothing to do with gender, so that through multiplying, we dissolve.

—*Judith*

Baruch Dayan Emet:
Translating Death into Life

Lynn Greenhough

Editor's Note

How does Judaism manage gender at the time of death? It turns out that gender follows a person after death, from the ritual cleansing performed by the chevra kadisha to the placement of the burial site in the cemetery. Lynn Greenhough's essay introduces end-of-life ritual, and then poses questions and proposes some responses to the encounter of traditional Jewish burial with sex- and gender-changed bodies.

Jewish tradition holds that when one hears of a death, one recites the following blessing: *Baruch dayan emet* (Blessed is the true judge).[1] These words encapsulate our recognition and resolve that even in death our relationship with God continues. As a longtime member of a *chevra kadisha*, a Jewish burial society, I am called upon to recite these three words regularly.

In this essay I will explore some of the emerging intersections of chevra kadisha and trans identities. I have a personal stake in finding a place within our Jewish burial traditions for those whose gender expressions do not necessarily conform to the sex of their bodies. I am married to Aaron Devor.[2] The complexities of gender have formed the core of Aaron's personal life and professional research for many years. We have spent many hours discussing gender, sex, and sexuality in every permutation imaginable. His research has taken us to gender conferences and celebrations where we have both made friends in the gender community.

Before, during, and after Aaron's own decision to transition, gender identity issues were never just an intellectual abstraction. They were also with us in our home life. One topic we have often discussed originates in my work with Jewish burial societies. Who will prepare Aaron's body for burial when he dies? Will it be a team of men, as is traditional for someone who is born male, or a team of women, as is traditional when someone who is born female dies? Or will some other configuration of a chevra kadisha, not yet imagined, be created? I am personally reassured by my knowledge and experience as a chevra kadisha member that Aaron's body and his wishes will be fully respected. But this is not to say there is not much room for broader education about these issues.

Historical Rituals and Contemporary Lives

Members of a chevra kadisha volunteer to care for the dying and for the dead prior to burial. At all times we are led by our obligation to uphold the honor of the deceased, an ethic known as *kavod ha'meit*. A chevra kadisha is very much a bastion of tradition, with procedures and rituals handed down from one generation to the next, usually literally from hand to hand. Members of a traditional chevra kadisha will probably hold traditional expectations about gender and bodies. A person's gender will be expected to be congruent with his/her apparent sex. A man should have a body that appears unambiguously male; a woman should have a body that appears unambiguously female.

How can these rituals, which are so deeply embedded in centuries of tradition, including gender congruency expectations, meet the needs of transpeople? The identities of transpeople often defy traditional understandings of masculinity and femininity, male and female, man and woman. How do we reassure transpeople that they will not to be seen as freaks? Do we even need to address questions raised by traditional Jewish halachic (legal) teachings when so many trans Jews choose to live their lives outside of such a traditional framework?[3] Yet, for those trans Jews who do observe halacha, what provision might be made? Ultimately, how do all these communities begin to work together and educate each other? My hope is that we will begin with a process of honest discussion within and between members of chevra kadisha groups and members of trans communities.

Chevra kadisha members are, by the very nature of their work, accustomed to being present in the hard face of death. We handle dead bodies. Every chevra kadisha member with whom I have spoken acknowledges the enormous privilege we have as chevra kadisha members. By the merit of our work, we often sense we are in the presence of a liminal soul hovering between death and afterlife.[4] Many of us have perceived such a soul-presence in the room as we attend to a deceased body.

Fluidity of gender identity, which many of us once assumed to be fixed, challenges us all to reflect on our own lives. Is our identity chosen? Is identity predestined? Some transpeople claim past-life influences, some claim identity from birth, some claim the right to freely choose identity in any particular moment.[5] This challenge to fixedness influences us all to more honestly understand the source of our own selves and our own identities. Might transpeople challenge us all to more stringently uphold *kavod ha'chai,* honor for the living, just as chevra kadisha upholds *kavod ha'meit,* honor for the dead?

Perhaps it will be this shared experience of liminality, of deep awareness of the delicate veil between life, death, and afterlife, between man and woman and all the realms of identity, that will bring chevra kadisha members and transpeople together. Perhaps, also, a shared ethic of honor for body and soul, for the living and for the dead, will cohere as a fulcrum for learning about each other.

"The way one dies is a reflection of the way one lives." Many who work with the dying have repeated this statement to me over the years, and while it is not entirely a truism, I have come to see it as one of the adages of dying. In continuation with this thinking, does not the chevra kadisha have an obligation to honor in death the identity and bodies of those who have lived in differently gendered ways?

Years ago, I wrote, "Many Jews who are no longer religiously observant may continue to cling to certain vestiges of communal ritual. The rites of burial and mourning may be personally significant even as the historical and/or cultural meanings may be mislaid or lost. However, exposure to a community that is still actively engaged in ritual practice may be a reentry point for some Jews. Ritual thus may carry an invocatory function that invites personal disconnection to be transformed into communal participation."[6]

As Jews, we are blessed with many rituals and traditions to provide care for those who are dying, for the dead, and for surviving mourners. These traditions hold tremendous wisdom; they guide us through some of the most destabilizing times of our lives. Yet, many Jews have sought community and connection beyond the traditional boundaries of Judaism and synagogue. Many live beyond the recognizable borders of community-based ritual. My experience is that there is potential for the inevitability of dying and death to open a door of return to these same Jews. Might the chevra kadisha also hold such a door open to trans Jews? And might transpeople bring their understandings of their identities into new forms of chevra kadisha ritual?

Halacha plays less of a role in the rituals of a chevra kadisha than does custom. I would suggest that a very similar situation holds for many Jewish transpeople. While the Reform, Conservative, and even Orthodox movements have ruled on issues concerning transgender people, many transpeople live with a high degree of social recognition and acceptance beyond that provided by halacha.[7] However, while some rabbinic authorities have officially recognized a change of sex and gender, such status is determined by completion of both upper and genital surgery (for both FTMs and MTFs), as well as continued hormone treatments. "Successful" gender transition is predicated on compliance with all possible medical interventions. Clearly, many transpeople live successfully in the gender of their choice, regardless of halachic or medical standards of completion. Many transpeople deliberately avoid invasive, complicated, dangerous, expensive, and often unsuccessful medical treatments. In light of this reality, halacha is often superseded by a broader social definition of success.

Yet, transitions that are generally viewed as entirely successful in normal everyday circumstances may be viewed by some as less successful when clothing is removed. Chevra kadisha members will confront unclothed bodies. Such nakedness inevitably invites complications of perception. Non-op (people who decide not to have surgical intervention), pre-op, and post-op transpeople may lie on the preparation table. However, rather than their once-lived gender, the deceased may be seen only as their body. In other words, a transperson may be seen in death as having a body whose gender is no longer recognizable. Any congruency between gender and body has become difficult to access, resulting in the possibility that an FTM might be seen as female and an MTF as male.

Members of a chevra kadisha, who are mostly uninitiated in gender variations, would typically hold an expectation that a (perceived) female body on the preparation table lived as a woman and therefore should be treated as a *meitah* (female deceased) rather than a *meit* (male deceased). In that moment, those expectations of chevra kadisha members may converge with certain visible sex characteristics and override the authority of any degree of surgical alteration. Traditionally, members of a chevra kadisha understand that their participation in this work is a *chesed shel emet,* a work of true lovingkindness for which there is no thanks possible. The dead cannot speak so there is also no argument. How will the hard-won identity choices of transpeople be securely honored by the chevra kadisha? Who should even be on a chevra kadisha team to ensure such honor of identity and person?

Traditionally, women have prepared only women's bodies, and men have prepared only men's bodies. While tradition allows women to perform the rituals for men if no men are available to do the job, the reverse is not permitted. The issue of modesty precludes men from seeing a naked *meitah.* But transpeople bring new questions into the room. Who is a man? Who is a woman? Will only halachic definitions of male and female hold sway on the preparation table? What are the naked determinants of identity? Will death change a person's chosen, lived reality in favor of the narrower strictures of halacha? Will a transman be honored as a man by a male chevra?

Most people assiduously avoid thinking about their death, never mind any possible rituals that may be linked to care of their bodily remains. However, even with all the many complications of identity in life, there is a growing awareness among some Jewish transpeople about the necessity to think ahead to end-of-life contingencies. Transpeople clearly face distinct challenges in this regard. Do transpeople believe that their identities will be understood and accepted, or rejected by non-trans chevra kadisha members? Perhaps transpeople offer unique opportunities to revisit this Jewish tradition.

One transman I spoke with said he would feel more comfortable with a women's team preparing his body. He feels they will approach his body with more compassion and more kindness. His experience of men (as a man) makes him reluctant to let the men's team encounter his differently bodied maleness. What does a chevra kadisha do with persons who have challenged the very words *man* and *woman?* How do the processes of identity continue beyond death?

Chevra Kadisha Practices

Do chevra kadisha members receive training about gender variance? I don't know of any chevra kadisha group that has had any actual training when it comes to variant gender expression. Even Kavod v'Nichum, an international organization to which I belong, an organization dedicated to teaching about these Jewish end-of-life rituals, has yet to teach about the needs of transpeople.[8] The GLBTQ community can be instrumental in helping to develop a set of guidelines to help those of us who work in a chevra kadisha.

What is that work? While many chevra kadisha groups are beginning to expand their mandate to include pre-death care, I am going to focus on the specifics of the washing and dressing rituals, which are generically called *taharah*. *Taharah* means "purification." The mandate of a chevra kadisha is to engage in symbolic rituals that act to purify the body and soul of the deceased. All procedures are virtually the same for the women's and men's teams, with a few minor variations of dress.

When someone dies in a community, the rabbi and the head of either the men's or the women's chevra are among the first people to be contacted. Funeral times are coordinated with the rabbi in consultation with surviving family members. When a funeral time has been set, members of the appropriate chevra kadisha are called. Ideally four to five team members are present for each *taharah.*

The overarching goal of a *taharah* at all times is to hold honor for the life and soul of the deceased *(kavod ha'meit)*. *Taharah* consists of three primary rituals: *rechitzah* (washing), *taharah* (purification), and *halbashah* (dressing). *Rechitzah* is the washing of the physical body. *Taharah* is the symbolic cleansing of the soul, and *halbashah* is dressing the deceased in ritual burial shrouds, or *tachrichim.*

These rituals usually take place in a preparation room in a funeral home. Usually, the *rosh* (the team member designated to be the leader in the room) will have consulted with their rabbi prior to the *taharah* if there are any indications of problems. Some chevra kadisha groups may also have a rabbi on their team. Once all of the equipment is in place, burial garments have been laid out in order, and team members have assured that health and safety protocols are in place, the *taharah* begins. Prayers are recited throughout. Team members begin and end by asking forgiveness of the deceased for any indignity they may have unwittingly performed upon them. I took the title of my thesis, "We Do the Best We Can," from a saying that is almost the mantra of chevra kadisha members. These words, "We do the best we can," guide the *rosh* and team members in making their decisions regarding the many challenging situations that can arise in the preparation room, while also holding the honor and dignity of the deceased at all times.

Each group has its own custom about how to proceed, but two general rules consistently hold. The body is always washed from the head down to the feet, and the right side always leads over the left. The body is washed carefully and gently, with every measure taken to not cause any blood flow. A variety of medical interventions may have taken place; there may be need to deal with colostomy bags, autopsy stitching, bedsores, or catheters, for example. Over the course of their years of service, chevra kadisha members encounter these and other medical interventions.

Once the washing of the physical body is complete, the actual *taharah* begins. This is a symbolic washing of the spiritual body of the deceased.

A measure of water (we use three full stainless steel buckets of cold water) is lifted over and then poured over the body in a continuous flowing stream. Our custom is to dry the deceased; others will begin immediately to dress the deceased in the burial shrouds.

Most groups use standard garments that include a head covering, a shirt, trousers, an overshirt, bands that tie on the leg and around the middle, and an apron. These garments, including the apron, symbolically reflect the garments worn by the *kohen gadol,* the high priest, as outlined in Torah (Exod. 28:1–43). These shrouds are white, and usually consist of seven different garments. Some groups have evolved their own set of garments. One group has developed a single-piece garment. Some groups have members of their communities sew their burial garments. Some groups purchase the shrouds.

Interestingly, the garments for men and women are virtually identical, the only variations being the location of the ties on the legs and the style of head covering. Men's heads are covered with a hood; women's heads are usually covered with a bonnet. Faces are covered either under a hood (men) or with a cloth face covering (women). Men are always buried with a prayer shawl, a *tallit.* The custom for women in our community, as in many, is that if a prayer shawl was worn in a woman's life, then her *tallit* will also be included among her burial garments. Finally, the deceased is gently lifted and placed on a white sheet in a simple unadorned coffin. The sheet is wrapped over the *meit/meitah,* and the lid is closed.

The actual ritual takes approximately an hour if there are no serious complications. Ideally, the person is then buried in a Jewish cemetery. The simplicity of these rituals acts to reinforce the democratic ideals of equality for all.

Yet, many questions emerge from this description. Many of these questions are being wrestled with today by members of chevra kadisha groups. Who is a Jew? Who can be buried in a Jewish cemetery? What if they cannot afford the cost? What if the person has chosen to be cremated?

Can persons who are not in a chevra kadisha do these preparations privately? Must they only take place in a funeral home? What are the legal limits to body preparation and disposal? What if family members intervene and state wishes that are contradictory to the wishes of the deceased and/or partner?

Gender Variance

And then there are the gender questions. What if the local rabbi or chevra kadisha has had no experience with gender variance? Who should make the decision regarding member participation in a *taharah* for a transperson? Who has a voice in this decision: the dying person in advance, the family, the rabbi, or the head of the chevra kadisha? Traditionally, a person could never request that particular members participate in his or her *taharah* (or not). There is also the added complication of timing. Ideally, Jewish burial should be held as immediately after death as possible—there isn't a lot of time for learning and/or negotiation.

To my knowledge there have never been mixed-gender chevra kadisha groups. As stated, when necessary, women may prepare men. But this would not be a mixed-gender group. Might women provide these rites for transpeople? If there were a GLBTQ chevra kadisha, as some have suggested, would lesbians perform these rituals for lesbians only, gay men for other gay men? Where do we draw the lines of acceptable identities? Must the chosen/given identity of the chevra members match up with that of the deceased?

What can we learn from other communities with similar rituals? Iran, for example, has a very large population of transpeople, largely because gay and lesbian sexuality is illegal. To live with their same-sex partner, many gay men and lesbians have been forced to change their sex. Medical interventions have enabled their survival but have also reinforced the Iranian heterosexual hegemony. Afsaneh Najmabadi is an Iranian-born historian and gender theorist now at Harvard. Najmabadi writes:

> The rules of washing the dead before burial are virtually the same in Islam (there is a huge degree of similarity between the two

traditions in many areas of ritual). If the transperson has had surgery to the extent that the body looks largely like a male or female body, then s/he would be washed by the same-gender washer. If not, it would follow the rule for intersex bodies: *the washing will be done by either washer (male or female) but the dead body would be totally clothed* (the usual rule is washing the body with no item of clothes).[9]

Of course this example invites other questions. What clothing? The clothing the deceased was wearing at the moment of death? Clothing can be a vehicle of gender defiance, of playfulness, or of conformity. Will the deceased be washed in their usual clothing of choice? Most commonly, the garment of death is a ubiquitous and revealing hospital gown. Most of us who have ever worn this usually skimpy garment would not consider ourselves to be dressed. I also have concerns that washing the body while it is fully dressed might be tantamount to creating the equivalent of an "untouchable" gender class.

That said, some chevra kadisha groups (both men and women) proceed throughout their *taharah* rituals with the deceased fully covered with a sheet at all times. This covering is to preserve the modesty of the deceased as fully as possible. While doing a *taharah* on a fully clothed body, as Najmabadi suggests, might not seem optimal, it does have the advantage of not revealing what the deceased might not want revealed.

In British Columbia, many First Nations peoples have preserved rituals very similar to those of Jewish tradition.[10] Anthony Black, a member of the Coast Salish nation, spoke with me about how his people still carefully wash their dead, dress them in burial garments, and bury them in the simplest of coffins. He spoke to me about how they deal with the situation of transpeople.

Within Black's traditional indigenous community individual autonomy continues to be subject to a greater communal authority. While individuals may choose surgical or hormonal changes to their bodies, social recognition of that chosen identity comes only with the approval of family and elders. Black spoke to me about one individual who was male-to-female. Only when the elders of her community had given her permission could she come to the tribal dance and participate as a woman in a dress. In Black's tribe, the authority of the family and the authority of the elders in counsel with each other ultimately determine the acceptance of any individual's change of identity. He also noted that today contemporary tensions exist due to many First Nations persons not growing up in traditional communities. Giving such weight to family and elder approval may run counter to their desire to actively define their own individual identities.

At death, First Nations men prepare men, and women prepare women's bodies. There are sets of other unique rituals that are oriented to the separate genders. A transperson will be prepared by either men or women, once elders and family members have agreed to their particular gender identity. Black also spoke of the small size of many communities today where there may be only fifty people, a size that enables everyone to know everyone. Such familiarity may enable and support recognition of that individual's gender choice well before death.

Black also spoke about how remnants of traditional beliefs continue to permeate the now largely Christianized First Nations peoples. He spoke about how most First Nations had understood gender as an almost infinite spectrum from the most hypermasculine to the most utterly feminine. While earlier, pre-Christian First Nations tribes held to such beliefs, today gender and sex conform more rigidly to the extreme ends of that gender spectrum. Where individuals once held a place of honor in their communities for holding multiplicities of gender expression, there is less room today for such recognition, never mind honor. Black finally suggested that there might be greater potential for acceptance of MTF than FTM persons for no other reason than the greater potential for complete and successful MTF genital surgeries.[11]

Working Together

Most Jewish transpeople also want to control authorship of their gender identities. They want those self-chosen identities to be consistently and correctly read in their social worlds. But such readings may be complicated. As the wife of a transman I have had to come to my own adjustments about changes to my husband's body and persona. This has not been easy at times. If this has been difficult for me, how much more so might this be for others who have had no contact with trans issues? While I have had years to adjust to these changes, members of a chevra may have hours if not minutes to understand this complexity. But it might not be as difficult as we think at first.

Clearly many seasoned chevra kadisha folks are used to dealing with death's finality. Many are also guided in their work by a belief in the presence of the disembodied soul of the deceased as they do their work. Many also hold faith in a life to come and find this work validation of a belief that we all transition from this world to the next. Perhaps by virtue of their experience, the hands of chevra kadisha members could serve all Jews. Perhaps they would gently wash, pour water over, and dress a transperson with as much gentle care as they would attend the needs of anyone. I suggest this while also recognizing that many of us hold fears about our bodies (which invariably we see as imperfect) being negatively judged.

I had one elder in our community speak with me about her *taharah* when her time should come. This woman was a much-beloved elder, a woman who had quietly and consistently sewn together the fabric of our community through its many rents and tears. This woman, who had once been a valued member of a chevra kadisha, was very concerned about her own *taharah*. Why? She had undergone many surgeries in her life. She was worried we might find her body repugnant, that we might find her many scars and lack of physical "perfection" difficult to face. I assured her that she would be cared for with the utmost of honor. She was. And I remember her fears to this day.

Chevra kadisha members are experienced in confronting all manner of bodies. Some bear witness to the ravages of long illnesses, some are scarred with deep bedsores, and some bodies have had multiple surgeries leaving an inevitable pathway of scars. We have prepared the bodies of persons who have had autopsies, of men and women who have committed suicide. We have held the bodies of children in our arms, our hearts breaking as we thought of the grief of their parents. We have prepared the bodies of those who have had cosmetic surgeries and those whose limbs have been amputated. Car accidents, fire, plane crashes—these are all circumstances that can end lives. Death can be messy, death can be kind. The rule, as always, is "What happens in the *taharah* room stays in the *taharah* room."

On some level, at the risk of sounding coldhearted, when we choose to enter a *taharah* room, we chevra kadisha members choose to set aside our personal identities and our affinities. We are there to do a job. We are there to wash, to cleanse, and to dress. We are there to place the deceased in a coffin, where no one will ever see them again. We are there to be final witnesses to a final transition. We are there to ensure that the deceased receive our fullest honor, as we tenderly cleanse the vessel that has housed their soul. We ask *teshuvah*, forgiveness, of the deceased at the beginning of these rituals and at their end. And finally we plead with God that by our example, God too will forgive that same soul.

My hope is that by beginning to build an understanding about the work of the chevra kadisha, we will begin to address some of the worries and concerns about body identity and gender identity among transpeople. Just as the very existence of transpeople helps all of us to come to deeper understandings of the living bodies we all call home, it is the work of the chevra kadisha to care for those same bodies in death, with honor and with dignity.

Notes

1. The blessing in full reads *Baruch atah Adonai, eloheinu melech ha olam, dayan ha'emet.* (Blessed are you God, King of the world, the righteous judge). This blessing is spoken in full by immediate family members, who are those most affected by the death: children, parents, spouses, and siblings. Others outside of the family generally follow the custom of omitting God's name from the blessing, and recite *Baruch dayan emet.* In Talmud, Berachot 59b, we learn that even when hearing bad news we acknowledge God as our judge.

2. Aaron Devor's essay "Narrow Bridge" is included in this anthology; his biography appears at the end of the book.

3. *Halachic* refers to the full corpus of Jewish religious law—biblical, Talmudic, and Rabbinic. While usually translated and understood as "law," the root letters (הלכה) can also be understood as "pathway," or "the way of walking."

4. *Liminal,* from the Latin word *limen*, "threshold," indicates a state of being in between. A liminal ritual involves some change to participants, or a rite of passage, that will affect their social status. For an in-depth examination of the range of these beliefs see Simcha Paull Raphael, *Jewish Views of the Afterlife* (Lanham, MD: Jason Aronson Publishers, 1996).

5. Harry Benjamin was an early sexologist who developed the idea of a continuum of transsexual identities. In 1966 Benjamin published *The Transsexual Phenomenon.* Interestingly, Benjamin referred to sex reassignment surgeries as "conversions," calling to mind similar questions of identity held by, and addressed toward, many Jews who have chosen to convert to Judaism.

6. Greenhough, Lynn, "We Do the Best We Can: Jewish Burial Societies in Small Communities in North America" (MA thesis, Royal Roads University, 2000), 48. See www.jewish-funerals.org/greenhough.htm for a partial reading of this thesis.

7. The details of denominational halachic responses to gender and identity are included elsewhere in this volume.

8. Kavod v'Nichum is a nonprofit Jewish educational organization. See hundreds of articles about Jewish death, *taharah,* chevra kadisha, cemetery management, and much more at www.jewish-funerals.org.

9. E-mail message to author, July 5, 2009 (italics added).

10. First Nations peoples are Canada's indigenous aboriginal peoples.

11. Personal communication, July 8, 2009.

CHAPTER THREE
Torah (Teaching, Instruction, Law)

Introduction

The first pillar of Judaism is Torah, the study of which is, in my opinion, one of the most important acts any transgender Jew can undertake. Knowledge is power. As I explained in the introduction to the first chapter, I chose to bring the third pillar (*gemilut chasadim*, acts of lovingkindness), to the front of the book. That is not to say that Torah is unimportant in the third position, but that recognizing the humanity of those who are different, and recognizing the Jewish *avodah* transgender people perform, *is also Torah*. Our actions are also Torah, in my opinion, because they are informed by our study of Jewish text, history, tradition, and ethics. Even as we move beyond history and tradition and into the realm of the singular, our innovations are guided by Torah.

One reading of halacha (Jewish law) says that transgender and transsexual body and clothing choices are forbidden.[1] In liberal Jewish practice, lives precede law as a matter of course, and even within traditional Jewish legal systems exceptions are made in the law to save a life (the principle of *pikuah nefesh*). For instance, if a complete fast is mandated by the law, exceptions are made for the sick and wounded, or for pregnant women. Under a strict interpretation of halacha, one may not drive on Shabbat, yet if a life is in danger that prohibition may certainly be relaxed.

Certainly, text study is a crucial Jewish practice that may be engaged not only by academics but also by activists as a tool for social transformation. Such study may be political as well as religious and scholarly, in that it includes reverence for the tradition's texts as well as serious engagement with the subject matter of social justice. Transgender Torah interpretation—Torah broadly interpreted here to include the entire spectrum of the creative Jewish world: the Five Books of Moses, the body of oral law, classical and modern commentary, but also secular Jewish literature, film, and other creative work—has the potential to transform the Jewish world.

Such a transformation is already well underway. Gender variance is certainly represented in Torah: ample evidence exists to suggest that Judaism's sages might have thought of a trait or two exhibited by the revered patriarchs and matriarchs of Jewish tradition in terms that we would today consider gender variant. One resource in support of this idea may be found on the Web site of Torah Queeries, a project of Jewish Mosaic: The National Center for Sexual and Gender Diversity. One Torah queery provides an example: the biblical patriarch Joseph was still called a boy or young man, *na'ar*, at age seventeen, long past the age at which Jewish boys are called men. The word *na'ar* in this context was disconcerting enough for classical commentators to attempt to explain its presence. In a Torah commentary, Gregg Drinkwater says that "in the midrash, the sages suggest that although Joseph was indeed seventeen, he 'behaved like a boy, penciling his eyes, curling his hair, and lifting his heel' (Genesis Rabbah 84:7) . . . Calling Joseph a boy is a way of feminizing him while also questioning his emotional and social maturity."[2] Setting aside speculations about Joseph's sexual preference based on present-day gender stereotypes, what we see in the story of Joseph is an effeminate, dreamy youth who was different enough for his odd gender presentation to be noted in our most sacred text.

Extraordinarily, Matriarch Rebecca, wife of Isaac, is also called *na'ar* five times (rather than *na'arah*, "girl," the feminine version). Classical commentators recognize this as a *ukere/ketiv*, a marginal note in biblical texts that marked what may have been a simple scribal error (literally, "read and written," which indicates that the text is read one way [*na'arah*, in this case] and written otherwise *[na'ar]*). Commentators often look for deeper meanings in such "errors." In another *Torah Queeries* commentary, Rachel Brodie suggests that the word *na'ar* is used intentionally to indicate our matriarch's female masculinity.[3] She suggests further (expanding on Rabbi Joseph B. Soloveitchik's interpretation of *ukere/ketiv*) that the *kere* (the text that is read) represents Rebecca's public feminine *(na'arah)* persona, while the *ketiv* (the text that is written) represents Rebecca's inner *(na'ar)* masculinity. Brodie concludes her *derash* (sermon) with a statement of a complex gender identity for Rebecca that might be recognizable to some transgender persons today: "Rebecca may have been physiologically and emotionally more of a *na'ar*, while presenting to the world the image of (making people 'read' her as) a *na'arah*." Brodie's inspired use of the common transgender parlance of "being 'read'" by one's physiology rather than by one's true gender puts transgender jargon into the very act of reading Torah.

In "God's Hidden Name Revealed" Rabbi Mark Sameth makes a connection between various gender-blending encounters with biblical patriarchs and matriarchs and moves to solidify the Reform movement's tradition of gender equality with a radical statement about the nature of God.[4] The gender-blending of our biblical forebears, he argues, is intentional, because the hidden name of God blends both genders, and humans are created *b'tzelem elohim* (in the image of God).[5] Sameth presents a compelling argument that *yud hay vav hay*, the four Hebrew letters that signify the unpronounceable name of God, are a "code" for the true name of God, which is *yud hay vav hay* read backwards (as a mystic might read a line of symbols), or *hay vav hay yud*. When read back to front, the letters spell out the Hebrew words *hu hi*, literally, "he, she." God is both sexes combined as a Whole Being. Sameth's reading utterly transforms the central prayer of Judaism, the Shema. *Shema Yisrael, Adonai Eloheinu, Adonai Echad*, which is usually rendered in English as "Hear O Israel, the Lord our God, the Lord is One," becomes "Hear O Israel, He-She is our God, He-She is One."[6] He concludes with the emphatic statement that gender equality for Reform Judaism is "*not* a modern and somehow less authentic invention, but emblematic of Judaism's most ancient conception of God."[7]

Gender variance is also surprisingly well represented in postbiblical Jewish texts. While Jewish legal texts specify a rigid two-gender grid, the discourse surrounding the law allows for a surprising amount of human variation. Many transgender and allied teachers have used the text of Mishnah Zeraim, Bikkurim, chapter 4, to teach about gender variance in texts from the rabbinic period of Jewish history.[8] These same teachers mention seven genders accounted for in the pages of Jewish law: *androgynos* (the hermaphrodite of classical literature and art, with one set each of female and male genitals), *tumtum* (whose genitals are hidden behind a flap of skin), *saris adam* (a eunuch castrated by humans), *saris chama* (a eunuch "of the sun" castrated by nature, that is, born, not made), *aylonit* (a female whose puberty is delayed for unknown reasons, whose voice and appearance may be masculine), *zachar* (man), and *nekevah* (woman).[9] Of course, considering these categories to represent nonbinary "genders" is a modern interpretation; the rabbis who wrote these texts probably thought of these outliers as differences that reinforced (and did not challenge) the binary.

Taken together, the powerful and persuasive recognition of gender variance in biblical and rabbinic tradition (as well as areas of the Jewish world I haven't touched on here, including Jewish mysticism, medieval texts, and the fiction of Isaac Bashevis Singer, to mention only three other examples), is a thread that extends the length and breadth of Jewish textual tradition. This strong thread compels the investigation of our cherished religious practices, *minhagim* (customs), and secular scholarship through the lens of gender variance and urges us to recognize and grant sufficient merit to the already existing Jewish spaces beyond and between the typical male/female binary. The sages have laid out the conceptual territory; those of us with eyes to see it are welcome to bring it to the fore so that our lives might be seen in the context of our tradition, rather than solely as unprecedented phenomena.

There are barriers to this push beyond the binary from expected and unexpected sources. The view of Orthodox halachists is an expected barrier, in which the rigid binary of male and female is unalterable; sex change even to save a life is forbidden.[10] A rabbinic tradition that bases the truth of gender on variable human perception notwithstanding (that is, the visible genitalia determine a single gender possibility), halacha rigidly interpreted prohibits the recognition of the true gender of a transsexual (the expressed gender identity that varies from the expected norm).[11]

The Jewish academic tradition, usually thought to be a liberalizing influence, offers an unexpected barrier to pushing beyond the binary, at least from the perspective of classic Talmudic interpretive traditions. In the instance of *androgynos* at least, even present-day feminist interpreters conclude that while sexual ambiguity exists in the legal tradition, modern conceptions of gender identity have no meaning for the ancients. Academics claim that the project of the rabbinic writers of the Mishnah was to test the limits of the law by imagining challenging test cases like the *tumtum* and the *androgynos*. Rather than being a document describing how an actual community might have lived in antiquity, the Mishnah was created as a teaching tool to train future rabbis, something like a textbook of case law that will establish a set of precedents for how the rabbi-as-interpreter-of-law should respond to legal questions. Academics are interested in recognizing how these texts were used in the context of ancient civilization.

Activists and religious leaders interested in creating space in the Jewish world for transgender lives, on the other hand, tend to ignore the opinions of the academics and the majority opinions of halachic decisors who recognize only prohibition and the establishment of legal limits of the law. The activists' and religious leaders' task is to happily and freely blend rabbinic characters and present-day transgender social agendas without restriction. This is not an active contest between academics and activists, wherein activists who "read gender into the text" are decried by academics; rather, to paraphrase feminist academics I've spoke to on this topic, "As an activist, any interpretation you make of the text is as valid as any other. Just don't call it scholarship." I can live with that, but I suspect someday activists and academics will meet in the productive and ambiguous middle. There is usefulness and opportunity in creative use of these texts.

This chapter contains text study, *derashim* (sermons), theological speculation, and halachic discussion.[12] The question this chapter attempts to engage is framed succinctly by Judith Plaskow in her essay "Dismantling the Gender Binary within Judaism": "If one can hardly say anything about the obligations of a Jew without immediately talking about gender, then what happens to a Jew whose gender is in principle undeterminable?"

A central focus of the chapter is the text of Mishnah Androgynos, which is considered from various perspectives: academic, activist, and pastoral. This text offers a glimpse at a rabbinic character who has both male and female genitals, and whose "differently gendered" obligations require hir to cross the mechitza *and* to take a position balanced on top. My own opinion echoes Dr. Plaskow's (from the essay referenced above): if activists, scholars, and religious leaders can find a way into text, the way beyond the binary will be open.

The translation I include of Androgynos at the beginning of the chapter is my own; I've coupled my translation with a sidebar providing an activist's reading of several significant parts of the text. This sidebar is followed by the conclusion from Charlotte Elisheva Fonrobert's "Regulating the Human Body," which provides a feminist academic reading of Androgynos.[13] The next essay, "An Ancient Strategy for Managing Gender Ambiguity," is also mine. Both this essay and the sidebar I mentioned above originate from the study I undertook as a Jewish studies graduate student of Mishnah Bikkurim chapter 4, Androgynos (Hermaphrodite). I intercut my work with Fonrobert's so readers would have an opportunity to identify the points of departure of both scholars and activists, and to think through the alternative viewpoints and methods of scholarship and activism. In "Created by the Hand of Heaven," Rabbis Reuben Zellman and Elliot Kukla employ the ancient text of Androgynos to challenge the present-day treatment of many intersexuals, whose ambiguously sexed bodies are surgically and hormonally altered to "fit" one of the two "acceptable" binary gender categories. In "Dismantling the Gender Binary within Judaism," Judith Plaskow indicates that, in the right hands, the text of Mishnah Androgynos could provide a lever long enough to move the world past the gender binary. Rachel Biale outlines for community leaders those aspects of the Jewish world that are affected by genders "Beyond the Binary Bubble," and in so doing pours the foundation of the road to change. "Judaism and Gender Issues" contains Beth Orens's summary of a minority Orthodox halachic opinion that enables transsexuals to move beyond prohibition to live an Orthodox Jewish life. Rabbi Jane Litman takes aim at the limiting, well-meaning, but misguided determinist argument that says GLBT people are "born that way." To wrap up the chapter and the book, Julia Watts-Belser offers the blessing of a "Transing God/dess."

This final chapter goes into the heart of the Jewish gender binary and explores the territory beyond.

Notes

1. For a discussion of Jewish law and trans embodiment, including the various positions of Jewish movements relative to transgender embodiment, please read Beth Orens's essay "Judaism and Gender Issues" in this anthology and the editor's note accompanying that piece.

2. Gregg Drinkwater, "Joseph's *Fabulous* Technicolor Dreamcoat," Parashat Vayeshev, Gen. 37:1–40:23, Jewish Mosaic Torah Queeries project, December 16, 2006, www.jewishmosaic.org/torah/show_torah/53.

3. Rachel Brodie, "When Gender Varies: A Curious Case of *Kree* and *Kteev,*" Parashat Chayei Sarah, Gen. 23:1–25:18, Jewish Mosaic Torah Queeries project, November 2, 2007, www.jewishmosaic.org/torah/show_torah/91.

4. Rabbi Mark Sameth, "God's Hidden Name Revealed," *Reform Judaism,* Spring 2009/5769. Among these is the midrashic recognition that the first created being, the Adam, was both male and female; Moses was "a nursing father" (Num. 11:12); Eve, the mother of all living, and Rebecca (who fetches water for the servant of Isaac) are referred to in Gen. 3:20 using the masculine pronoun.

5. Ibid.

6. *Adonai* (Lord) is a substitute for YHVH *(yud hay vav hay).*

7. Sameth, "God's Hidden Name Revealed," 33.

8. Elliot Kukla, "Terms for Gender Diversity in Classical Jewish Texts," *TransTorah,* www.transtorah.org. Mishnah is an early legal code. Talmud is (to put it simply) an

explanation of the Mishnah. There are 149 references to sex- and/or gender-variant persons in Mishnah and Talmud (first through eighth centuries CE); 350 in classical midrash and Jewish law codes (second through sixteenth centuries CE).

9. Ibid. *Tumtum* is referred to 181 times in Mishnah and Talmud; 335 in classical midrash and Jewish law codes.

10. Other than the minority opinion of the Tzitz Eliezer, whose work is described in Beth Orens's essay "Judaism and Gender Issues" later in this anthology.

11. The Tzitz Eliezer is the only dissenting opinion.

12. For many essays in this chapter, sufficient context is provided in the chapter introduction. Therefore, not every essay in this chapter includes an editor's note.

13. Charlotte Elisheva Fonrobert, "Regulating the Human Body: Rabbinic Legal Discourse and the Making of Jewish Gender," in *The Cambridge Companion to the Talmud and Rabbinic Literature,* ed. Charlotte Elisheva Fonrobert and Martin S. Jaffee (Cambridge: Cambridge University Press, 2007). The entire chapter was too broadly focused to include here, but I highly recommend reading it in its entirety.

Intersexed Bodies in Mishnah: A Translation and an Activist's Reading of Mishnah Androgynos*

Noach Dzmura

[Concerning the hermaphrodite]: There are in him manners[1] equivalent[2] to men, there are in her manners equivalent to women, there are in hir manners equivalent to men and women, and there are in zir[3] manners equivalent to neither men nor women.[4]

Manners equivalent in them to men: he conveys Levitical impurity in semen like men; he may marry but may not be married to a man, like men; like men he may not be alone with women; he may not be sustained with the daughters in matters of inheritance like men; he is obligated to all the mitzvot proclaimed in the Torah, like men; he may not put on female clothing or cut [his hair as women do]

The first paragraph to the left acts as a table of contents for a set of communal obligations, organizing the material that follows in the next four paragraphs by topic sentence. The hermaphrodite may exhibit behaviors that signal maleness, femaleness, "both sexes," and "neither sex" to the community.

His external appearance is male. His public behavior is male. He behaves toward women as a heterosexual man. However, his male exterior conceals female genitalia. He is not a man, but his community may see a man when they look at him.

---

*A translation of Mishnah Zeraim, Bikkurim, Perek Dalet, Androgynos (Mishnah Seeds, First Fruits, Chapter 4, Hermaphrodite).

like men; he may not make himself impure by corpses like men; he may not transgress "you shall not round off," "you shall not mar" like men.

Manners equivalent in them to women: she may become Levitically impure with menstrual blood like women; she may not be alone with men like women; she may not contract a levirate marriage like women; like women she does not receive a portion [of the inheritance] with the sons; she may not share in the holiest things like women; she is unfit to give any testimony mandated in the Torah like women; if she had prohibited intercourse her sons are prohibited from qualifying for priesthood like women.

Manners equivalent in them to (both) men and women: s/he is obligated for damages incurred as though s/he were a man or a woman; the one who kills hir intentionally is put to death; if unintentionally the murderer receives asylum in the cities of refuge; hir mother will observe, on account of hir birth, the period of blood purification as if she had borne both a female and

She may be capable of pregnancy, so her behavior toward men is female (avoiding one-on-one social contact). Because she appears male, observers of her female-coded behavior toward men might not know how to interpret her behavior; perhaps it would seem a gender-variant masculinity. Since this is the way she is obligated to behave, her gender-variant form of masculinity might eventually be viewed as "another acceptable type of man"—that is, unless she is mistakenly perceived as (simply) male. To prevent such mistakes, some form of perception management is required.

This paragraph insures that s/he receives basic human rights, just as both men and women do. "Both" in this paragraph indicates equivalence to men and women, "sameness." "Neither" (in the next paragraph) indicates "otherness" or dissimilarity to other humans.

*The last two paragraphs of Androgynos are peculiar in that they spell out obligations **for others** in the community rather than for the hermaphrodite: "hir murderer" is men-*

a male child, and brings an offering on account of the child as though both a male and female child had been born; s/he inherits all (if s/he is an only child) the inheritance like men and women; s/he eats holy things eaten outside of Jerusalem like men and women; if one said, "I am a Nazirite if this is both a man and a woman," then he is a Nazirite.

Manners equivalent in them to neither men nor women: they are not obligated on account of hir uncleanness; they do not burn (an offering) on account of hir uncleanness; zie cannot be subject to valuation like neither men nor women; zie cannot be sold as a Hebrew slave like neither men nor women; and if a person said, "I am a Nazirite if this is neither a man nor a woman," then he is a Nazirite. Rabbi Yosi says, "*Androgynos* is a being created in zir own image and the sages could not decide whether he was a man or she was a woman, but *tumtum* is judged either a doubtful man or a doubtful woman."

tioned, as is "hir mother," and an anonymous "they" who incur no obligation because of hir action or inaction, and finally the "one" who takes a Nazirite vow on the condition of hir "bothness" or hir "neitherness."

The writers of this text involve others in the process of ritually calling attention to the hermaphrodite as a human who exhibits "bothness" and "neitherness"—characteristics which would otherwise be hidden under hir slightly feminized (as described on the previous page) masculine behavior and appearance. The hermaphrodite is a special case—no other set of religious obligations crosses gender boundaries or requires the assistance of other community members to help realize the truth about a person's communal behavior.

To this activist (who often engages in managing communal perceptions about transgender "bothness" and "neitherness" that is hidden under a single-sex appearance), the writers of this text appear to have performed the postmodern task of managing perceptions about this dual-sex being, so that the community might recognize the truth of a complicated sex, rather than make a mistake and misinterpret a being who looks and behaves in public like a man.

Notes

1. Alternative translations for the Hebrew word *derachim:* "manners," "ways," "things."

2. Alternative translations for the Hebrew word *shaveh:* "equivalent to," "similar to," "like."

3. *Zie* and *hir* are gender-neutral pronouns. Hebrew is a binary-gendered language, and the hermaphrodite is referred to in the masculine. I use this and other gender-neutral pronouns in my translation. I got the idea to use male, female, binary gender inclusive *(s/he),* and binary gender exclusive *(zie, hir)* pronouns from Reuben Zellman.

4. Charlotte Elisheva Fonrobert translates this passage: "[As far as the] androginos [is concerned]: there are *with* regard to him [grammatical gender] *ways* in which he is *similar* to men, and there are ways with regard to him in which he is similar to women, and there are ways with regard to him in which he is similar to both men and women, and there are ways in which he is dissimilar from both men and women" (emphasis mine). Fonrobert, "Regulating the Human Body," 273. I include this substantially similar translation here to emphasize differences (*with* vs. *in; ways* vs. *manner; similar* vs. *equivalent*). See my essay "An Ancient Strategy for Managing Gender Ambiguity" later in this volume for more about these choices.

Regulating the Human Body: Rabbinic Legal Discourse and the Making of Jewish Gender

Charlotte Elisheva Fonrobert

Editor's Note

This essay is a reprint of the two-page conclusion of Fonrobert's chapter in The Cambridge Companion to the Talmud and Rabbinic Literature on how the body is presented in rabbinic literature. The summary presents a feminist academic view of androgynos (the hermaphrodite). While for the surrounding Greek and Roman cultures the term hermaphrodite was often used as a way to speak about gender variance, especially effeminate masculinity, rabbinic literature uses hermaphrodite to talk about anatomical variations. Fonrobert's argument is that for rabbinic thought, sex variation is recognized and included within the legal fabric, while gender remains a constant binary. The point of including sex variations in rabbinic legal thinking is not to demonstrate the tolerance of the Jewish religion nor to "embrace human diversity," as transgender activists might like to read into these texts, but rather, to demonstrate that halacha is robust enough to contain even these anatomical outliers.

Rabbinic thinking about the body as articulated in the early discussions of a legal nature can be summarized in this way then: predominantly the rabbinic sages project an assumption of the existence of two kinds of human bodies as far as their sex is concerned, male and female. At the same time, rabbinic legal thinking admits to a greater variability of human bodies. There are male and female bodies, and bodies that are both, others that are neither, to name those that we have discussed here. To expand the list a bit more, there are eunuchs, and their female counterparts, whom we did not discuss here.

The question remains why the rabbinic sages devoted so much space to discuss the legal repercussions of sexual ambiguity in the figure of the hermaphrodite. If this were simply a sign of their anxiety about the stability of the dual-gender grid of their lawmaking, it might have been easier for them to simply ignore this figure and go about their ways. Perhaps this was not an option, due to the omnipresence of the hermaphrodite in all kinds of discursive contexts. At the very least we are confronted with an interesting constellation, especially in view of the feminist theoretical argument mapped in the beginning of this essay. The rabbinic sages admit to a significant degree of sexual variability. This hardly amounts to the scale of sexual identities that contemporary advocates for intersexuality point to, where human bodies and their sexual identity are considered to be as variable as can possibly be imagined along the scale of "intersexuality." Still, contrary to the situation theorized by [gender theorist Judith] Butler where the duality of genders in a "heterosexualist" economy of gender is rooted in a promotion of a two-sex system, the rabbis' legal thinking did indeed allow for a variety of sexual ambiguities. In fact, we have to take note that the rabbis maintain a legal system with a dual-gender grid in spite of ambiguous bodies. And they did not consider these as external to the system they crafted, but they integrated them into the system. Hence, hermaphrodites are not only human, but they are Jews, something that must be emphasized in view of the cultural alternatives also available in the Roman world. They are to be circumcised (if not on the Sabbath), and they can marry.

Contrary to the sophists, the rabbinic sages hardly ever deploy the hermaphrodite as a term to designate effeminacy, of deceptive masculinity, a masculinity that only pretends to be one but really is not. Such patterns of thought the rabbinic sages refuse. The baby may not be considered male enough to justify something as severe as transgression of the Sabbath for his circumcision, but in the end this is more a question of whether the biblical law that explicates "male" applies to him as it does to a male baby than of whether he is really "male enough."

There is a stark juxtaposition between the variability of bodies, admitted into legal consideration, and the absolute insistence of the gender duality of law. Sex is variable, but gender is not. In the end, perhaps, it only makes sense that the hermaphrodite could not be considered "a creature in its own right" by the rabbinic sages. It was much more important to demonstrate that the Torah, in the form of law or halacha, could absorb everything under its mantle. Thus, the repeated insistence on fitting the hermaphrodite into the legal conditions as instituted by the rabbinic sages could only serve to demonstrate the viability of their law.

An Ancient Strategy for Managing Gender Ambiguity

Noach Dzmura

Western cultures deal with gender in terms of binary norms, instantaneous categorization, and certainty. Transgender people force us to confront gender in a more complicated way, tacitly or overtly positing a hard to define "third space" that exists outside the gender binary. It can be hard to categorize a person in a gender category, and harder still to remain certain about gender as a person transitions. Transgender ideologies ask us to recognize and grow comfortable with ambiguity and uncertainty. Transgender ideologies ask us to support transpeople in both their binary and their nonbinary self-identifications—even when such identifications occur simultaneously. How do we develop the tools to see the world in this unfamiliar way? These challenging postmodern propositions are not entirely without precedent in the ancient world. Mishnah Androgynos introduces and reifies three postmodern ideas about the management of gender ambiguity:

1) Ambiguity or indeterminacy can serve as a valid category of recognition, a "third space" in the context of a binary norm. In the same way, an electron in particle physics is said to be located within a cloud of possibilities rather than in a specific, predeterminable position. All possible positions within a common set are equally likely, equally true. Rather than certainty, this category of recognition is characterized by doubt. In other words, like Schrödinger's cat, which is both dead and alive until such time as an observation is made, the Mishnaic hermaphrodite is single-sexed and double-sexed and neither-sexed all at the same time— at least until the law requires a movement toward one state or another.

2) The category of third space embraces each pole of the normative binary and recognizes a space beyond it. A common set of options co-

exist within this third space, from which situational or relative truths may be extracted. These situationally applied truths do not invalidate the third space's overarching ambiguity. Rather, the situation-specific truths (certainties like "male," "female," "both," or "neither") exist for a brief time in a longer-term container of indeterminacy (an uncertainty that contains "male," "female," "both," and "neither"). Interestingly, third space introduces the idea of *time* to the consideration of gender.

3) In order to collectively recognize an ambiguous or indeterminate third space alongside a recognized binary requires training (in the form of a statement of identity followed by reinforcement by another member of the community and renegotiation of terms between community members) about two simultaneous realities: a situational truth plus the recognition of third space as an overarching category. When such reinforcement occurs in Mishnah Androgynos, the rabbis seem uncharacteristically to be showing us that social role is not the sole determinant of gender; rather, the community participates in constructing the hermaphrodite's nonbinary gender identity.

The essay below shows how, against academic convention, I imagined these postmodern ideas in an ancient text. The subheading "It Takes a Village" takes readers past the surface to the underlying tensions in Androgynos, and shows how time and communal assistance are implicated in gendering the hermaphrodite. The subheading "Doubt and Difference: Translation Notes" shows how ambiguity-over-time acquires the stability required to comprise a category of recognition.

It Takes a Village

Since God commanded two genders ("male and female created he them," Gen. 1:27), the rabbis were limited in how they could approach the obligations of another human type. The strategy they arrive at is almost unique in rabbinic literature. S/he is to perform some behaviors in the way a man does, some behaviors in the way a woman does, some behaviors in the way both men and women perform them, and some behaviors as they are performed uniquely by a person who is neither man nor woman.[1]

On the surface, Androgynos appears to describe a separate human category that is strikingly balanced, covering each of the gender possibilities equally (equivalent to men, equivalent to women), and also seeming to see past the binary sex/gender system to encompass a being who embodies both genders, or neither (that is, equivalent to both men and women, equivalent to neither men nor women). Once one looks carefully at the way Androgynos is structured, this apparent democratic instinct seems much more complicated, and tells us that the rabbis maintained masculine dominance even within a dual-sex individual.[2]

Jewish religious obligations in antiquity circumscribed a wide range of personal behaviors, including such things as hair and clothing styles, the type of offerings one brought to the temple, laws of inheritance, and avoidance of the opposite sex before marriage.

These obligations were markedly different for members of each sex. If an observer did not know a person's gender in this ancient society from the clothing they wore (hard to imagine this situation, since clothing was gender-coded, but play along with me in this thought experiment), the observer would soon be able to identify a man or a woman via their daily duties. Mishnah Androgynos (translated above) organizes a set of religious obligations for a person with two sexes—two sets of genitals, one male and one female. Historically, such a person was referred to as a *hermaphrodite*. True hermaphroditism is mythical, but a condition called *pseudohermaphroditism* does occur (rarely), and other intersex conditions (genitalia that exhibit some aspects of both sexes) are quite common. If these ancient words might be said to apply to any modern persons Androgynos applies to intersexed people.[3] I think it is also helpful to classify some transpeople (including myself) in the same category as the intersexed, because our hormonally and surgically altered bodies retain characteristics of both sexes.

The authors of Androgynos didn't think of gender as a set of rules that could be modified according to a personal truth of an incongruent relationship between the physical sex of a body and the gender identity one expresses, but there's nothing to prevent readers of that ancient text today from thinking that way. This text, studied in synagogues today, can be useful in sharing with one's community those complicated personal truths about gender, which might then be incorporated into communal perceptions. In this essay, I want to put forth the idea that the ancient authors of Androgynos seem to have understood that it takes a village to communicate a complicated truth, in surprising agreement with the postmodern idea that perceptions of reality are socially constructed—and communally altered.

The Mishnah did not outline a distinct "third gender space" for the hermaphrodite that was easy to identify. Instead, the authors borrowed some behaviors from men and some from women, and cobbled together an ambiguous dual gender characterized by doubt.[4] The intersexed person the Mishnah is concerned with has a set of prescribed obligations that intentionally cross gender boundaries. Nevertheless, Mishnah Androgynos sets out a consistent prescription of behaviors such that, if an observer watched such a person long enough in the performance of hir daily duties, that observer would be able to correctly identify the person as a hermaphrodite, having distinguished both male- and female-coded behaviors. An observer's *certain* classification of the person as a hermaphrodite could only be made when other community members were observed together with the presumptive hermaphrodite. Those behaviors in Mishnah Androgynos that label a hermaphrodite as belonging to a category that is "both male and female" or "neither male nor female" are performed by other community members on behalf of the presumptive hermaphrodite (see paragraphs four and five of the translation, above).

How does such confused gender-coding play out socially? There was no real community governed by Mishnaic law; rather, in the Mishnah the rabbis constructed a legal fiction to flesh out and test the law. Engaging the imagination to construct a hypothetical social life for this fictitious ancient community can be a useful activity for thinking about gender in present-day society. Rather than being simple to decode and mutually exclusive, like the obligations for men and women, the gender identity for the intersexed person is ambiguous and challenging to decode. It takes time and observation in context to understand the hermaphrodite's behavior. Because this being's obligations required hir to cross genders, s/he might have been difficult to "read" and thus hard for a hypothetical observer to correctly and infallibly identify. If one did not observe the presumptive hermaphrodite for a long period of time together with other community members, one could make a mistake in identifying the sex and gender of the hermaphrodite.

An example: Hir dress and public behavior are patterned after male behavior. Hir external appearance follows a male pattern. Hir public behavior is male. S/he avoids one-on-one contact with women like any other unmarried man. However, hir male exterior conceals female genitalia. S/he is not a man, but hir community may see a man when they look at hir, because most of the public behavior s/he is required to perform marks hir as a man. However, since the hermaphrodite may be capable of pregnancy, s/he is required to avoid one-on-one social contact with men, too. Hir avoidance of both male and female companionship might appear strange and uncategorizable. If the hypothetical observer saw only a few public behaviors, such an observer might mistakenly identify the hermaphrodite as a man, since, according to the rabbinic prescription in Androgynos, s/he dresses like a man and only performs a few, relatively private female-coded behaviors.

To prevent such mistakes (and such mistakes were directly linked to divine displeasure in the hypothetical construct of Mishnaic "society"), it seems to me that the authors of the Mishnah obligated other people to reinforce the gender of the intersexual—by publicly identifying the hermaphrodite's dual-sex status. One example: Hir mother is required to bring an offering to the temple when s/he is born. Rather than bringing the offering for a male child or a female child, she brings both sorts of offerings. Her community, who knows she did not give birth to twins, will get the message that her child is intersex. The mother's offering is a gender code. Another example: On certain unspecified occasions, a person is required to stand up and make a claim (supported by a vow of increased piety if the statement is true—called a Nazirite vow) that a hermaphrodite has male and female genitals, and therefore is neither male nor female. Nazirite vows were often made to support the truth of a statement that might otherwise be contested. In a culture where gender is a rigid binary, gender variance is invisible. Gender-variant bodies have no specific language, no categories of recognition. If what we talk about shapes and defines our reality, gender variance is wraith-like, visible only as deviation or *averah* (transgression). So it seems that even the ancients who wrote the Mishnah recognized as we do today that it takes a village to construct, reinforce, and police collective understanding of a nonbinary gender identity.

Today in Western cultures, many people mix or cross the binary lines of culturally specific gender-identifying behaviors. While we still attempt to classify people in gender boxes based on their behavior choices, transgender reality tells us that's no longer possible. Sight alone cannot tell us the entire truth about a person's gender. When I walk down the street, for example, people see a large bearded man. The reality of my female history is not apparent to the casual observer. To really understand my gender identity (if I didn't tell you outright), you would have to observe me and my community for a longer period of time, and allow the community to tell the story. Just like the hermaphrodite, whose story of dual sex must be told to the community by hir mother (when she makes the offerings at temple for both a boy child and a girl child) and by the Nazirites (who make the claim that s/he is both male and female and therefore not simply male or female), my story is told by my mother (who remembers her long-ago daughter with longing but speaks of her present-day son with love) and by my community (who know me as FTM and as an openly transgender activist). It takes a storyteller's eye to put together the full tale of a complicated gender identity.

Doubt and Difference: Translation Notes

Gender is what we do rather than what we are. Gender is a complex set of negotiated performances that indicate or divert attention from our hidden sexual organs and broadcast our sexual roles and preferences, rather than a simple binary code for what is between our legs. What gender is occupied by a person who has two sets of genitals? Since gender can also be described as one's sociosexual role, I think Mishnah Androgynos is an attempt to find a solution to that problem.

As an activist, I embrace this small corner of the Jewish canon as the core text for transgender inclusion.[5] While some academics and many present-day rabbis hold that the rabbinic hermaphrodite is a mythical creature not unlike the *koi* (an imaginary animal that is half domestic and half wild), I'd like to push this text out front and into our communities to discuss how gender variance can be accommodated within the existing binary, but also may push our capacity to recognize more than two genders in a sustained and systematic way.[6] More than any generic biblical text proclaiming the need for treating all people fairly "even to the stranger in your midst," the text of Mishnah Bikkurim chapter 4 says *of what fairness might consist,* and assures basic human rights are granted while "what is fair" is negotiated between members of a compassionate community. Mishnah Androgynos introduces the postmodern idea that—for all genders—one's social role is not the sole determinant of gender, and that certain negotiated alliances can foster recognition of a variant gender identity.

My version of Androgynos (appearing on pages 163–66) contains several key differences from typical academic and religious translations. The Hebrew word *derachim* (ways, manners, things) and the word *shaveh* (like, equivalent to) open interpretive possibilities in the text. Take for example the translations by classical commentators Pinchas Kehati and Herbert Danby. Pinchas Kehati translates *derachim* as "ways": "The *androgynos* is in some ways *(derachim)* like to men, in some ways like to women, and in some ways like to both men and women, and in some ways like to neither men nor women."[7] Herbert Danby translates *derachim* as "things": "The *androgynos* is in some things *(derachim)* like men, in some things like women, and in some things like both men and women, and in some things like neither men nor women."[8]

A reader of the Kehati or the Danby translations may be confused. A question remains as to whether "ways" refers to the physiology of the hermaphrodite, or hir behavior. One might ask the same question of Danby's "things"—must a body perform a certain way because one is equipped with certain things (a penis, perhaps, or both a penis and a vagina), or do the "things" refer to the behaviors one performs? A reader may also question the meaning of the word "like." Does it convey the meaning of identity (that is, "the same as"), parody or charade (almost, not quite), similarity (resemblance or approximation), or identity of behavior across differences of physiology? In reference to the text of Androgynos, if a hermaphrodite performs behavior assigned to women, does s/he *become* a woman, for that moment, under the law? Is she a half woman, whose male half remains unobligated during that momentary span of time? Or, is zie obligated like a woman and like a man at the same time, with halves of hir body compelled by different obligations? Or, is s/he truly "a creature in hir own image" only able to perform a parody of the behavior a (complete/whole/real) woman (or man) would perform?[9] Is the hermaphrodite who inherits from hir father's estate "acting like a man" or "really a man?" How much of that assessment depends on who is looking? I ask these questions to explore how an activist only peripherally influenced by scholarship (or halacha) might conceive of one kind of Jewish gender, the relationship between bodies and behaviors, and the communal implications of the hermaphrodite's carefully constructed gender performance.

In my translation, I chose to translate *derachim* as "manner" over "ways" or "things" to emphasize that the text is speaking primarily of behavior, although behavior almost always links to a particular anatomy. For the word *shaveh*, I chose "equivalent" over "like" to emphasize what I believe is the text's focus, which is not at all a matter of resemblance or parody, but rather, a matter of an authorized approximation. The hermaphrodite "does masculine" with the masculine half of hir body while the female half remains null. The result, rather than absolute ambiguity, is a limited (ephemeral?) typology: for the duration of the performance of the masculine act, there are two kinds of masculinity, one hermaphroditic, one male. The same applies to feminine acts.

As long as these categories are equivalent *(shaveh)* rather than hier-

archical, the idea that there might be recognized, authorized, or negotiated "kinds" or "types" of masculinity and femininity is liberating for
gender-variant persons in the present day.

The cumulative result of these word choices is to recognize in this
text not simply a body of legal precedents (as some academics and some
rabbis might view it), but to see the establishment of normative behavior and appearance of a hermaphrodite. Norms of behavior and appearance are actions that we perform—or performatives—for gender
expression. Rather than an abstract legal document, the text describes
norms of behavior and elucidates the ways the community may respond
to enforce or police those norms.

In my translation, I substituted gender-variant pronouns (s/he and
hir) because they help a reader of present-day American English (with
its strict binary gender system) to keep the hermaphrodite's dual gender
in mind. This option is not available in Hebrew, which defaults to a normative masculine gender (and therefore genders the hermaphrodite
masculine). When reading the Hebrew I found it easy to let the hermaphrodite's male gender pronouns enable him to "pass for male."
I think the loss of visibility of hir female aspects and dual nature
were rabbinic concerns as well (see my translation of Androgynos for
a discussion).

Perception is crucial to Jewish notions of gender. In fact, one minority Orthodox ruling on the "true gender" of a postoperative transsexual is based on the idea that perception carries halacha.[10] According to
this *possuk* (rabbinic legal decision maker), a transsexual woman is a
woman.

Safek (in the final paragraph of the translation) can mean both
"divided" and "doubtful." The word *safek* is used in Androgynos to
describe the sex of the *tumtum* (*safek zachar v safek n'kevah*—a "doubtful man or a doubtful woman").[11] What the phrase means is that the
tumtum might be a man or a woman, but there is no way to be sure
until/unless surgery to remove the skin flap over the genitals is performed. *Safek* is later used in the Talmud to describe the sexual status
of the hermaphrodite when considering whether s/he should be cir-

cumcised on the Sabbath. In this instance, the hermaphrodite is referred to as *safek zachar* (a "divided man," or the male half of a dual-sex person). Reading the modern world onto an ancient text in the way only an activist can, both senses of the word *safek* (as "doubtful" and as "divided") could be used in the case of the hermaphrodite, as a descriptor for gender that is uncertain. The hermaphrodite is a divided man/woman whose obligations to society variously express any of the following: sexual doubling, common asexualized humanity, maleness, or femaleness. Any of hir prescribed behaviors may result in the perceiver's doubt. If she is obligated according to hir "bothness" her masculinity and her femininity are covered over. If she is obligated according to her masculinity, her femininity and her "bothness" are covered over. There are additional permutations, but I won't spell them all out.

For academics, the modern concept of gender should not be brought into discussion of ancient texts; it's a modern construct and therefore irrelevant. As an activist outside of the academy, I am free to offer the word *safek,* inclusive of the connotations of both division and doubt, as a word that might describe the gender of a hermaphrodite.

The idea of official sanction of "true gender" that may be perceived as multiple, and "stable gender" that may be perceived as ambiguous *(safek)* offers potentially transformative options to the present day. In addition, it is liberating to recognize the hermaphrodite's gender as an expression of productive ambiguity rather than as a place of binary fixity, oppression, and/or repression.[12]

I'd like to put forward the idea that the perception of doubt or ambiguity about a person's gender is as valid a perception as is certainty. I'd like to hold up the irresolvability of the *androgynos's* gender identity as a desired condition. The irresolvable discomfort of the perceiver and the perceived that is inspired by doubt when one is confronted by a gender outside the ordinary is exactly the state that should be nurtured in Jews seeking to include transgender lives in their midst. It is a state wherein the participants are awake and aware to truth and human compassion, and the ability to relate as human companions is opened.

Notes

1. *S/he* is a pronoun that combines both male and female pronouns.

2. Fonrobert, "Regulating the Human Body."

3. Elliot Kukla and Reuben Zellman assert that intersexed people are a present-day analog of the Mishnaic hermaphrodite in the essay "Created by the Hand of Heaven" later in this anthology.

4. The last line of Mishnah Androgynos bears repetition here: "Rabbi Yosi says, '*Androgynos* is a being created in zir own image and the sages *could not decide* whether he was a man or she was a woman.'"

5. The Mishnah is the core text upon which is built the three hundred years of Rabbinic discussion that forms the Gemara, and together the Mishnah and Gemara are commonly known as the Talmud, a collection of halacha (law) and aggadah (story). The Mishnah was collected earlier than the Talmud (circa 200 CE), and not everything in the Mishnah became a subject of the Gemara. The Mishnah was studied in its own right, too, as training material for aspiring rabbis. For these and other reasons it is still studied today. Mishnah Androgynos is a five-paragraph text tacked (in a late redaction) onto the tail end of the tractate concerning agricultural matters, called Zeraim, or Seeds. Mishnah Androgynos deals in a sustained way with the ritual obligations of a hermaphrodite, conceived by the rabbis as a human in possession of a set of male genitals and a set of female genitals. While Androgynos appears only in some versions of the Mishnah, it always (and perhaps more properly) appears in an earlier collection of legal writings called the Tosefta. I refer to it as Mishnah here simply because it was this context in which I first found Androgynos. The texts are substantially the same from both sources; the only changes are to the number and order of listed obligations. The overall structure of the hermaphrodite's social role (and masculine gender presentation) is the same in all the texts. Mishnah Androgynos does not have a corresponding Gemara, but its subject (the hermaphrodite) is referenced close to three hundred times in the Talmud as a "special case" whose obligations vary from those of normative men and women.

6. The rabbis specify that the *koi* (Tosefta Bikkurim 1) is to be treated in some things like a wild animal, in some things like a domestic animal, in some things like both a wild and a domestic animal, and in some things like neither a wild nor a domestic animal. The *koi* is a mythical creature (sometimes described as half goat and half cow) employed by the rabbis to test the limits of the law.

7. Pinchas Kehati, *The Mishnah: A New Translation with a Commentary by Rabbi Pinchas Kehati,* trans. Rafael Fisch (Jerusalem: Eliner Library, Department for Torah Education and Culture in the Diaspora, 1996), 52.

8. Herbert Danby, *The Mishnah* (New York: Oxford University Press, 1933), 97–98.

9. Tosefta Bikkurim 2:7, *"androgynos biria bifnei atzmo hu."*

10. Tzitz Eliezer; see Beth Orens's essay "Judaism and Gender Issues" in this volume for more information.

11. A *tumtum* is a second human of variable gender in rabbinic texts. The *tumtum* is either a man or a woman whose sex cannot be known until/unless a flap of skin covering the genitals is removed.

12. I owe the idea of productive ambiguity to Ann Burlein's article "The Productive Power of Ambiguity: Rethinking Homosexuality through the Virtual and Developmental Systems Theory," *Hypatia* 20, no. 1 (Winter 2005): 21–53.

Created by the Hand of Heaven: Making Space for Intersex People

Reuben Zellman and Elliot Kukla

God spoke to Moses, saying: Speak to the Israelite people thus: When a woman at childbirth bears a male, she shall be unclean seven days ... She shall remain in a state of blood purification for thirty-three days ... If she bears a female, she shall be unclean two weeks as during her menstruation, and she shall remain in a state of blood purification for sixty-six days. On the completion of her period of purification, for either son or daughter, she shall bring to the priest, at the entrance of the Tent of Meeting, a lamb in its first year for a burnt offering, and a pigeon or a turtledove ... Such are the rituals concerning her who bears a child, male or female.

–LEVITICUS 12:1–7

After eighteen hours of labor, Eliana gave birth at 4:37 a.m. on the Tuesday before Passover. Over the baby's piercing cries, Eliana tilted her head upward and strained to hear the midwife's most important news. "Is it a boy or a girl?" The long months of pregnancy were finally over. Now, the midwife's answer would mean everything. Eliana (like all new parents) knew that, from the moment of birth onward, most facets of her child's life—the clothes it would be told to wear, the activities it would be anticipated to like, the careers and hobbies it would be encouraged to pursue, the loving relationships it would be expected to have—would be guided by the answer to this one crucial question.

Parashat Tazria opens with instructions to the Israelites regarding the birth of a baby. There are two separate sets of instructions to expectant parents, and they must begin following one of them immediately after their child is born. How to proceed is dependent on one factor: whether the baby is a girl or a boy. In the worldview of the Bible, as in the twenty-first century, it is usually assumed that there are two possible answers to this one crucial question. It is also assumed that this answer is immediately apparent from our first moments on earth—every person has either one body or the other one.

It isn't true.

The Intersex Society of North America states that one out of every one to two thousand infants are born intersex—they are born with physical traits that cannot be easily classified as male or female.[1] Many more people discover at the onset of puberty that they have ambiguous hormonal or chromosomal status. Intersexuality is quite common. But the twenty-first century is structured to allow two, and only two, sexes. There are two locker rooms, two gender boxes to choose between on every form we fill out, two diagrams in the science book, and two kinds of birth announcements: "It's a Girl" and "It's a Boy." So what do we do when someone doesn't "fit"?

We fix it.

Modern medical science has provided a "solution" to this challenge. If visible anatomy does not identify the sex of a baby, a surgeon operates to transform the infant into an unambiguous boy or girl. If an individual's body takes an alternate route to maturity at puberty, we promote hormone therapies to create conformity. Perhaps for the first time in history, our society today has the know-how—as well as a powerful desire—to force real people into one of the two categories found in this week's *parashah* (portion).

Andie, an intersex teenager, says: "I have not suffered because of my birthright, which is really how I now feel about being intersex. I have suffered because of well-intentioned intervention along the way that was meant to shape me into a person that someone else wanted me to be, that someone else believed I should be, that someone else thought was best for me. I was prodded and poked, photographed, examined and cut. I was six years old."[2]

This modern "solution" may seem like the only way to handle intersexuality in a strictly sexed and gendered society. But Jewish sacred tradition offers us a very different approach.

The Mishnah (Bikkurim 4:1) explains: "The *androgynos* in some ways is like men, and in some ways is like women, and in some ways is like both men and women, and in some ways is like neither men nor women." Among other things, we learn in this chapter of the Mishnah that if a woman gives birth to an *androgynos*—an intersex child with both male and female characteristics—then she is to observe the ritual laws for *both* a son *and* a daughter.

Like the Torah, the early rabbis of the postbiblical period were very concerned with defining the roles and expectations of women and men. But they also understood that humankind was not as simple as two sexes. The rabbinic sages struggled to understand the sometimes abstract or terse teachings of the Bible, and how those teachings applied to the complexity of the actual people that surrounded them. By the third century of the Common Era, Jewish civil and sacred law had begun to address the question of how to integrate intersex people into the gendered society of Jewish antiquity. This chapter of the Mishnah is just one of many texts that discuss the *androgynos* and the *tumtum*—two of the labels that the rabbis applied to intersex people in their time. The *tumtum* and the *androgynos* appear over three hundred times in the Babylonian Talmud alone! The Mishnah, the Talmud, and the later codes of Jewish law address questions about intersex people in every aspect of society: marriage, property, commerce, dress and conduct, puberty, inheritance, sex, conversion, and religious duties. Throughout our multivocal Jewish tradition, one teaching is clear: intersex people are to receive equal protection from harm, and their lives are to be sanctified, just like any other person.

In the twenty-first century, we confront those who don't "fit" and endeavor to change them. In antiquity, our rabbis took people as they really were and went on from there. There are many ways to read these texts, and the sages' approach is very far from perfect. They certainly do not advocate the overthrow of binary gender systems; they do not argue for sex and gender liberation, as some of us might wish that they had. But they also never question whether intersex people really exist, or whether these "conditions" were better eradicated. They do not advocate operations to transform a child's body to better fit a gender category. They understand that intersex people are created *"al y'dei shamayim"* (by the hand of heaven), and that every divine creation is entitled to be seen, considered, and included—exactly as they are.[3]

Today, we've gone back to the more simplistic worldview of *Parashat Tazria*. We have forgotten the more complex and humane approach of our classical thinkers toward intersex people. Modern medical science has created a world of intersex invisibility, perhaps more than any culture in any other era. Suzanne Kessler, a contemporary scholar who writes about intersexuality, states: "Genital ambiguity is corrected not because it is threatening to an infant's health, but because it is threatening to an infant's culture." As Jews, our sacred tradition provides us with both the resources and the mandate to transform our culture into one that is no longer threatened by God's creative hand. Our heritage asks us to speak out to stop the exclusion of intersex experiences, to celebrate the diversity of real bodies, and to challenge a culture of medical interventions on intersex people when they do not choose them for themselves. Traditional Jewish approaches toward intersexuality are complex and imperfect. But if we look back toward them, they can lead us forward, toward a society that has space for all of our unique identities, whether we are male, female, intersex, or something else.

In the Mishnah, Rabbi Yosi makes a radical statement: *"Androgynos bria bifnei atzma hu"* (The *androgynos*, he is a created being of her own). Our sacred texts frequently blend male and female pronouns, poetically expressing the complexity of intersex identity. The term *bria bifnei atzma* is a classical Jewish legal term for exceptionality. This term is an acknowledgment that not all of creation can be understood within binary categories. It recognizes the possibility that uniqueness can burst through the walls that demarcate our society. The Hebrew word *bria* (a created being) explicitly refers to divine formation; hence this term also reminds us that all bodies are created in the image of God. People can't always be easily defined; they can only be seen and respected, and their lives made holy. This Jewish approach allows for genders beyond male and female. It protects those who live in the places in between, and it opens up space in society for every body.

To challenge the myth of binary sex is to ask our society to reconsider some of the fundamental assumptions that we have all been taught since the day we were born. And yet this is exactly what Jewish sacred texts ask us to do. What if instead of asking "Is it a boy or a girl?" we simply celebrated that a new person has been created in the image of God? What if, whenever we are asked about a child's sex, we simply responded: "It's a created being of its own"? Jewish tradition recognizes that intersexuality is part of the beauty of the created world. Like our sages, we must insist upon telling the full truth about the diversity of God's creation.

Notes

1. Although the Intersex Society of North America (ISNA) is now defunct, their Web site remains a valuable resource for information about intersexuality. See www.isna.org.

2. Bodies Like Ours: Intersex Information, www.bodieslikeours.com (site now discontinued).

3. *Maggid Mishneh,* commentary on Rambam's *Hilchot Shofar* (2:1–3).

Dismantling the Gender Binary within Judaism: The Challenge of Transgender to Compulsory Heterosexuality

Judith Plaskow

Gender is one of the fundamental categories through which we order and interact with the world. Most people absorb the fundamental "rules" of gender at an early age, and these rules provide the basis for all relationships with others. There are two and only two genders, we are taught, male and female; all human beings who have ever lived are one or the other; gender is determined through visual inspection of a baby's genitals at birth, and remains unchanged throughout life; female/male dimorphism is natural, having nothing to do with social criteria or decisions, and so is individual membership in one gender or another.[1] These assumptions are so basic to the way in which we understand reality that anything that threatens them—a baby with ambiguous genitalia, a person on the street whose gender is difficult to determine, a man who is cross-dressed, a butch woman—may evoke both anger and a profound sense of vertigo. Violations of gender norms seem to endanger the foundations of the earth, the walls of our only safe and certain home in the universe.[2]

I would argue that we cannot comprehend the virulence of homophobia or the power of compulsory heterosexuality apart from these deep-set assumptions about gender. Homophobia and a binary understanding of gender are intertwined aspects of the same hierarchical system, and dismantling one requires exploring and attempting to dismantle the other. The very way gender is defined in U.S. society assumes the alignment of gender assignment, gender identity, gender role, and sexual desire. To be female or male is to be recognized as such from birth; to affirm this identity; to behave in certain expected ways in terms of emotional characteristics, interests, activities, and skills; and to be attracted to members of the "opposite" sex.[3] To be a proper woman or a proper man is to be heterosexual—to establish one's own gender through differentiation from the gender of the desired partner.[4] The same complex web of ideologies and institutions, of expectations, rewards, and punishments that teach us what it means to be a man or a woman also teach us that we will someday fall in love with someone of the other sex, marry, and create a family.[5] Gender roles guarantee that the smallest viable social unit will consist of one man and one woman whose desire must be directed toward each other, and that men have rights to women's sexuality, time, attention, and labor that women do not have either in relation to men or to each other.[6]

There have always been individuals and groups who have challenged this tightly ordered gender and sexual system, but their existence has often been interpreted in ways that reinforce heterosexuality and the gender binary. When the concepts of homosexuality and heterosexuality emerged in nineteenth-century Europe, for example, homosexuals were understood as inverts—those with marked characteristics of the other sex. The notion of the masculine lesbian and the effeminate homosexual man managed to combine gender and sexual variance into one neat package that preserved a dichotomous view of gender and desire.[7] The concept of homosexuals as wishing they were the other sex still shapes popular stereotypes and images of gays and lesbians and leads people to label and harass as gay those with nonstereotypical gender role self-presentations. The treatment of intersex infants—those born with ambiguous genitalia—has similarly been aimed at maintaining heterosexuality and a dichotomous understanding of gender. Doctors have been concerned not only to "correct" intersex children's genitals so that they can grow up as clearly female or male, but also to do so in a way that holds out the possibility of their living a "normal" adult heterosexual life. A child assigned as female must have a vagina that can receive a normal-size penis, while a child assigned as male must have a penis that can satisfy a female partner.[8] An analogous set of medical criteria has been used for the past fifty years to treat transsexuals. The protocols for sex reassignment surgery, like those for intersexuals, assume the existence of two and only two "opposite" genders. Those seeking surgery often find that they must demonstrate a firm commitment to heterosexuality, constructing compelling and "authentic" personal histories of exclusively heterosexual desire, whether or not these accord with their experiences.[9]

In each of these cases, a potential threat to a binary gender and sexual system is integrated back into the system, demonstrating its enormous power and flexibility and the stake of medical and other social institutions in maintaining it. But at the same time that these exceptions have been used to bolster the system, they still have the capacity to complicate and ultimately undermine it—particularly as various social movements over the last four decades have explicitly challenged the naturalness of both gender and heterosexuality. The feminist movement has demonstrated the socially constructed and damaging nature of gender roles, and certain strands within feminism have attacked the very notion of two genders as a tool for the oppression of women.[10] The lesbian, gay, and bisexual liberation movement has rejected the notion of inversion, claiming that there is no necessary correlation between gender and the contours of desire. A growing intersexual rights movement has called for an end to infant surgery and demanded that intersexed persons be able to make up their own minds about gender identity and surgery as they mature.[11] Increasing numbers of transsexuals, by refusing to live seamlessly and invisibly in their new gender identities, are rejecting the demand that they uphold the two-gender system. A new "transgender" movement is emerging that highlights the kinship among gender-variant identities and celebrates a multiplicity of ways of challenging the gender and sexual binaries.[12] This movement has the capacity to extend and deepen the feminist critique of gender roles and gender hierarchy by enacting and embodying the disruption of gender dimorphism.

In the rest of this essay, I will explore the relationship between moving beyond the gender binary and dismantling compulsory heterosexuality in the Jewish context. While rabbinic Judaism definitely maintains a hierarchical, dichotomous gender system and a notion of male/female marriage as a universal norm, the rabbis also seem to have been aware of the existence of gender-variant persons who threatened the stability of this system. Contemporary Jews committed to a nonsexist and non-heterosexist vision of Jewish life may be able to use rabbinic discussions of gender variance as a jumping-off point for a radical critique of gender and the compulsory heterosexuality with which it is intertwined.

Judaism, Gender, and Heteronormativity

Until the invention of the concept of heterosexuality in the modern era, Jewish culture was certainly heteronormative, but it was not explicitly homophobic. Male/male anal intercourse was forbidden and regarded as an "abomination," but it was the sexual *act* that was proscribed, not intimacy or attraction between men, which was in fact an important part of rabbinic culture.[13] Sex between women was also prohibited but was seen as a minor infraction. There is no evidence that the rabbis categorized people on the basis of the gender of their sexual object choice.[14] The relatively sparse legal literature dealing with same-sex sexual relations manifests none of the anxiety or horror that marks modern debates. It is clear that some Jews engaged in same-sex sex, and it seems that they were treated in the same way as those who violated any other legal prohibition. Contemporary statements that condemn "homosexuality" as prima facie disgusting and unnatural and that depict gays as threatening the Jewish family and all of civilization should be read in the context of recent gay demands for legitimacy and equality, rather than as expressions of an unchanging Jewish position.[15]

While Jewish tradition has not necessarily singled out same-sex sex for special opprobrium, however, it has been thoroughly heteronormative, in that it prescribes highly differentiated gender roles, develops elaborate legislation for preventing illicit sexual contact between women and men as if heterosexual sex were the primary temptation for everyone, and assumes that all Jews should marry. As one feminist scholar of rabbinics points out, "Jewish law is based on a fundamental assumption of gender duality."[16] Although there are many commandments (especially negative commandments or "thou shalt nots") incumbent on both women and men, it is virtually impossible to talk about Jewish legal obligations without talking about gender. The Mishnah, the second-century code of Jewish law that is the foundational text of rabbinic Judaism, frames and attempts to categorize individual laws in terms of a tightly gendered schema. The general principle it enunciates is that women are exempt from positive commandments that must be performed at particular times. While this principle is riddled with exceptions and contradictions, the rule holds that women are excused from certain crucial religious duties, such as praying three times daily and wearing tzitzit (fringes) and phylacteries, while adult men are never excused. The reason for women's exemption is not stated in the Mishnah and has been the subject of extensive interpretation and debate, but its effect is to release women from many of the ritual practices that constitute the center of a positive Jewish religious identity. It is possibly for this reason that the traditional Jewish man recites the infamous morning blessing thanking God for not making him a woman—because he carries the full burden and benefit of obligation, while women do not.

Even the briefest consideration of the gendered nature of Jewish law makes clear that the gender binary is asymmetrical. Indeed, it is impossible to talk about halacha (Jewish law) and gender without talking about hierarchy. Because those obligated to perform any commandment have a higher status in its performance than those who are not obligated, people who are exempt cannot perform religious acts on behalf of others—even should they choose to take on particular commandments for themselves. Thus, according to halacha, women cannot lead religious services or read publicly from the Torah when men are present. They are also exempt from Torah study, the quintessential form of Jewish religious expression. Traditional Jewish law views women as "enablers": they perform the tasks that allow men and boys to engage in regular prayer, observe numerous special rituals connected with the holidays, and have time to study, but women themselves are "peripheral Jews."[17] Not only are they secondary in the public realm, but they are also subordinate within marriage. A woman "is taken" or acquired in marriage, but she herself does not "take" or acquire a husband; her sexuality is sanctified to her husband, but his is not set apart to her; he has the right to divorce her by writing a bill of divorce, and, according to rabbinic law, he has the right to take other wives, but these rights are not reciprocal. Women's sexuality and reproductive functions constitute a central, though not exclusive, locus of anxiety for the Mishnah, which is deeply concerned to regulate and control these functions in the interests of a patriarchal system.[18]

A number of recent articles on the Jewish prohibition of male/male intercourse have argued that one of its key purposes is to maintain gender hierarchy. Leviticus 18:22 condemns the active partner in male anal intercourse, while Leviticus 20:13 sentences both the active and passive partners to death. As the rabbis elaborated on the laws of Leviticus, they dwelled on the humiliation of the man penetrated "like a woman," but they also continued to see the penetrator as guilty of a transgression.[19] His fault seems to lie in mixing or confusing kinds: a man who penetrates another man violates the gender binary, treating another man as one should treat only a woman, and thus moving a male body into the category of female. Like cross-dressing, which Leviticus also forbids, sex between men confuses borders that are meant to be kept clear as part of the order of creation. The weight of this violation is underscored by the fact that the very word for female in biblical and rabbinic Hebrew means "one with an orifice," as if being penetrated is natural to females but not to males.[20] Thus male/male intercourse endangers gender boundaries in two different ways: it "unmans" the particular man who is the penetrated partner, but it also threatens the notion of penetrative intercourse as a defining aspect of gender difference.[21]

The rabbis may have regarded sex between women as a less serious infraction than sex between men both because it is not explicitly prohibited by the Torah and because they did not see it as intrinsically threatening gender hierarchy. The brief Talmudic discussion of female homoeroticism revolves around whether women who "rub against each other" have lost their status as virgins and are forbidden to marry priests. The majority opinion is that such behavior is "mere indecency" and does not count as a disqualification. The argument assumes that "lewdness" *(mesolelot)* between women is not incompatible with marriage to men. Indeed, the one other Talmudic passage that touches on sex between women concerns a rabbi who forbids his daughters to sleep in the same bed together, lest they become accustomed to a foreign body. His worry seems to be either that the daughters are not yet ready for marriage or that they need to get used to sleeping alone during the period of menstrual impurity when married sex is forbidden. But unlike female homoeroticism, which evokes only mild anxiety, the possibility of marriage between women is roundly condemned by later sources. A midrashic commentary on the book of Leviticus interprets the "practices of the land of Egypt and the land of Canaan" referred to in Leviticus 18:3 as a man marrying a man and a woman marrying a woman. As medieval codifiers understood this text, marriage between women is forbidden by the Torah. The possibility of a woman taking on the role of husband is as unacceptable as a man taking on the role of wife because it threatens gender hierarchy and the institution of heterosexual marriage.[22]

The prohibition of male anal intercourse and marriage between women makes the relationship between heteronormativity and sharply differentiated gender roles very clear. But even where same-sex sex is not the explicit topic of rabbinic discussion, there is still a mutually constitutive relationship between dichotomized gender roles and the cultural insistence on male-dominated marriage. Whether we look at the work roles and obligations of women and men, the religious division of labor, issues of property rights, or the rabbinic conception of marriage, gender differentiation is part of a system in which the very meaning of being a woman or a man depends on taking certain roles within a heteronormative framework. The Mishnah's principle that I mentioned earlier of exempting women from positive time-bound commandments both presupposes and helps create a social structure in which women's primary obligations are to fathers, husbands, and children. In caring for small children, observing the dietary laws, preparing for holy days by readying their homes and cooking special foods, women free men for their own prayer and Torah study and enable them to observe the dietary laws and the Sabbath and holidays fully. At the same time, women need men to take on ritual roles in the home that they themselves are neither obligated nor educated to assume. Thus laws that seem to concern only religious obligations are also an important node in the construction of heterosexual marriage. The same point applies to other aspects of gender role division that appear only peripherally connected to the compulsion toward marriage. Just as a man is forbidden to violate gender boundaries by having sex with another man, so he is advised not to transgress gender norms by teaching his son a craft that is practiced among women. The rabbis seem to have been concerned both with preventing men from laboring alongside women and thus being tempted by illicit (heterosexual) sex and with protecting men from becoming like women by doing labor coded as feminine. The ultimate male work was Torah study, work that was limited to men by definition, and that marriage allowed them to pursue.[23]

Hermaphroditic Disruptions

Given the fundamental place of the gender binary in rabbinic thought and legislation, it is both surprising and understandable that the rabbis were fascinated by "exceptions" that might potentially disrupt the dichotomized gender system. Rabbinic texts describe a number of categories of persons who in some way extend or challenge the dominant schema of gender roles or gender dualism. The rabbinic classifications of *aylonit* (barren woman) and *saris* (eunuch), for example, refer to persons who are clearly female or male, but who confound gender role expectations by being unable to reproduce, and who thereby stand in a complicated relationship to the elaborate laws of marriage. The *aylonit* is defined as a woman who fails to produce two pubic hairs by a certain age, who never develops breasts, who finds sexual intercourse difficult, who does not have the lower abdominal curve of a normal woman (the meaning of the Hebrew is uncertain), and who has a deep voice that is indistinguishable from a man's. The *saris* is a man who likewise fails to produce two pubic hairs by a certain age; who has soft, smooth skin and no beard; whose urine does not froth, ferment, or form an arc; whose body does not steam when he bathes during rainy season; and whose voice is so thin, it is hard to tell whether he is male or female.[24] Within the Jewish legal framework, it was crucial that families be aware of these signs of infertility before arranging a marriage because the reproductive status of the partners affects important areas of marriage law. Both the *aylonit* and *saris* are exempted from levirate marriage, for instance (marriage with a deceased wife's sister as specified in Deuteronomy 25:5–10), because the purpose of such a marriage is to ensure progeny for a deceased man who has left no children. Similarly, since a man is legally required to have children, he should not marry a barren woman unless he already has children or has another wife who is fertile.[25]

In Roman culture, which generally had a profound impact on rabbinic Judaism, the eunuch was often depicted as less than male and associated with all kinds of vices. It is interesting, therefore, that the rabbis never ask whether the *saris* or the *aylonit* is a "real" man or woman; nor do they generally regard them as untrustworthy. The laws which refer to the eunuch and the barren woman treat them in almost all cases as having the same rights and responsibilities as anyone else of their gender—save where their infertility becomes important for the laws of marriage.[26] This suggests that the rabbis read gender off the basic morphology of the body. Just as in U.S. culture, gender is assigned on the basis of a baby's genitals at birth, so for the rabbis, the genitals were "the place from which it can be recognized whether s/he is male or female."[27] The presence or absence of secondary sex characteristics such as breasts or body hair in no way affected the status of the individual in Jewish law. Thus, it seems that the rabbis preferred tolerating a certain range of gender ambiguity to challenging gender dimorphism. They were willing to stretch the boundaries of femaleness and maleness to accommodate a deep voice in a woman or the absence of a beard in a male, and even to accept the maleness of a eunuch, rather than to entertain the notion of a multiplicity of genders.[28]

The rabbis also discussed two other categories of persons, however, whose bodies presented different and more ambiguous gender possibilities. The *tumtum* and *androgynos* (hermaphrodite), whom today we would label "intersexed" persons, are categories that often appear together in rabbinic literature.[29] The rabbis defined the *tumtum* as an individual who is actually a man or a woman, but who appears to have no genital organs because his or her genital area is covered over at birth. If the covering is later opened, and the person is found to be male, then he is considered a full male, or if she is found to be female, then she is considered a female in every respect. The *tumtum* raised a practical problem for the rabbis but not a theoretical one, because s/he fell within the binary system, though the rabbis might not know where. The *androgynos* is the more interesting category because s/he has the genitals of both sexes, and it can never be determined whether s/he is male or female.[30] S/he thus posed a serious challenge to a legal system thoroughly structured around a dichotomized understanding of gender. If one can hardly say anything about the obligations of a Jew without immediately talking about gender, then what happens to a Jew whose gender is in principle undeterminable? Rabbinic debates about the hermaphrodite shed interesting light on the rabbis' understandings of gender, gender hierarchy, and heteronormativity.

There are several different views of the *androgynos* in rabbinic literature. The majority position was that s/he is of uncertain sex, either male or female. Others argued, however, that s/he is part male and part female, others that s/he is definitely male, and still others that s/he is a creature sui generis. Some sages suggested that there are three doubts about the hermaphrodite: whether s/he is a distinct creature, a man, or a woman.[31] The question for the rabbis, then, when discussing any particular area of legal obligation, was how to define the hermaphrodite in such a way that, whatever her or his "true" status might be, no laws would be violated.[32] One passage in the Mishnah, for example, lists the ways in which the *androgynos* falls into the halachic (legal) category of men, the ways s/he falls into the category of women, the ways s/he straddles the two, and the ways s/he fits neither. The most important way in which s/he functions legally like men is that s/he can take a wife but not be taken (note the passive) as a wife. Also like men, s/he must perform all the commandments of the Torah and dress like a man.[33] S/he functions like women in that s/he contaminates with per[34] menstrual flow, must not be alone in the company of men, does not need to perform levirate marriage, and does not receive a share in inheritances with sons. S/he fits both categories in that anyone who maims per incurs guilt or who kills per is subject to punishment; per mother must bring an offering at the time of the birth, and s/he receives a share of sacrifices to be consumed outside the temple. Unlike men and women, however, s/he incurs no penalty for entering the temple unclean; s/he cannot be sold as a Hebrew slave, and s/he cannot be evaluated for the purpose of making an offering (see Lev. 27:2–7).[35] Clearly, the rabbis struggled to fit a doubly sexed person into the limits of a binary system without undermining any of the rules of that system.

The ingenuity with which they addressed this task can be seen from a couple of specific examples. According to Jewish law, girls reach maturity at twelve years and a day, while boys reach maturity at thirteen. Thus, in case s/he is a woman, the hermaphrodite is obligated to any precepts incumbent on women from twelve years and one day. S/he is exempt from any precepts not incumbent on women until the age of thirteen, however, because if s/he is a man, s/he is still a minor, and if s/he is a woman, s/he is exempt from these laws altogether. Rules of inheritance pose especially complicated issues for the rabbis, because these rules depend on overall family configuration, as well as the size of the estate. The majority view is that an only child who is a hermaphrodite inherits per father's whole estate. If an estate is large, and the father leaves a son and a hermaphrodite, the son inherits because he is clearly an heir, whereas the hermaphrodite is doubtful, but the hermaphrodite has a right to be maintained with the daughters. If the estate is small enough that everything would normally go for the daughters' maintenance, the daughters can relegate the hermaphrodite to the category of sons and say s/he has no right to a share. If a man leaves daughters and a hermaphrodite, they share the estate equally. The rabbi or rabbis (the texts are unclear) who see the hermaphrodite as sui generis, on the other hand, rule that s/he is not maintained with the daughters, because s/he is not a daughter; whereas those who see the hermaphrodite as a definite male say s/he inherits equally with a son.[36] Because the rabbis insist on fitting the hermaphrodite into the available, gendered, legal categories, rather than questioning those categories, the laws concerning the hermaphrodite help to clarify the ways that gender distinctions operate in relation to various areas of halacha.[37]

The gender ambiguity of the *androgynos* produces numerous shifts in per status, but where the rabbis must make a choice as to whether the *androgynos* is male or female, per default status seems to be male. This is suggested by the fact that the *androgynos* can marry a woman but cannot be taken as a wife, and that, in a culture in which cross-dressing was a serious violation, s/he must dress as a man. Of all the ways in which the hermaphrodite is "in some ways like men and in others like women," these are the ways that would have the greatest impact on daily life. The presence of testes carries more signifying weight than the presence of a vagina. Or as one contemporary Orthodox authority says in discussing the treatment of intersex infants, "The presence of testes, either external or internal, is an absolute indication that the child is not a female."[38] It is interesting to compare the default maleness of the *androgynos* with the "one drop rule" for determining race in many states in the American South. Light-skinned Americans with African ancestry have been defined and generally raised as black, as if "one drop" of so-called black blood were sufficient to contaminate their lineage. In the case of the hermaphrodite, however, the dominant status trumps the subordinate status. It would be unthinkable to treat as female someone who might be male or to make such a person into a wife.[39]

A central reason to treat the hermaphrodite as male has to do with the issue of preventing halachic violations. Because men are fully obligated to all the commandments and women are not, to treat a potential male as female is to run the risk that the *androgynos* might incur a long list of legal transgressions. Among the laws that the hermaphrodite must not infringe is the commandment not to lie with a man as one lies with a woman. A hermaphrodite cannot be taken as a wife because in the event s/he is male, marriage with per would constitute lying with a man. The rabbis are clear that men are liable for stoning for intercourse with a hermaphrodite, just as for intercourse with a male, but they debated whether men incur this penalty for *any* intercourse with a hermaphrodite, or just through the male orifice.[40] On one view, the hermaphrodite is counted as a male for sexual purposes, so any intercourse with per is forbidden. Indeed, one rabbi interprets Leviticus 18:22's prohibition on lying with a man as with a woman as referring specifically to the hermaphrodite, since only the hermaphrodite has two places of cohabitation.[41] The opposing view is that a man incurs the penalty for lying with a man only "when he comes upon him [the *androgynos*] in the way of males, but if he does not come upon him in the way of males, he is not liable."[42] For the rabbis who hold this position, the hermaphrodite is sufficiently male that s/he must not be penetrated by another man; yet its female genitalia retain independent significance. A similar debate about whether the hermaphrodite is fully and completely male occurs around the issue of circumcision, and whether one should circumcise a hermaphrodite on the Sabbath if it is the eighth day after birth. While all the sages agree that a hermaphrodite must be circumcised, some argue that circumcision overrides the Sabbath only in the case of a definite male, but not in the case of one whose status is in doubt. The alternative view is that the hermaphrodite should be circumcised on the Sabbath if necessary, because Genesis 17:10 reads "Every male among you shall be circumcised," and "every" includes the hermaphrodite.[43]

Implications

The figure of the hermaphrodite plays a paradoxical role in rabbinic thought, as it does in other cultural contexts. On the one hand, the hermaphrodite poses a problem that a binary gender logic must find a way to erase; it is a "necessary irritant" that ultimately serves to consolidate and stabilize the two-gender system. On the other hand, the hermaphrodite is the "vanishing point" of the gender binary; it "embodies the dissolution of male and female as absolute categories."[44] While the fundamental approach of rabbinic texts is to use the *androgynos* as a kind of thought experiment that serves to clarify and shore up a rigid gender grid, the rabbis differed among themselves in the extent to which they were willing to entertain the notion of a dual-sexed person.[45] For the majority of the rabbis, the hermaphrodite must be either male or female. Because they did not know which, they tried to manage their ignorance by ensuring that the hermaphrodite would transgress as few halachic norms as possible. For practical purposes, s/he was treated as a male, except where such female bodily functions as menstruation made this impossible. At least one rabbi, however, understood the hermaphrodite as a third-sex being who was forced to function in a binary system.[46] This dual-sex person was "a creature unto itself": a creature who could be both a prohibited passive male in sex and a permitted passive female, a creature who could exempt others of its own kind from certain legal obligations such as hearing the shofar blown or reading the Megillah, but who could not exempt either men or women.[47] The minority view did not upend the gender grid, but it seemed to presuppose a map of the world that allowed genuine exceptions to it.

The challenge for contemporary Jews is to find ways to use the opening provided by rabbinic categories that potentially extend or undermine a binary understanding of gender to question our own gender dimorphism. Just as the rabbis tried to fit the *androgynos* into a bifurcated system, so modern Western culture has found ways to force a range of gender outlaws—from homosexuals, to intersexuals, to transsexuals—into the same binary system. It has used a variety of strategies to read the psychology, experience, and bodies of those who might threaten gender dualism to reinterpret and restabilize it. As the rabbinic concepts of *aylonit* and *saris* suggest, the very imprecision and malleability of the concepts of male and female have aided in this task, helping to sustain a dimorphic understanding of gender. None of the characteristics that supposedly differentiate males and females is always and without exception found in only one gender. Many—perhaps most—people fail to fit at least some of the stereotypical expectations concerning their gender. Yet the traits that allow someone to be labeled a man or woman are so elastic that very few people present themselves as entirely ambiguous.[48] When we meet someone previously unknown to us, we generally attribute gender to them automatically and at first glance. We then interpret all further evidence to support our initial ascription, and explain away any cues that fail to fit.[49] Like the rabbis, we have a profound stake in maintaining our picture of human beings as dichotomously gendered.

This picture, however, which has been under attack by feminists and gays for over three decades, is now facing criticism from a new angle—that of transgender activists. The notion of transgender was added to the nomenclature of the gay, lesbian, and bisexual (g/l/b) rights and liberation movement in the mid-1990s, and it has a complicated, if short, history. There is not space here to discuss the "border wars" between different groups within the g/l/b/t coalition or the permutations that the concept of transgender has itself undergone.[50] Transgender persons have often been suspicious of gay and lesbian hegemony within the g/l/b/t struggle, while being gay does not necessarily entail openness to people who consider themselves transgender. Some gays have seen transgenderism as threatening to "queer" a movement that has increasingly sought assimilation into the U.S. mainstream. On the other hand, because the term *transgender* has often been identified with transsexuals—people who experience themselves as having been born the "wrong" gender and who seek sex change surgery—some feminists and gays have criticized transgender people for buying into traditional gender roles and accepting heteronormativity.[51]

I am interested in the concept of transgender in its recent and broad meaning as designating anyone who challenges the gender binary. Understood in this sense, the term refers first of all to transsexuals, especially those who claim a transsexual identity, and who may be many places along a continuum of taking hormones and undergoing surgery, or have no interest in medical intervention. But it also includes cross-dressers; drag queens and kings; bi-gendered people who are one gender by day and another by night; intersexuals who define themselves as such; the many gays, lesbians, and bisexuals who perceive themselves or are perceived by others as transgressively gendered; as well as straight masculine women and feminine men. It can potentially embrace the youth who adopts an androgynous look or who experiments with shifting gender presentations, the stay-at-home dad who has no interest in fulfilling the traditional male role, and, indeed, anyone who has rebelled against traditional gender stereotypes and refused to accommodate to them.[52]

I recognize that using the notion of transgender in this inclusive way is potentially problematic. It erases important inequalities in social power and location along different points on the continuum, downplays the very real physical dangers faced by only some of those who threaten gender dimorphism, and obscures the disagreements among groups with distinct and sometimes conflicting agendas. But the strength of a broad definition lies in making clear the great range of people who potentially have a stake in dismantling the gender binary. As the rabbis recognized in their own inadequate way, our restricted gender categories do not work; they neither exhaust the spectrum of human gender variation nor create the foundations for a just society. They do not work because, as feminists have been arguing for several decades, they make a socially constructed, hierarchical relationship appear to be natural and divinely ordained, giving men economic, political, sexual, and religious power over women and constricting the possibilities of what it means to be human. They do not work because, as advocates of gay, lesbian, and bisexual liberation have recognized, they lock people into particular family structures and forms of desire, rewarding and punishing them based on the gender of their sexual object choice. They do not work because, as transgender activists make clear, there are those who embody multiple and shifting gender possibilities for which we as yet have no names or generally available conceptual frameworks.

To admit the inadequacy of a binary concept of gender is to enlarge the boundaries of our conceptual and social universes by beginning the process of expanding notions of gender. To be sure, there is no easy way to dissolve or vault over the categories of male and female, both because they thoroughly shape the world in which we live and because they are interstructured with profound inequalities in power and access to resources that cannot be wished away. Yet we can think concretely in the Jewish and larger contexts about what it might mean to move toward dismantling gender dimorphism. In part, it involves reclaiming that part of the original feminist vision that called for a radical critique of gender dualism. As Jewish feminism has unfolded over the last thirty years, its enormous impact on Jewish life has been largely confined to women gaining access to formerly male modes of religious expression. Even in the liberal Jewish community, there has been little attempt to seriously shake up gender categories. Men have been reluctant to take on so-called women's commandments such a candle-lighting; women have "feminized" male ritual garb in the process of adopting it; and feminists have as often celebrated gender differences (by creating new ceremonies for important biological events in women's lives, for example) as sought to overcome them.[53] Synagogue life is still organized around heterosexual couples; "singles' events" are organized with the purpose of getting heterosexuals married; gays and lesbians are accepted insofar as their relationships approximate heterosexual marriage. Meeting times and expectations of Jewish professionals still presuppose a traditional division of labor in which someone in the role of wife—generally a woman—attends to family obligations to free the other member of the couple for outside commitments. It is time to undertake a thorough, critical investigation of the persistence of gender roles, leading to a new phase in the transformation of Judaism in which the liberal community takes a hard look at the ways its structures continue to assume and support the gender binary.

Transgender awareness and activism are crucial elements in moving to this next stage. Feminists must maintain a difficult tension between presupposing the existence of women, reconfiguring the meaning of that category, and seeking its demise. It is neither possible nor sensible to stop talking about men and women in a society in which gender inequality is a pervasive reality and in which "women" must band together to demand basic rights. But precisely for this reason, it is important to embrace transgenderism as a movement that gives concrete and embodied meaning to the notion of dismantling the gender binary by breaking the connection between body and gender and proliferating gender possibilities.

I do not know what the ultimate role of gender should be in a society that abandons gender dualism. But it seems to me that the most effective way to make clear the socially constructed nature of gender dimorphism is to begin by multiplying genders. Feminists have argued that we can experience the reality of a God who transcends maleness only by using a wide variety of gendered and nongendered images.[54] Calling on God as Goddess, she, mother, queen, Shekhinah, birth giver, wellspring, source, and so on breaks the hold of dominant male images of God in a way that cannot be achieved simply through theoretical discussion. Similarly, we can fully understand the inadequacy of the gender binary only by beginning to name the many ways of being in the world that fall outside the dual-gender version of reality. The rabbis were our forerunners in this regard, in that they were at least willing to think about the existence of persons who threatened their gendered universe. Our awareness of gender and sexual inequalities enables and requires us to go well beyond their tentative and male-centered experiments with expanding gender categories. The Jewish community must make synagogues and other Jewish communal institutions safe places both for people who consider themselves transgender and for all those who transgress gender norms. It must engage in (another) round of basic consciousness-raising to explore the ways in which gender norms fail almost everyone. Jewish organizations should support the goals of the Intersex Society, which calls for ending genital surgery for intersexed infants, surgery that has less to do with helping children than upholding society's two-gender system.[55] They should support the elimination of gender categories from basic identification documents such as licenses and passports and, most importantly, cease using such categories themselves on job and Jewish school applications and other forms.[56]

Because gender dualism supports and is supported by compulsory heterosexuality, moving beyond gender also entails rethinking the nature of sexuality and family. The categories of man and woman presuppose the heterosexual matrix to give them substance and make them meaningful. Heterosexuality as an institution has persistently assumed the existence of men and women linked in hierarchical social units that model and prepare us for other forms of social hierarchy. If gender is no longer the defining criterion of sexual normalcy, then we need to find new ways of imagining and structuring desire. If the family is no longer rooted in gender-role differentiation, then we need to become aware of the many constellations of intimacy that provide ongoing contexts for mutual support and childrearing. When a married male-to-female transsexual continues living with and making love to her wife, or two intersexuals enter into a long-term relationship, or a bisexual woman insists that she desires and seeks out people with dark, curly hair more than the "opposite" gender, the links between gender and an obligatory heterosexuality are disrupted.[57] These identities and family forms are not supposed to exist, and yet they do exist all around us. Like the *androgynos*, they invite us to imagine ways of living and loving outside the gender binary and summon us to create a world without the hierarchies of gender and sexual orientation.

In the context of the Jewish community, rethinking sexuality and family means ceasing to promote marriage as the universal norm for adult Jews. For some Jewish groups, especially those that have the strongest commitment to differentiated gender roles, this goal is still unthinkable.[58] In many Reform and Reconstructionist and some Conservative congregations, on the other hand, lesbians and gay men are fully integrated members of the community. But part of what has made this significant change possible is the assimilationist path taken by many gay and lesbian Jews whose relationships are like marriage except for the gender of their partners. While the choices of these Jews and the new openness of parts of the Jewish community should be welcomed and affirmed, their joint effect is to allow the umbrella of marriage to be enlarged a bit at its edges. Marriage remains the norm for Jewish life, and gender remains central to marriage, only now its definition includes committed relationships between two women or two men. This move continues to marginalize people who are obviously transgressively gendered. It also does not yet take up the challenge of imagining sex and relational intimacy in a world of many, possibly shifting, genders.

It is frightening to try to free ourselves from a two-gender system and to explore the new understandings of sexual desire that arise from such a change. It entails living in that liminal period, as necessary as it is unsettling, that is part of any transition to new ways of organizing the world. Attempting to dismantle gender is an extraordinary challenge that signifies a new phase in both the feminist and g/l/b/t movements. But heterosexism and homophobia cannot finally be overcome without moving beyond the gender binary.

Notes

1. Harold Garfinkel, *Studies in Ethnomethodology* (Englewood Cliffs, NJ: Prentice Hall, 1967), 122–28, cited in Suzanne J. Kessler and Wendy McKenna, *Gender: An Ethnomethodogical Approach* (Chicago: University of Chicago Press, 1978), 113–14. Note that while the distinction between (biological) sex and (cultural) gender was an important contribution of feminist theory, this distinction has come under increasing criticism. I am following Kessler and McKenna (7) and many other recent feminist theorists in including so-called biological sex as part of the gender system.

2. Kate Bornstein, *Gender Outlaw: On Men, Women, and the Rest of Us* (New York: Routledge, 1994), 72; Judith Shapiro, "Transsexualism: Reflections on the Persistence of Gender and the Mutability of Sex," in *Body Guards: The Cultural Politics of Gender Ambiguity,* ed. Julia Epstein and Kristina Traub (New York: Routledge, 1991), 249; Steven Greenberg, *Wrestling with God and Men: Homosexuality in the Jewish Tradition* (Madison: University of Wisconsin Press, 2004), 138.

3. Kessler and McKenna, *Gender,* 8–12; Kate Bornstein, *My Gender Workbook* (New York: Routledge, 1998), 27; Judith Butler, *Gender Trouble: Feminism and the Subversion of Identity* (New York: Routledge, 1990), 6–7, 17.

4. Butler, *Gender Trouble,* 22–23.

5. Adrienne Rich, "Compulsory Heterosexuality and Lesbian Existence," *Signs: Journal of Women in Culture and Society* 5/4 (1980): 63–60.

6. Gayle Rubin, "The Traffic in Women: Notes on the 'Political Economy of Sex,'" in *Toward an Anthropology of Women,* ed. Rayna Reiter (New York: Monthly Review Press), 178–83. See my essays "Sexual Orientation and Human Rights: A Progressive Jewish Perspective" and "Authority, Resistance, and Transformation: Feminist Reflections on Good Sex," in Judith Plaskow, *The Coming of Lilith:*

Essays on Feminism, Judaism, and Sexual Ethics 1972–2003 (Boston: Beacon Press, 2005), 186–188 and 196–201.

7. Anne Fausto-Sterling, *Sexing the Body: Gender Politics and the Construction of Sexuality* (New York: Basic Books, 2000), 14; Judith Halberstam, *Female Masculinity* (Durham: Duke University Press, 1998), 76, 82.

8. Fausto-Sterling, *Sexing the Body*, 71–2; Suzanne J. Kessler, "The Medical Construction of Gender: Case Management of Intersexed Infants," *Signs: Journal of Women in Culture and Society* 16/1 (1990): 19–20; Suzanne J. Kessler, *Lessons from the Intersexed* (New Brunswick, NJ: Rutgers University Press, 1998), 105–6.

9. Bernice L. Hausman, *Changing Sex: Transsexualism, Technology, and the Idea of Gender* (Durham: Duke University Press, 1995), 6–7, 146, 460. This demand is not part of the Benjamin Standards of Care for Gender Identity Disorders, but it has been the reality at many clinics beginning with the case of Agnes in 1958.

10. See Monique Wittig, "One Is Not Born a Woman," *Feminist Issues* 1/2 (Winter 1981) for an early and important example of this position.

11. See the (now defunct but still informative) Intersex Society of North America Web site, www.isna.org.

12. Kate Bornstein is an important spokesperson for this movement; see her books cited in notes 2 and 3. Also Anne Bolin, "Transcending and Transgendering: Male-to-Female Transsexuals, Dichotomy, and Diversity," in *Third Sex, Third Gender: Beyond Sexual Dimorphism in Culture and History,* ed. Gilbert Herdt (New York: Zone Books, 1994), 260–85.

13. Daniel Boyarin, *Unheroic Conduct: The Rise of Heterosexuality and the Invention of the Jewish Man* (Berkeley and Los Angeles: University of California Press, 1997), 14, 16–17.

14. Michael Satlow, "'They Abused Him Like a Woman': Homoeroticism, Gender Blurring, and the Rabbis in Late Antiquity," *Journal of the History of Sexuality* 5/1 (1994): 18, 24.

15. Greenberg, *Wrestling with God and Men,* 129–30, 133–34, 136. For examples of the contemporary homophobic position, see Greenberg's discussion on 137–8 and Norman Lamm, "Judaism and the Modern Attitude Toward Homosexuality," in *Jewish Bioethics,* ed. Fred Rosner and J. David Bleich (New York: Sanhedrin Press, 1979), esp. 204.

16. Charlotte Fonrobert, "Gender Identity in Halakhic Discourse," in *Jewish Women: A Comprehensive Encyclopedia,* ed. Paula Hyman and Dalia Ofer (Jerusalem: Shalvi Publishing Company), online version housed at the Jewish Women's Archive, http://jwa.org/encyclopedia/article/gender-identity-in-halakhic-discourse.

17. This is Rachel Adler's language in her classic essay, "The Jew Who Wasn't There: Halakhah and the Jewish Woman," in *On Being a Jewish Feminist: A Reader,* ed.

Susannah Heschel (New York: Schocken Books, 1983), 13–14. See also Paula Hyman, "The Other Half: Women in the Jewish Tradition," in *The Jewish Woman: New Perspectives*, ed. Elizabeth Koltun (New York: Schocken Books, 1976), 105–13. Contemporary liberal Judaism no longer follows any of these laws.

18. Fonrobert, "Gender Identity in Halakhic Discourse"; Judith Romney Wegner, *Chattel or Person? The Status of Women in the Mishnah* (New York: Oxford University Press, 1988); but compare Miriam Peskowitz, *Spinning Fantasies: Rabbis, Gender, and History* (Berkeley and Los Angeles: University of California Press, 1997), who points out that there are many loci of rabbinic control in addition to sexuality.

19. Satlow, "'They Abused Him Like a Woman,'" 9–15.

20. Daniel Boyarin, "Are There Any Jews in 'The History of Sexuality?'" *Journal of the History of Sexuality* 5 (1995): 340–47. See also Greenberg, *Wrestling with God and Men*, 178–79.

21. Greenberg, *Wrestling with God and Men*, 179.

22. For discussion of rabbinic sources on lesbianism, see Rebecca Alpert, *Like Bread on the Seder Plate: Jewish Lesbians and the Transformation of Tradition* (New York: Columbia University Press, 1997), 29–33; Rachel Biale, *Women and Jewish Law: An Exploration of Women's Issues in Halakhic Sources* (New York: Schocken Books, 1984), 192–97; Greenberg, *Wrestling with God and Men*, 86–89; Satlow, "'They Abused Him Like a Woman,'" 15–17.

23. Peskowitz, *Spinning Fantasies*, 60–74.

24. Charlotte Fonrobert, "The Semiotics of the Sexed Body in Early Halakhic Discourse," in *Closed and Open: Readings of Rabbinic Texts*, ed. Matthew Kraus (Piscataway, NJ: Gorgias Press, forthcoming); Isaac Klein, trans., *The Code of Maimonides, The Book of Women* (New Haven: Yale University Press), chap. 2. On the *saris*, see Sarra Lev's doctoral dissertation, "Genital Trouble: The Figure of the Eunuch in Rabbinical Literature and the Surrounding Cultures of the Period" (New York University, 2004).

25. Fonrobert, "The Semiotics of the Sexed Body"; *Encyclopedia Talmudica* (Jerusalem: Talmudic Encyclopedia Institute, 1972), s.v. "Eylonith."

26. Sarra Lev, "Excerpt from 'Genital Trouble'" (paper delivered to the Jewish Feminist Research Group, January 2005), 3–5, 14. While Lev focuses on the eunuch, the same applies to the *aylonit*. See Fonrobert, "The Semiotics of the Sexed Body." The *saris* is forbidden to judge capital cases, but Lev thinks the reasons for this are related to his absence of parental responsibility rather than gender (22–24).

27. Genesis Rabbah 46:5, 13. Cited in Fonrobert, "Gender Identity in Halakhic Discourse."

28. Fonrobert, "The Semiotics of the Sexed Body." See J. David Bleich, *Judaism and Healing: Halakhic Perspectives* (Jersey City, NJ: KTAV Publishing House, 1981), 76.

29. Fonrobert, "The Semiotics of the Sexed Body." Fonrobert sees the notion of the *androgynos* as a "figure of thought" that allowed the rabbis to elaborate the gender binary. While it certainly served that function, I see no reason to believe that the rabbis were unfamiliar with people who exhibited a range of primary and secondary sex characteristics.

30. Klein, *The Code of Maimonides,* chap. 2, 24–25.

31. *Encyclopedia Talmudica,* s.v. "Hermaphrodite."

32. Thanks to Sarra Lev for this important point. Conversation, January 2005.

33. Mishnah Bikkurim 4:1–5. I am listing only a few of the ways in which the *androgynos* fits each category for purposes of illustration.

34. I am using *per* as a neutral pronoun to avoid cumbersome phraseology.

35. Mishnah Bikkurim 4:1–5.

36. *Encyclopedia Talmudica,* s.v. "Hermaphrodite."

37. Fonrobert, "The Semiotics of the Sexed Body."

38. Bleich, *Judaism and Healing,* 78.

39. Satlow, "'They Abused Him Like a Woman,'" 18.

40. Talmud Yevamot 83b. See Joshua Levinson, "Cultural Androgyny in Rabbinic Literature," in *From Athens to Jerusalem: Medicine in Hellenized Jewish Lore and in Early Christian Literature,* ed. Samuel Kottek, Manfred Horstmanshoff, Gerhard Baader, and Gary Ferngren (Rotterdam: Erasmus Publishing, 2000), 127–28; Satlow, "'They Abused Him Like a Woman,'" 17–18.

41. Talmud Yevamot 83b.

42. Tosefta Yevamot 10:2; Satlow, "'They Abused Him Like a Woman,'" 18.

43. *Encyclopedia Talmudica,* s.v. "Hermaphrodite."

44. Ann Rosalind Jones and Peter Stallybrass, "Fetishizing Gender: Constructing the Hermaphrodite in Renaissance Europe," in *Body Guards* (see note 2), 80.

45. Fonrobert, "The Semiotics of the Sexed Body." In using the phrase "thought experiment," I do not mean to suggest that the *androgynos* was only that, but simply that the rabbis' fascination with *androgynos* serves a particular role in their system.

46. Greenberg, *Wrestling with God and Men,* 188–89; Levinson, "Cultural Androgyny," 128.

47. It's R. Yose who holds that a hermaphrodite is sui generis; Talmud Yevamot 83a. See also *Encyclopedia Talmudica,* s.v. "Hermaphrodite."

48. Halberstam, *Female Masculinity,* 20, 27; Kessler and McKenna, *Gender,* 1–2.

49. Kessler and McKenna, *Gender,* 161–62.

50. The term "border wars" is Halberstam's, *Female Masculinity,* chap. 5. See Bolin, "Transcending and Transgendering" for a discussion of shifts in the meaning of *transgender.*

51. Halberstam reviews some of the large literature on this issue, *Female Masculinity,* chap. 5. See also Bornstein, *Gender Outlaw,* 134–35. Janice G. Raymond's *The Transsexual Empire: The Making of the She-Male* (Boston: Beacon Press, 1979) remains the strongest feminist critique of transsexualism, and one that has been roundly criticized by the transgender community.

52. Bornstein, *Gender Outlaw* and *My Gender Workbook.*

53. Rebecca Alpert, "Challenging Male/Female Complementarity: Jewish Lesbians and the Jewish Tradition," *People of the Body: Jews and Judaism from an Embodied Perspective,* ed. Howard Eilberg-Schwartz (Albany: SUNY Press, 1992), 368.

54. See my *Standing Again at Sinai: Judaism from a Feminist Perspective* (San Francisco: Harper SanFrancisco, 1990), chap. 4, for one of many examples.

55. Kessler, "The Medical Construction of Gender," 25.

56. Fausto-Sterling, *Sexing the Body,* 111.

57. See Bornstein, *Gender Outlaw,* 31–40 and *My Gender Workbook,* 90–106 and Bolin, "Transcending and Transgendering," 460–82, for discussion of breaking the ties between gender and desire.

58. See Maurice Lamm, *The Jewish Way in Love and Marriage* (San Francisco: Harper & Row, 1980), 67, for a description and affirmation of the connection between gender differentiation and heterosexuality.

Beyond the Binary Bubble: Addressing Transgender Issues in the Jewish Community

Rachel Biale

Editor's Note

This essay can be used to guide decision makers in Jewish organizations as they consider the ramifications of including gender-variant persons. This essay goes beyond the often-mentioned issue of creating public restrooms in which all persons might feel welcomed and safe to the creation of a broad schematic of the organized Jewish world and the Jewish life cycle to see where and how issues of gender variance might arise.

A nonbinary palette of gender and sexuality can dislocate familiar assumptions. Once you begin to entertain possibilities between and beyond the conventional binary of gender norms ("male and female He created them" [Gen. 1: 27]) and heterosexuality ("therefore shall a man leave his father and mother and cleave to his wife" [Gen. 2:24]), doors and challenges open in every facet of Jewish life. Educational programs, Jewish culture and learning, ritual practice and religious institutions, social services, advocacy and social activism, vocational and psychological services—you name it and transgender issues emerge.*

---

*For the sake of economy, I will use the term *transgender* in this essay in its broadest implications (*trans* as "beyond" rather than "cross to the other side") to include all gender-variant people: those who change their gender only in psychological identification, and/or appearance and/or social behavior, and those who undergo surgical or chemical treatments; those who identify as "neither" traditional male or female; those preferring the terms *queer, gender-fluid, gender-ambiguous,* etc., and those identified as nonconforming with any socially recognized gender definition, except their own fluid and evolving one.

"Good morning boys and girls," the daily greeting at preschool, becomes problematic. The bar or bat mitzvah dilemma is no longer how to get the right date on the synagogue's busy schedule, but how to maneuver the "either/or" gender assumptions. An Orthodox synagogue may need to create a tripartite mechitza separating men, women, and some transpeople (other transpeople would be under the radar, choosing to remain hidden among the men or women in their gender of choice). Would a Jewish day school allow a male teacher to remain in a male gender role but wear a dress to work? Would a Jewish business association welcome a woman wearing a men's pinstripe suit? Once you let your imagination loose, the list goes on and on.

These thoughts that follow on the implications of transgender identity and the transgender rights movement began in informal meetings of individual San Francisco Bay Area transgender activists and three Jewish community organizations: Jewish Mosaic: The National Center for Sexual and Gender Diversity (www.jewishmosaic.org), the LGBT Alliance of the Jewish Community Federation of San Francisco, the Peninsula, Marin and Sonoma Counties (www.sfjcf.org/groups/lgbt), and Progressive Jewish Alliance (www.pjalliance.org). As the Bay Area regional director of the latter, a Jewish social justice education and activism organization, my participation in the conversation was based on a conviction that transgender issues should be positioned as a community-wide concern. These issues must be addressed not simply to meet the needs of a small group whose members often feel marginalized and pained, but as challenges to our overall identity as a just and caring community. How we listen to and address the concerns of transgender people and how we think about the implications of a post-binary gender identity will determine the character of our community as a whole. Interactions based on gender affect all of us, whether or not we identify as transgender.

The Jewish community has been engaged with the issue of homosexuality for well over twenty years and has made great strides. These would not have been possible, in my view, without the foundational work of feminism, which continues to undergird today's conception of gender identity. While homosexuality provided a challenge to the mainstream Jewish world, transgender issues upset the conceptual apple cart much more dramatically and challenge personal and institutional comfort zones more daringly. Accepting lesbians and gays—individuals, couples, and families—as fully recognized and valued members of our community requires truly accepting that any sexual behaviors between consenting adults are ethically and morally sound Jewish choices. Addressing and accepting transgender identity requires changing the foundational boy/girl, man/woman categories we find familiar and "safe," and accepting new, nonbinary public manifestations of those categories. It involves challenging and countering gender-coded behavior such as dress, hairstyles, mannerisms, public bathroom designations, names, and titles, to name just the most obvious.

The task of this essay is to begin to outline the implications of transgender awareness and openness for the Jewish community and its institutions, in the United States in general, and with some particular reference to the Bay Area Jewish community. The essay's somewhat schematic outline is intended to lay out a road map for considering how transgender issues emerge in all facets of life in the Jewish community.

Transgender issues affect individuals and our community at every stage of Jewish life: birth, childhood, bar/bat mitzvah, young adulthood and leaving home, marriage, childbirth and adoption, aging, and death. Transgender issues will manifest along a variety of vectors:

- communal education institutions and programs
- religious life (organized in synagogue and individualized/alternative)
- ritual practices
- social service programs and economic support service
- cultural programs
- political and advocacy work
- social justice activism and community organizing

Embracing Challenge: Considering How Transgender Issues Emerge in Your Jewish Community

This template can help to guide decision makers as they consider changes that increase welcome and inclusion for transgender people. This schematic may help community leaders navigate the unfamiliar decision spaces that emerge when Jewish gender variance meets Jewish gender norms.

I. Birth and Early Childhood

1. **Support for transgender expectant and new parents**—going beyond the expectant mom/expectant dad model.
2. Welcoming **Bris and covenantal** rituals for infants (utilizing the now commonly celebrated "Brit Bat") that deemphasize the boy/girl dichotomy and introduce new, more open and inclusive language with terms such as *newborn*. Creating welcoming covenantal rituals for infants of indeterminate gender, when the parents opt to keep the options open until the child defines her/his own gender.
3. Supportive **early childhood educational environments** that allow young children to develop their own gender identities and do not box them into uncomfortable traditional modes, while also providing acceptance and support for children of transgender parents.
4. **Support services** for extended family members of transgender parents and young children who evidence nontraditional, fluid gender identity.
5. **Acceptance of early childhood education professionals** who identify as transgender, whether openly or "stealth." This might include teachers who transition during employment at a given school, or wish to cross-dress on the job or outside of work. This would also include developing appropriate language to explain these situations to children in the school.

6. **Curriculum** modifications and new content that allow for more open categories of gender and family stories that include families with transgender members.

II. Jewish Education: Religious School, Day Schools, and Informal Jewish Education

All of the above issues pertain to elementary and middle school education, but school activities and curriculum reassessment needs become more pressing as the division between boys and girls becomes more pronounced, starting in third or fourth grade.

1. Educators must develop **teaching materials** that include Torah and midrash passages that include androgyny as a model alongside stereotypical masculinity and femininity, not as a counter to tradition, but as a tradition also found in Torah (for example, the Adam was created male and female; the rabbis called that being androgynous; God is described at one point as having breasts, indicating a desire to nurture Israel like a mother nurtures her child, and so forth).

2. **Physical education activities and after school sports teams,** which are often divided into boys' and girls' groups and school teams, must be reexamined and reorganized.

3. To the extent that Jewish religious and day schools offer **sex education** (and they all should!) the curriculum needs reevaluation and re-creation to allow room for sensitive discussions of gender identity and gender variances. It may include bringing speakers to classrooms to give the issues a human face and a personal story.

4. **Bar and bat mitzvah** preparations need thorough reexamination, from the actual content of the preparation to the emotional investment, family participation, and group excitement. In all these areas we need to make room for transgender children. This must begin with the gender-specific terms *bar* or *bat* and extend to the content of the ceremony, the emphasis on

adult-gendered dress (suits for boys, dresses for girls), and the more trivial (but often pivotal for the bar/bat mitzvah celebrant) traditional gender-biased themes for the party.

5. **Jewish summer camps** must take on the same challenges in programming as do religious schools. But sleepaway camps face a much greater challenge in addressing the traditional division between girls' and boys' cabins. Especially as children approach adolescence and have growing concerns with body image and sexual attraction, making room for trans-identified children, as well as gay teens, in the close quarters of camp is undoubtedly complicated and delicate. Both the children and their parents need assurance from camp personnel and materials that they will be welcomed and given protection, dignity, and support.

III. Entering Adulthood and Young Adult Services

1. **College preparation:** As Jewish educational institutions participate in preparing their graduates for college, they should equip them with social and life skills that will help them navigate more diverse and often less hospitable environments.

2. **College** is often the time when many young adults first recognize or experiment with alternative gender identities, so specific programs such as presentations, support groups, and ritual services that address and welcome this exploration are vital.

3. **Campus Hillels** should see their role as providing a welcoming, supportive place for transgender Jewish students, especially those far away from home. Programming, curriculum, publicity materials, and staff training are all necessary components in creating such an environment.

4. **Jewish community programs for young adults** heavily emphasize heterosexual matchmaking with an eye to marriage and childbearing, from the popularity of "speed dating" to the messages, both overt and subliminal, of the Birthright Israel trips (many participants jokingly refer to the trip as "Birthrate Israel."). All these programs must be reread with a "queer eye"

and redesigned to be welcoming to transgender persons and
to gay men, lesbians, and bisexual Jews and offer a broad,
inclusive vision of becoming an engaged member of the Jewish
community.

IV. Adult Social Services

1. **Health care services** to address the needs of gender-variant children, young people, and adults are of paramount importance to
   the transgender community. In many cases, even if a person is
   insured, the costs of transitioning (necessary pharmaceutical
   and surgical interventions) are considered cosmetic. Ongoing
   health maintenance is often problematic because, for example, a
   person who has an *M* in the gender box on medical forms will
   not automatically be scheduled for routine examinations of his
   still extant female organs. It is also important to consider the
   education of health care providers around transgender issues,
   and patient advocacy in the face of biased or bigoted health care
   providers. There is also a need to lobby for insurance coverage
   of surgical and pharmacological interventions during transition. All medical personnel at Jewish hospitals and other health
   care establishments supported by the Jewish community should
   be educated and receive sensitivity training.

2. **Vocational services** offered by the Jewish community need to
   create special tracks for training and support for transgender
   people seeking employment within and outside the Jewish community. These programs need to develop specific plans to
   address the high rates of both unemployment and underemployment in the trans community.

3. In tandem, Jewish Vocational Services need to provide **training
   to Jewish agencies and employers** on ways to address the needs
   of transgender applicants and employees.

4. **Economic support** services are vital for transgender Jews and
   their families in light of the high rates of unemployment and
   underemployment in this community. In addition, alienation

from family of origin, which is more common for transgender people, often contributes to greater economic strains as loving grandparents are not there to step in and help with day school tuition, summer camp fees, trips to Israel, and so forth.

5. **Counseling and psychological services agencies** should develop special services for both individuals and families, as well as group counseling for transgender people. For example, these agencies should provide couples therapy when one member of the couple is transgender and counseling for persons considering or undergoing transition-related distress. Such agencies should also include transgender issues in staff development and clinical training.

6. Specialized **grief and healing** support for transgender people needs to be developed to address loss of intimate and supportive relationships that do not fit into conventional heterosexual models.

7. Services to **aging adults and their families** must address transgender needs, which may include special issues in arranging for in-home personal care and institutional living. In addition, services are needed to support transgender children of aging parents, addressing both deep emotional issues, such as reconciliation with alienated parents at the end of their lives, and practical ones, such as navigating bureaucracies and services that do not recognize transgender identity.

V. Religious and Ritual Life and Life-Cycle Events

1. **Synagogues** need to recognize that for a large proportion of the Jewish transgender community their doors are forbidding. They need to develop special **outreach plans to connect with transgender Jews** and make them feel respected and welcome. This includes reviewing gendered language, reassessment of ritual practices such as mechitza and *aliyah laTorah,* and openness to transgender clergy. Additionally, synagogues need to examine the organizational structure of their communal/social life (men's clubs and Sisterhoods, for example).

2. The Jewish community needs to support **religious life outside of the synagogue** and welcome life-cycle ritual options offered by independent clergy and lay leaders. These are critical in the effort to reach out to the transgender community. For many transgender Jews, these frameworks, rather than synagogues, will be a first entry point into Jewish life.

3. **Conversion:** A significant portion of the transgender Jewish community is made up of converts. Recognition of the often intertwined journeys of gender and religious identity transformation is important for making them feel welcome. Public discussions, special outreach programs, and new rituals to mark this dual transition are all needed to address the needs of trans converts.

4. **Marriage** (and divorce) presents perhaps the most challenging arena for including transgender people in legal and communal practices. Heterosexual marriages in which one partner has legally changed gender and the other has not are legal. Heterosexual marriages where both partners have legally changed gender (going in opposite directions, an FTM with an MTF) are legal. Marriages in which one formerly heterosexual partner changes sex but not sexual preference (for example, the husband in a traditional heterosexual marriage becomes a woman who continues to love her wife) retain their validity as legal homosexual marriages. This state of affairs exists with very little legal scrutiny at present. However, the surviving spouse's right to inheritance or parenting rights can be successfully legally challenged after the death of a spouse. Marriage equality struggles in the GLBT community should be inclusive of these "under the radar" options so that marriage rights, rather than being piecemeal, may be extended to all.

5. **Adoption** and foster care options for transgender children are limited; there is no guarantee that a child's gender choices will be respected by adopting or fostering parents.

6. **Parenting:** Transgender parents have children before or sometimes during transition (as was made famous in the story about an FTM who gave birth to a child in 2008), so issues and concerns of transgender parents must be addressed in parent/teacher interactions at school and with all social services.

7. **Death and Dying:** The *chevra kadisha* movement, funeral directors, and bereavement counselors must be educated about transgender *taharah* (preparation for burial) and the process through which new customs may be introduced before death occurs, thus ensuring *kavod ha guf* (honor of the body).

VI. Jewish Communal Institutions

1. The **"flagship" Jewish communal institutions** in the Bay Area that represent the organized community both internally and to the general non-Jewish world, such as the Jewish Community Federation and its LGBT Alliance, the Jewish Community Relations Council (JCRC), and Jewish Community Centers (JCCs), all need to evaluate and redesign their staff and lay leadership appointments, their public positions on issues of the day, and their publicity materials to make them attuned to and supportive of transgender inclusion.

2. Jewish communal institutions should take the lead on creating models for **professional and lay leadership training** on transgender issues and support the development of educational curricula, media materials, and a cohort of highly proficient trainers who can be available to all Jewish (and interested non-Jewish) institutions.

3. **Advocacy organizations** need to join existing campaigns to advance the rights of transpeople and include support for them in their public positions. The Jewish community ought to see itself and act to be a leader in the general public discussion of these issues.

4. The Jewish community should advocate and lobby for **health care** services that address the special needs of trans patients,

especially inclusion of surgical and hormonal treatments in standards of care and health insurance coverage.

5. **Social justice** organizations need to address the interconnection between social marginalization and economic disempowerment of transgender people and communities in their advocacy and education campaigns. They should work in coalition with other trans empowerment organizations outside the Jewish community to ameliorate these conditions. In addition, they should support advocacy campaigns related to freedom to marry, domestic partnership rights, and other issues that extend equal protections and benefits to all people.

VII. Jewish Culture and Intellectual/Academic Life

1. The Bay Area Jewish community offers an extraordinarily rich palette of **Jewish cultural programs.** Planning of these programs should reflect transgender Jewish identity and related cultural artifacts and performing arts. This should include films presented at the San Francisco Jewish Film Festival, visual art presented in our museums and galleries, and music and theater presented in Jewish cultural festivals and ongoing cultural programming.

2. **Adult Jewish Education** through Bay Area–wide institutions like Lehrhaus Judaica and lectures and classes at synagogues and JCCs should all include attention to transgender issues through both the content of courses and lectures they offer as well as the engagement of transgender Jewish scholars as teachers and public speakers.

3. **University Jewish studies programs** in the Bay Area and Northern California are rich with innovative scholars and courses on gender issues. We are, in fact, the "cutting edge" region for this work. The **academic institutions** as well as the **Jewish community foundations** that provide support for these institutions should engage transgender issues in course offerings and invite appropriate visiting scholars and lecturers.

Foundation support of graduate students in the Jewish studies field should also see it as an important goal to support new research in this area.

VIII. Israel and Israel Programs

1. Presentations of **Israeli life and culture** through the Israel Center, the Israeli Consulate, and the myriad community groups and institutions that offer Israel-related programs should include information and cultural representation of transgender issues in Israel. The Federation's bringing Israel's most prominent transgender person, the singer Dana International, to the San Francisco Bay Area event Israel in the Gardens was a very significant step, and it should be followed with additional programming.

2. Jewish **community trips to Israel:** Trips for teens, young adults, synagogue groups, and Federation and JCRC missions and delegations should all undertake to address transgender issues in Israeli society in their itineraries and teachings and discussions related to the trips.

3. Funding priorities for our community for **projects in Israel,** which already emphasize pluralism, support of marginalized groups, and equal rights, should expand to include Israeli transgender support services and programs.

Conclusion

There are so many areas of investigation and so much work to be done in addressing transgender issues in the Jewish community, it can seem daunting, if not undoable. We face issues that have daily and profound impact on people's lives and dignity, on their rights for equality, economic viability, and community security. It may seem unrealistic to change our community within a time frame that will reflect the sense of urgency among transgender Jews, but we must begin now.

Pirkei Avot (The Teachings of the Fathers) 2:15 states: *"Hayom katzar ve'hamelchha merubah"* (Time is short and there is much to do). Further, it continues—"And the landlord is pressing." The "landlord," be it God or an ethical, compassionate community, is indeed pressing, because *tzedek* and *hesed* (justice and lovingkindness) are at stake. It may not be possible to make as rapid a change as some of us may wish, but we must start, remembering that "it is not incumbent upon you to finish the work, but neither are you free to desist from doing it." (Pirkei Avot 2:16).

Judaism and Gender Issues

Beth Orens

Editor's Note

For Orthodox communities, determinations about issues of halacha (Jewish law) that affect daily life are made by rabbis called poskim *(singular* possuk*) who spend a great deal of time studying the minutiae of halachic decision making. The issue can be as simple as whether a chicken is kosher, or as complicated as whether or not a sex change operation may be undertaken. The* possuk's *ruling is a community guideline, and the best (or most prolific)* poskim *publish volumes that discuss how they arrived at their decisions. This ever growing and changing body of literature is the slow and measured mechanism through which Orthodox halacha, which is often seen to be eternal and unchanging, evolves.*

Often, Orthodox halachic decisors in the area of medical ethics claim that changing one's sex is not permitted by halacha.[1] Rendering oneself sterile is prohibited. Surgical alteration of one's genitals is prohibited. ("And that which is mauled or crushed or torn or cut you shall not offer unto the Lord; nor should you do this in your land" [Lev. 22:24].) Wearing the clothing of the opposite sex is prohibited. ("A woman shall not wear that which pertains to a man, nor shall a man put on a woman's garment" [Deut. 22:5].)

According to the principle of pikuah nefesh, *when a life is in danger even the strictest of prohibitions may be lifted. May this principle be applied to transsexuals? Orthodox* poskim *typically say no. To save a life, other options would be employed to correct the person's wish to end life. Within the mainstream Orthodox world, transsexuality and transgender identity are considered medical and psychological illnesses.*

Given these rigid legal walls, it seems impossible to imagine that there would be transsexuals who embrace Orthodoxy, yet there are many frum *preoperative, nonoperative, and postoperative transsexual men and women. I have heard and read claims from* frum *transmen and transwomen that permission to undergo SRS (in the case of a specific transwoman), or to receive hormone treatment without undergoing SRS (in the case of a specific FTM) was granted by individual rabbis; yet no rabbi has yet publicly acknowledged that such a decision (in favor of transsexual or transgender expression and in support of the new sex and gender) has been made.*

After a sex change, whether that decision was made with legal consent or not, most poskim *say that the sex-changed person is still counted as belonging to their birth sex. In the most famous example, a 1998 Israeli bet din (panel of judges) ruled that Israeli pop star Dana International counted in a traditional* minyan *(prayer quorum), even though she no longer possessed the requisite genitalia.[2] In fact, there is only one Orthodox* possuk *who takes the position that sex-changed persons may be counted among their gender of preference. In the essay below, Beth Orens, a* frum *transwoman, summarizes the Tzitz Eliezer's famous minority position.*

Notes

1. Olivia Wiznitzer, "Transitioning: The Halachic Ramifications," *The Observer: The Student Newspaper of Yeshiva University,* December 3, 2008, http://media.www. yuobserver.com/media/storage/paper989/news/2008/10/03/features/ transitioning.the.halakhic.ramifications-3467993.shtml (accessed May 21, 2009).

2. Leah Koenig, "The Wondering Jew: Judaism and Gender Identity," *New Voices: National Jewish Student Magazine,* December 2004.

Rabbi Yehuda Waldenberg, also known as the Tzitz Eliezer, wrote two responsa relevant to transsexuality.[1] The first, in the Tzitz Eliezer's eponymous volumes of collected responsa, volume X, part 25, chapter 26, section 6, is a responsum dealing with transplants, particularly heart transplants. At the end of this responsum, Rabbi Waldenberg sets out to deal with "other significant/organic alterations of the body, such as a person who changes from male to female, or vice versa." He mentions that such surgery is done in special cases, adding the comment "rare, of course."

Rabbi Waldenberg brings sources from centuries ago into the discussion, citing women who changed into men. Exactly what phenomenon effected the change is not clear from what he writes, but it is clear that to the naked eye, persons who were female by appearance became male by appearance.

Discussing whether such a person, if married, would require a writ of divorce from his/her husband, one of the sources cited by Rabbi Waldenberg writes that he/she does not: "Because this woman has many signs of being a man which are apparent to the visual sense, she does not require a writ of divorce, because she is truly a man."

The source continues to say that in the morning blessings, where a man says, "Blessed are you, Lord our God, King of the Universe, who has not made me a woman," such a man should end the blessing instead "who has changed me into a man" (Rabbi Waldenberg states elsewhere that a male who becomes female would say "who has changed me according to his will," rather than the standard "who has made me according to his will," which is said by women).

Rabbi Waldenberg discusses the strange case mentioned in the Bible, of Elijah the prophet ascending to heaven. According to Jewish tradition, Elijah was transformed into an angel. During the Middle Ages, the question was asked whether Elijah's wife would have been permitted to remarry, since her husband had neither died nor divorced her. The conclusion was that since a woman is barred from remarrying so long as she is a man's wife, and in this case she was no longer a man's wife, but an angel's wife (a status which doesn't exist in Jewish law), her marriage would be automatically nullified. Rabbi Waldenberg states that the same would be the case if a man becomes a woman, as the wife of a woman is not a recognized status in Jewish law.

Important elements of this responsum are, first, that a change of sex that results in the individual appearing mostly to be a new gender actually changes that individual's gender in the eyes of Jewish law. And second, that this is obvious enough that it can end a marriage without either death or divorce, which is an extreme position in Jewish law. Of well-known Orthodox decisors in the present day, Rabbi Waldenberg's responsum presents a minority opinion that is nevertheless maintained in the corpus of responsa.

The second responsum is in volume XI, part 78. It begins with a letter sent to Rabbi Waldenberg by a doctor who read the first responsum and wanted to ask about a case that occurred in the hospital where he worked. The case seems to have been one of androgen insensitivity syndrome. A child was born mostly female in appearance. Labia and what seemed to be a clitoris were present. But there was a single testicle in one of the labia. When tested, the baby was found to be XY, genetically male. An invasive examination was performed, and there were no male organs inside the baby's body. The doctor's two questions were whether it was permissible to operate in order to make the genetically male child functionally female and whether it was permissible, in light of the prohibition against castration, to remove the single testicle. Rabbi Waldenberg begins by noting that the fact that there were no male organs inside the infant's body is irrelevant. "The external sexual organs of the newborn in question, as you have described, appear as those of a female, and it has no external indications of male organs. Only the special examinations [genetic testing] showed that male cells were present. And therefore, in my opinion, even if we were to leave it as it is, it would have the status of a female, since the external organs which can be seen by the naked eye are the determinant in Jewish law."

There is more to the responsum, including a discussion of whether the prohibition of castration applies when the testicles are not functional (there are views in both directions), and I should emphasize that the significance of these responsa applies only to post-op transsexuals. There is no implication that actually undergoing hormone therapy and surgery are permissible.

It would be interesting to compare this to Rabbi Waldenberg's responsum regarding abortion. Jewish law is not pro-choice, as that is generally understood; nor is it pro-life, as that is generally understood. Rather, abortion is considered to be highly undesirable, and possibly close to bloodshed. Nevertheless, the mother's life always takes precedence, and when there is risk to her, rabbis will almost always permit abortion.

Rabbi Waldenberg recognized psychological factors as real ones. He recognized psychological trauma as a danger to a woman that could be grounds for permitting abortion even when no physical danger existed. In light of this, and in light of the terribly high rate of clinical depression and/or suicide among transsexuals, a case might be made for permitting hormone therapy and surgery in certain cases. This is conjecture, however, and I don't believe it has been addressed in those terms and in the context of Rabbi Waldenberg's determination that surgery actually results in a gender change.

Note

1. A *responsum* is a Rabbinic decision concerning a halachic (Jewish legal) issue. Responsa are often written by Rabbis who are known for their ability to think through legal precedent in conjunction with a community's cultural or social necessities. The Tzitz Eliezer is an affectionate and respectful nickname given to Rabbi Eliezer Yehuda Waldenberg, a contemporary rabbinic decisor in Jerusalem. Tzitz Eliezer is also the title of his most famous halachic treatise. Rabbi Waldenberg, who died in 2006, is well-known for his opinions on medical ethics.

Born to Be Wild: A Critique of Determinism
Jane Rachel Litman

One common political strategy of contemporary gay and trans rights advocates is to maintain that people who are variant from the norm in their sexual or gender identities are "born that way," and have no volition in the matter. This strategy is a response to years of oppressive theory that pathologizes LGBT identity as an illness, or—worse still—vilifies it as a sin. Homophobes assert that if variant sexual/gender identity is understood as an illness, it can be "cured," and if it is conceptualized as a sinful lifestyle choice, it can be repented. LGBT-identified people don't want to be medically cured or religiously redeemed, and so might rather prefer to eliminate those possibilities from the discourse. Indeed a number of studies have shown that presenting gender/sexual variance as a condition determined from birth is a convincing response to such homophobic tropes. According to the Quinnipiac University Polling Institute, voters in North America who believe that people are "born gay" are much more likely to support gay rights ordinances.

However, though the determinist argument may afford short-term political gains, I believe that a mindful examination of this claim is important. In my view the secular political doctrine that gender/sexual identity is invariably determined (the mechanism remains unspecified) at birth has unintended and detrimental consequences for both LGBT people and the movement for gender/sexual identity freedom.

There are also several Jewish versions of the deterministic discourse. One Jewish approach rests on the rabbinic doctrine that if one is physically unable to perform a certain mitzvah, one is not obligated to do so. The classic example is a person without hands. Such a person is not halachically obligated to perform the mitzvah of laying tefillin (putting on the ritual objects associated with Jewish prayer) (Shulchan Aruch,

Orach Chayim). Proponents of this idea argue that male homosexuality (they are not concerned with lesbianism since it falls into a different Jewish legal category) is a physical bodily disability that renders a man unable to engage in a fulfilling sexual relationship with a woman. He is therefore not required to engage in one, just as the person with no hands is not required to lay tefillin.

Rabbi Steven Greenberg, in his book *Wrestling with God and Men*, presents a similar though not identical approach. Greenberg suggests that homosexuality falls into the halachic (Jewish legal) category of *oness*, a compulsion or power beyond control. In certain cases, for example a Sabbath medical emergency, an *oness* allows a transgression of normal halachic boundaries. It is not my aim to engage either of these arguments halachically, but rather to note their determinist foundation and to examine the moral implications of any determinist approach for LGBT, and, in particular, transgender people.

According to secular and halachic "born that way" arguments, both gender and sexual identity are binary categories. There are two and only two genders—male and female—and two and only two sexual identities, heterosexual and homosexual. Anyone who does not fit the sexuality binary (such as a bisexual person) is either discounted as "transitionally bisexual," or told to deny any nonheterosexual impulses and pass as heterosexual. Similarly, transpeople are only acceptable as long as their goal is to make a complete and full switch from one existent binary category to the other. Any other life path undermines the binary determinist discourse. Self-identified trannies and genderqueers need not apply.

What's wrong with a determinist "born that way" approach? Most importantly, it doesn't reflect reality. It displaces real human experiences with a political theory. I'm reminded of the midrash about the sin of Sodom (Sanhedrin 109b). According to Jewish tradition, the people of Sodom had a community guesthouse with a single bed. If a guest to the city was too short for the bed, the citizens of Sodom put the person to the rack. If the person was too tall, they cut off the guest's feet and legs to fit. This gruesome story is particularly ironic in the context of this essay. The transgression of Sodom wasn't homosexuality but literally and brutally forcing human beings to fit an already existing rigid structure.

Human beings simply aren't merely male and female, heterosexual and homosexual. People are complex aggregations of hormones, genes, body structures, social mores, cultural contexts, and personal styles. As early as 1948 sex researchers such as Alfred Kinsey expressed sexual identity as a spectrum rather than two rigid categories. In 1978, Fritz Klein went even further to create a multidimensional system for describing complex sexual orientation. Klein proposed seven different vectors of sexual orientation and identity (sexual attractions, sexual behavior, sexual fantasies, emotional preference, social preference, lifestyle, and self-identification) as they relate to a person's past, present, and ideal future.

Like the researchers who examine sexual identity, gender theorists are also increasingly understanding gender identity as a spectrum or multidimensional grid, rather than two separate and discrete binary categories. It turns out that we humans are more than our chromosomes, more even than our chromosomes and hormones. The determinist argument of the "born that way" crowd reduces the humanity of all people by ignoring our complexity.

Another midrash (Mishnah Sanhedrin 4:5) teaches that while in Caesar's mint all the coins are the same, in God's mint each coin emerges unique. "Born that way" theorists want God's mint to be a slightly different version of Caesar's mint. This is sad. Human beings are wonderfully and miraculously diverse both in their individual selves and in their cultures.

In addition, people change and transform over the course of their lives. Trans activist Kate Bornstein (as described in the essay "HOOWAHYOO?" in this anthology) has identified as a male, a female, and neither male nor female. How can the "born that way" argument square with Kate's authentic life experience? Was Kate really and essentially born a man who then mutilated himself? Or born a woman trapped in a male body who liberated herself? Why not actually listen to Kate, who self-identifies as neither? Not only does the "born that way" argument avert its eyes from reality, it reduces the richness of authentic human difference into an unnatural and humanly constructed sameness and conformity.

It's also a very sad political strategy. The likening of trans or gay identity to a birth defect or a compulsion has a certain "vale of tears" quality. It is true that coming to grips with a homosexual or trans identity can generate feelings of great loss, particularly if one is Orthodox or committed to traditional heterosexual familial structures. However, some people willingly and happily choose to be queer or trans, despite external oppression. Just as in the seventies, some feminist women chose lesbianism as the socio-expression of their deeply held political values, today some people actually prefer to identify as tranny or genderqueer rather than female or male, as a profoundly held expression of their discontent with the rigid gender categories of our society. The "vale of tears" view of queer life negates the reality of queer experience.

The "vale of tears" reminds me of the preeminent Jewish historian Salo Baron's critique in a 1928 *Menorah Journal* article of much of Jewish historiography as "lachrymose." Though Jews have unquestionably experienced extraordinary oppression, the Jewish people are resilient, creative, and productive. I am reminded of how many Jews-by-choice tell me that they are asked, Why would anyone choose to be Jewish? Despite anti-Semitism, many thousands of people do choose to become Jews. They do so because they find a richly textured culture and value system. Judaism is not a lachrymose vale of tears; it's often quite a lot of fun. Jews sometimes have a tendency to present ourselves as pitiable victims. That is a false representation of Jewish life and furthers our own collective oppression. It is important for Jews to articulate the positive aspects of Jewish life, culture, and spirituality, in order to support our own sustainability as a people.

Similarly, LGBT life has its attractions. The LGBT community is more tolerant of difference, supports authenticity of expression, and has a certain joie de vivre. LGBT culture tends to be progressive and humanistic and to affirm the worth of community in a world in which caring community is undervalued. Queer life is not a vale of tears; we are not simply the passive victims of oppression. We are a vibrant creative community that is attractive both to people who understand themselves as having been born gay or trans and also to people who understand themselves as having a choice. Indeed, many gay outreach synagogues have a credible percentage of straight members who like being part of the LGBT community.

The determinist strategy, with its unstated assumption that anyone with a choice would prefer to be heterosexual and gender-conforming in a homogenous society of hetero and gender-conforming people, shifts and deflects accountability from the true source of trans and queer disease, that is, oppression. The biggest problem with being queer isn't some essentialist lack, but mistreatment by society at large. Discrimination isn't an unchangeable fact of existence; it's a set of social norms that can be changed. In my view, there is relatively little hassle about being LGBT that equality and acceptance wouldn't fix.

It is particularly ironic and painful to see Jews make the secular "born that way" argument. As I understand the point, it's not okay to oppress people who are born that way and thus cannot help their condition. This implies that it is acceptable to stigmatize or coerce people who merely choose to be different and could change their condition. What if we made the same argument in terms of ethnic difference? Obviously it would not be okay for the white majority to oppress the—let's say— Asian minority, because they can't help it. They're born looking Asian and can't choose to change their variant condition. However, following this logic, it would be okay to insist that light-colored African Americans identify and live as white people, because they can. If they choose to be different, to affirm their unique heritage, that is viewed as an affront to the majority. Minority status is only tolerated when it is biologically determined.

What does this idea say about Jews as a religious minority? That the Jewish minority perversely chooses to be different even though they could live as Christians and fit into the majority category? Jews aren't "born that way"; they have to be raised and socialized as Jews. If a child born of Jewish parents is raised in a Christian home, it is completely possible that the child will never know that he/she is of Jewish heritage. In North America, at least, Jews are Jewish because we make a choice. If we follow the logic of the "born that way" political argument, that the choice to be different is not valid in and of itself, we find ourselves returning to the days of medieval disputations in which Jews had to prove the worth of their religious choice to a hostile Christian majority.

In summary, some gay and transpeople believe they have been born into one of two specific gender and/or sexual orientation categories. Good for them. I support their right to self-determination and complete equality. However, other LGBT people do not have this experience. They experience gender and/or sexual orientation as fluid, complex, and/or a choice.

Accurate abstract theories do not erase and distort on-the-ground evidence. Constructive political tactics do not divide the very people they claim to support. Positive strategies do not portray their own adherents as perpetual victims trapped in a condition lacking any appeal or positive aspects.

There are better approaches. LGBT people and our allies must assert an unconditional right for all individuals to identify as they see fit. I believe that in particular, Jewish activists must challenge any notion based on determinism or binary categories. As Jews we claim the right to pursue our varied Jewish paths without coercion from the majority or claims of biological determinism; I suggest that as queer people and allies, we must do the same.

Transing God/dess:
Notes from the Borderlands

Julia Watts-Belser

As a child, I grew up with a strong mystical bent: whispering to the *neshama* of the willow tree behind our Alabama home, singing to the crepe myrtles that blossomed brilliant pink, drawing companionship from the holiness I felt running through the world, as tangible as a cloak of wind. Growing up a hungry, yearning soul in the midst of a family who didn't have much place for the spiritual, I found my closest kin among the trees. Behind our house, by a tiny little creek-turned-drainage-ditch that crawled with black snakes and water moccasins and other critters I didn't have the sense to fear, the willow tree swept her weeping branches against the grass. She was my refuge, the safest, deepest place I knew. I had no words in those days for religion or for prayer. No one taught me anything about the spirit, so I found my own way: barefoot and brazen against the branches of the old souls of this world.

I met my God unexpectedly, as a teenager one summer afternoon, leaning out over a balcony rail and watching the sunset turn the sky into violet gold. I remember the pulse of the small rocks in my hand, the way they thrummed against my skin with life. I recall the wind, crisp and bright against my face, the feel of my own body discovering center, stumbling into joy. *She* was none of that and all of it: the Presence that flooded through me, the press of the stones in my hand, the strange, sudden wideness of the sky. Even now, the memory takes me back to a profound, primal knowing. That moment of encountering Presence tuned me to relationship, to the possibility that life could be lived in *service* to Her. Like a pebble tossed once into a vast pool of water, that moment is forever rippling out across the texture of my life. And into that pool a thousand other stones have dropped: moments of meeting, moments of connection.

This Presence—this divine She—lives at the heart of my story.

For several years, I practiced with a small, spiritual community of pagans with wide-ranging lineages and traditions, finding kin who were as deeply devoted and fiercely eclectic as I was. Through creative ritual and long nights of yearning, I taught myself to pray—sometimes in silence, sometimes in song, self unfurling like a fiddlehead fern turning her tender head toward the kiss of sun. In this company, I began a lifelong practice of learning to listen to the Holy and a commitment to radical authenticity, to honoring the living pulse of Spirit as it moves in my life.

That listening led me to Judaism. Some people become Jewish because they are drawn to the soul-stirring prayers or the ancient traditions, because they connect with the rich, complex narratives of the Hebrew Bible, because they fall in love with a Jew. I became Jewish because I *was* Jewish. When I entered my first Shabbat service, accompanying a friend who didn't feel like going alone, I was nearly bowled over by an uncanny, undeniable sense of belonging. It was a matter of recognition, deeper than the bones, older than memory.

Jewishness went wild with me. I stumbled into the sea of Talmud and found a complex conglomeration of text and tale and holy argument that lit up my heart and mind. I swallowed so much Hebrew in those first years that it started running loose in my dreams. Medieval texts unfolded for me like love letters, a heritage from which I had somehow become estranged. The tragedies and tenacity of Jewish history claimed me. My own rhythms resonated with the cycle of Jewish time, with the holidays bound up with the land and the moon and the sacred moments of ancient story. The vibrant depths of the liturgy gave me anchor while I reached out for Presence, as my own yearnings and memories tumbled out alongside whispered, chanted Hebrew prayers.

But I didn't become Jewish because it fit my life or synced up nicely with my beliefs. When I became Jewish, I had a God problem. Throughout much of written Jewish history, God's gender has been profoundly and unabashedly masculine. Prevailing metaphors for the Holy from the liturgy and the classical texts are suffused with male imagery:

God as Father, God as King, God as warrior, God as ruddy youth and ancient sage. The feminine was not absent from divinity entirely—and at certain periods of Jewish history, a female divine presence was a strong, vibrant part of Jewish piety and practice. Still, the feminine was understood as a part of God—often as an exiled part, a part that needed redemption and yearned for reunification with the male Source. '

Faced with the immensity of Jewish masculine God language—which I loved, which nourished and nurtured my heart and my knowledge of Presence—I let my own knowledge of Goddess go underground. I spoke of Her in whispers, amidst the candlelit softness of my early morning prayers. I feared exposing that which was most vital in my life to the scorn or judgment of the gatekeepers of good behavior. The silence nearly strangled me. Slowly, barely noticing, I lost myself from the Holy and so I got lost from myself, all the while polishing an outward practice and prayer that might pave over the broken place in my midst.

But there is always a road that leads home.

During my final year of rabbinical school, I wrote a Jewish thealogy[1] of Goddess, in which I articulated how Goddess as a whole and holy being was a viable Jewish option for understanding and encountering the Divine. I examined how theological rejection of Goddess as a Jewish possibility grows out of often-unexamined cultural patterns that demonize the feminine, the pagan, and the earth—and declare them separate from holiness and from God. It was invigorating, terrifying, soul-stretching work. I listened to the stories I had gathered from other Jews who loved Goddess, these gifts of rare confidence and profound trust, determined to do them honor. I sat at the computer each morning, daring to bring my worlds together, trusting the twin realities of my life to dance with each other, if I could but spin the right words.

Very little of that work will fit into this present essay. What I want to explore here is the ramification of one of the insights that emerged from that time: the idea that Jewish experience of Goddess can and does live alongside our traditions of masculine God. Let me be clear: I choose the word Goddess, rather than a myriad of other more palatable Jewish names for the divine feminine, because names like Shekhinah come with a cultural, theological heritage that emphasizes their partiality and their receptivity to the masculine. The Shekhinah, as a friend of mine once said, is like God's feminine side. The word Goddess is more provocative. It speaks of a primal feminine reality. A divinity who is whole and integral unto Herself. Goddess is not easily assimilated. She has the power to shake us up.

But let me be equally clear in another direction: I am not interested in hearkening back to ancient Israelite traditions of YHWH and Asherah. I don't want a God with a girlfriend, even if She is an awesome presence and holy source in Her own right. I believe, as do many Jews today, that there are myriad manifestations and expressions of divine reality—that the Holy has many faces and expresses itself in more ways than I or you will ever know. And I affirm the power and promise of Jewish understandings of divine *ehad*, a profound unity and vast, all-encompassing reality that runs through all existence.

To further complicate the picture: I'm not interested in replacing God with Goddess. Jewish thealogies of Goddess need not reject Jewish theologies of God. We need not pit Goddess language against God language, setting the feminine in competition with the masculine. The feminine complements and complicates experiences mediated through masculine symbols—as well as those expressed in neutral or nongendered forms.

In a binary gender system, in which beings are either ultimately male or female (with no crossing over the line!), a Divine Being that is male, female, and trans at one and the same time would pose a serious logical problem. But when we recognize that binary gender is a limited cultural construction that tangles up human and holy truths all the time, then my three realities can live together in all their brilliant, paradoxical complexity. Just as human genders come in a variety of expressions, divine gender is not a stable, reified finality. Jewish tradition speaks of God in masculine, feminine, and nongendered ways: as *Tsur* (Rock) and *HaMakom* (The Place), alongside *Melekh* (King) and *Av HaRahamim* (Compassionate Father), as *Hakhamah* (Midwife), *Shekhinah* (Indwelling Presence) and *Rahamena* (Compassionate One). Rather than splitting off the feminine from the masculine and declaring them distinct and separate spheres, Jewish affirmations of divine unity and wholeness suggest that God *is* Goddess. A Goddess who is God who is Goddess.

In contemporary Jewish contexts, it has become commonplace to assert that God is beyond gender. Ultimately, I suspect, in a realm that is far removed from our own, gender *is* actually insignificant. *Ehiyeh Asher Ehiyeh*—the ultimate divine force that will be whatever it will be—has neither a womb nor a penis to tangle our thoughts. But we live in a world in which gender matters. We live in a world scarred by the denial of the feminine sacred, wounded by the loss of Goddess. Reclaiming symbols and metaphors of the divine feminine offers a powerful way to counter androcentric religious tendencies that affirm men as the sacred center and relegate women to the periphery. Opening ourselves and our communities to Goddess experience can bring powerful spiritual transformation to contemporary Jewish life.

This transformation also pushes us beyond the binary dichotomy of Goddess and God, to an awareness of the Holy that turns gender inside out and sets it awhirl. Opening ourselves and our communities to the *transness of God/dess offers vital, imperative thealogical insights for the present day. First, connection with the *trans*ness of God/dess acknowledges the way in which our efforts to "gender" the divine are both profoundly meaningful and inherently incomplete. The transgender community offers witness to the significance of gender in terms of expressing identity and mediating relationships—the fact that gender *matters.* At the same time, the trans community also testifies to the reality that the binary gender system fails to capture the full range of human expression, and that our cultural investment in having people play by the rules of socially constructed "normative" genders does a profound violence to the human spirit. I suspect it does the same to God.

*Trans*ing God/dess also offers profound resources for resisting the idolatry of grasping too tightly to any single image or idea of the Divine. A trans God/dess is characterized by fluidity, a shifting nature that refuses to resolve itself into a single manifestation or gender expression. Feminist theologians commonly point to a vitality of shifting images and multiple metaphors as a way of guarding against the idolatrous tendency to cling too firmly to any single mode of speaking about God. Rachel Adler points to the quicksilver metaphorical poetry of Moses's farewell words in Deuteronomy 32 as a prime example of this type of speech, where "God is imagined in rapid succession as a rock, a father, a mother eagle, a birth giver, and a warrior."[2] The plurality of images and metaphors for God present in the Torah and the diversity of divine names and epitaphs likewise speak to the inability of a single name or image to adequately represent divine nature. Poet and liturgist Marcia Falk draws upon this diversity to critique what she calls "single image monotheism," since "all images are necessarily partial and the exclusive use of any part to represent the whole is misleading and theologically inauthentic."[3]

Goddess language and imagery can be as idolatrous as any other human language that claims to capture our experience of the Divine. But *trans*ness, by its very nature, rejects the static single imagery characteristic of idolatry. *Trans*ness suggests that a fundamental characteristic of the Divine is an unwillingness to be pinned down to a single manifestation, to a single form, to a single image. Perhaps Goddess is God is "Androgydess"—God/dess expresses Hirself in a myriad of gender-complex ways. The Divine draws us into an encounter with mystery, toward a Presence who will never be the same twice. God/dess refuses to ever be fully and finally known. Divine vitality is manifest in His unfolding, in Hir boundary-breaking, in Her transformative Presence. May that *trans*spirit bless you, as it has blessed me. May it bless us all.

Notes

1. Study of the feminine divine.
2. Rachel Adler, *Engendering Judaism: An Inclusive Theology and Ethics* (Boston: Beacon Press, 1998), 88. Adler notes that "even those who use diverse images can betray unwillingness to relinquish some characteristic associated with a particular image. In Bible and liturgy, that characteristic is likely to be God's maleness. Thus, in Deuteronomy 32, God as mother eagle and birth-giving rock retains grammatical masculinity."
3. Marcia Falk, "Toward a Feminist Jewish Reconstruction of Monotheism," in *Contemporary Jewish Theology: A Reader,* eds. Elliot Dorff and Louis Newman (New York: Oxford University Press, 1999), 131.

Contributors

Rachel Biale is the author of *Women and Jewish Law: An Exploration of Women's Issues in Halakhic Sources* (Schocken Books, 1984), which received the Kenneth Smilen Award of the Jewish Museum of New York in the category of Jewish Thought in 1985 and, now in its second edition, is used widely in university courses on Judaism, women, and gender studies. She has worked in various positions and organizations in the San Francisco Bay Area Jewish community. Presently she is the Bay Area regional director of Progressive Jewish Alliance (www.pjalliance.org) and also the director of Bible by the Bay, a project of Lehrhaus Judaica.

Kate Bornstein is an author, playwright, and performance artist. Her work recently earned her an award from the Stonewall Democrats of New York City, and two citations from New York City Council members. Her latest book, *Hello, Cruel World: 101 Alternatives to Suicide for Teens, Freaks, and Other Outlaws* (Seven Stories Press, 2006), is a runaway underground best seller. Other published works include the groundbreaking women and gender studies books *Gender Outlaw: On Men, Women, and the Rest of Us* (Vintage, 1995) and *My Gender Workbook* (Routledge, 1997). Her books are taught in over 150 colleges around the world.

Aaron Devor is dean of graduate studies and professor of sociology at the University of Victoria, British Columbia, Canada. He specializes in the study of gender, sex, and sexuality in transmen, female-to-male transsexuals, transgendered females, and lesbian women. He has written numerous articles on trans issues and two books, *Gender Blending: Confronting the Limits of Duality* (Indiana University Press, 1989) and *FTM: Female-to-Male Transsexuals in Society* (Indiana University Press, 1997). See http://web.uvic.ca/~ahdevor.

Chav Doherty completed his MS in counseling with a concentration in marriage, family, and child counseling in 2008. He holds a prior MA in Jewish studies from the Graduate Theological Union, where he studied feminist Judaism and Jewish mysticism. He has been involved in the transgender community in the San Francisco Bay Area for over ten years. Chav has written articles on FTM identity and health care, and is participating in an ongoing research project with San Francisco State University faculty on gender identity and adolescence. His current research interests include identity formation, the social construction of gender, and spirituality in therapy.

Noach Dzmura's essays have appeared in the anthology *Torah Queeries: Weekly Commentaries on the Hebrew Bible* (New York University Press, 2009) and in *Genderqueer: Voices from beyond the Gender Binary* (Alyson Books, 2002), and in periodicals such as the *Jewish Daily Forward, Sh'ma, Zeek,* and the *Jewish Chronicle* (UK). He holds an MA in Jewish studies from the Graduate Theological Union. He serves as online projects consultant at Jewish Mosaic: The National Center for Sexual and Gender Diversity. In that capacity, he edits the weekly online Torah commentary, also called Torah Queeries. He operates a communications consultancy serving Jewish and interfaith nonprofits. Dzmura is a member of Kol Tzedek, a San Francisco Bay Area collective supporting marriage equality and transgender inclusion in the Bay Area Jewish community.

Charlotte Elisheva Fonrobert teaches in the Department of Religious Studies at Stanford University, and currently serves as the codirector for the Center for Jewish Studies there. Much of her work has focused on gender issues in rabbinic literature and culture. Her first book, *Menstrual Purity: Rabbinic and Christian Reconstructions of Biblical Gender* (Stanford University Press, 2000) focused on the representation of women's bodies in rabbinic and to some degree early Christian literature. Beyond her earlier feminist work, Charlotte became interested in transgender and intersex discussions because rabbinic texts betray just such an interest, namely with the creation of legal categories for people that range from doubly sexed (the *androgynos*) to non- or not-yet-sexed people (the *tumtum*). Charlotte contributed some of that work to the *Cambridge Companion to the Talmud and Rabbinic Literature,* which she also coedited (Cambridge University Press, 2007). She is also supervising the dissertation work of Max Strassfeld, who writes on the Talmudic discourse about these categories.

Ari Lev Fornari currently lives in Boston, Massachusetts, where he is a rabbinical student at Hebrew College and a recipient of a Davis-Putter Scholarship. In summer 2006, he worked with Birthright Unplugged in Palestine, and continues to support pro-semitism, anti-zionism, and anti-racism. Before moving to Boston, Ari Lev completed the Anne Braden Anti-Racist Training Program with the Catalyst Project, which continues to ground his involvement in grassroots social justice movements. Ari strives to weave his spiritual practices with his political work in a vision of our collective liberation. Ari enjoys studying Talmud with SVARA, riding a bike, and cooking for a crowd.

Lynn Greenhough lives in Victoria, British Columbia. She has been a member of the local *chevra kadisha* for over thirteen years. In 2000, at age forty-nine, she completed her master's degree and her thesis, "We Do the Best We Can: Jewish Burial Societies in Small Communities in North America." Even as she continues to learn about rituals involving the *chevra kadisha*, she has also expanded her research to include the evolution of Jewish cemeteries. She is a member of the board of Kavod v'Nichum, an international organization devoted to teaching about Jewish rituals of death, burial, and mourning. Greenhough has taught about these rituals locally, at Kavod v'Nichum conferences, and in other communities. Married to Dr. Aaron Devor, Greenhough is a mother and the delighted *bubbe* of Zoey and Jacob.

Eliron Hamburger was born in Los Angeles to immigrant parents and spent several formative years in Buenos Aires, Argentina. Ey worked as a professional for the past twenty-five years on developing physical surroundings (housing, in particular) to serve low-income families as a resource-rich environment, not simply shelter. Now Eliron is dedicating the second half of eir life to re-creating a home for eir body and soul. Ey holds a masters in urban and regional planning and a masters in gerontology, both from the University of Southern California. Eliron lives in Albany, California.

Elliot Kukla is a rabbi at the Bay Area Jewish Healing Center in San Francisco and provides spiritual care to those struggling with illness, grief, or dying. His writing on Jewish spirituality and gender has appeared in numerous magazines and anthologies and has been featured nationally in the media. He lectures across the United States on stigma and diversity in Jewish sacred texts, and his new life-cycle prayers are published widely and have been implemented in congregations across the country.

Joy Ladin (formerly Jay) is David and Ruth Gottesman Professor of English at Stern College of Yeshiva University, of which she is the first openly transgendered employee. This essay is drawn from an unpublished collection of autobiographical reflections on transition entitled *Inside Out: Confessions of a Woman Caught in the Act of Becoming,* excerpts of which have appeared or are forthcoming in *Prairie Schooner, Southwest Review, Parnassus, The King's English,* and other publications. Her prose and poetry has been widely published, and her third book of poems, *Transmigration,* was published by Sheep Meadow Press in 2009, which also brought out her first two collections, *Alternatives to History* (2003) and *The Book of Anna* (2007). She is currently working on a book of psalms, a new collection of poems, and *Trans Poetics,* a book-length essay reflecting on how being transgendered has affected her development as a poet.

Tucker Lieberman was interviewed about his experience at the Ari Mikveh for *Tikkun* (May/June 2006). His story about wearing a yarmulke was included in the anthology *Nobody Passes: Rejecting the Rules of Gender and Conformity* (Seal Press, 2006). A graduate of Brown University and Boston University, he won Brown's Casey Shearer Memorial Award for Excellence in Creative Nonfiction in 2002. He co-organizes TranScriptions, an open mic in Boston.

Jane Rachel Litman is the western region director of the Jewish Reconstructionist Federation and the rabbi of Congregation Kolot Mayim. She has served Reform, Reconstructionist, Conservative, and gay outreach congregations, and has taught in academic institutions including the University of Judaism, California State University Northridge, and Loyola Marymount University. She is the author of numerous articles and essays on feminism, queer rights, creative liturgy, and contemporary theology. She edited the award-winning *Lifecycles 2: Jewish Women on Scripture in Contemporary Life* with Rabbi Debra Orenstein (Jewish Lights, 1998). The next volume in the series, *Lifecycles 3: Jewish Women on Holy Times and Seasons,* is due out in 2010. She enjoys gardening, river rafting, and Japanese art. She lives in Berkeley, California, with her partner, Stewart Schwartz, and their two children, Sophie and Asher.

Catherine Madsen is the author of *The Bones Reassemble* (Davies Group Publishers, 2005), a study of the elements of strong liturgical language; *In Medias Res: Liturgy for the Estranged* (Davies Group Publishers, 2008), a liturgical cycle; and a novel, *A Portable Egypt* (Xlibris, 2002).

Beth Orens is an Orthodox Jew living in the United States. Prior to transitioning, she attended a rabbinical seminary in Israel. She transitioned in the mid-1990s and is doing her best to live happily ever after.

Judith Plaskow is professor of religious studies at Manhattan College and a Jewish feminist theologian. Cofounder and for ten years coeditor of the *Journal of Feminist Studies in Religion,* she is author or editor of several works in feminist theology, including *Standing Again at Sinai: Judaism from a Feminist Perspective* (HarperOne, 1991) and *The Coming of Lilith: Essays on Feminism, Judaism, and Sexual Ethics, 1972–2003* (Beacon Press, 2005).

Rachel Pollack is the author of thirty-one books, most recently the "trifecta" of *Tarot of Perfection* (fiction) (Magic Realist Press, 2008); *Tarot Wisdom* (nonfiction) (Llewellyn Publications, 2008); and *Fortune's Lover* (poetry) (A Midsummer Night's Press, 2009). Her books have been published in fourteen languages. Rachel transitioned from male to female in 1971. She had an adult bat mitzvah exactly forty years after her bar mitzvah.

Martin Rawlings-Fein is a second-year Jewish Studies graduate student at Hebrew College in Boston. As an out bisexual transman, he is a queer community documentarian and runs his own media company, A Fein Mess Productions (www.afeinmess.com). When Martin is not writing papers, reading texts, or organizing in his various communities, he is blessed with the privilege of being a husband and father.

Jhos Singer (www.jhossinger.com) has served as the service leader at Coastside Jewish Community in Half Moon Bay, California, since 2000. He received *s'micha* (ordination) from his community to act as their rabbi in 2002, and at the same time his teacher, Rabbi Gershon Winkler, conferred upon him the title of *maggid*. He is a frequent contributor to Jewish Mosaic's Torah Queeries commentary (www.jewishmosaic.org). He lives in Berkeley, California with his lovely wife, Julie Batz (www.jewishmilestones.org), and their three delightfully wily children and one lazy cat. He is a Koret Jewish educator fellow and is in the midst of pursuing his master's degree in Jewish studies at the Graduate Theological Union.

Max K. Strassfeld is a genderqueer activist working toward a dissertation on transgender and intersex categories in the Talmud at Stanford University. Ze has taught classes on queer Talmud and gender diversity in Judaism, sex positivity, and sexual communication (when he was a sex educator at Good Vibrations), and workshops on the intersection of racism, sexism, classism, and homophobia.

Ri J. Turner holds a BA in anthropology from Cornell University. Starting in college, ze has been heavily involved in building queer Jewish community, especially through NUJLS (the National Union of Jewish LGBTQQI Students) and Nehirim: GLBT Jewish Culture and Spirituality. Ze is also a frequent contributor to Jewish Mosaic's online Torah Queeries commentary.

Julia Watts-Belser is the assistant professor of Judaism at Missouri State University. She was ordained at the transdenominational Academy for Jewish Religion, California, in Los Angeles. She received her PhD in rabbinic literature from the University of California, Berkeley, and the Graduate Theological Union. In addition to cultural studies of the Talmud, she is passionate about feminist Judaism and Jewish environmentalism. A strong advocate for social justice, she serves on the advisory board of Nehirim: GLBT Jewish Culture and Spirituality and recently coauthored an international grassroots health guide, *A Health Handbook for Women with Disabilities* (Hesperian Foundation, 2007).

Tobaron Waxman is an interdisciplinary artist specializing in performance and digital media. He completed an MFA at the School of the Art Institute of Chicago, where he also taught voice in the Performance Department. He has been a visiting artist/lecturer at the University of California, Irvine; Parsons; the School of Oriental and African Studies; Hampshire College; and Tel Aviv University. Waxman also studies and performs Jewish liturgical music as a cantorial soloist. He has conducted mourning ceremonies and services on Yom Kippur, as well as provided spiritual support for the homeless, the sick, and the dying. He has been a grateful recipient of awards including the Van Lier Digital Artist Residency, an ACO Hong Kong Art and Culture Outreach Residency, a Franklin Furnace Performance Art Award, and a Berlin Institute for Cultural Inquiry Fellowship, and he was an invited artist at Siggraph Asia 2009.

Margaret Moers Wenig has served as rabbi of Beth Am, The People's Temple in New York City (1984–2000), as its rabbi emerita and High Holiday rabbi (2002–present) and as instructor of liturgy and homiletics at Hebrew Union College – Jewish Institute of Religion (1985–present). She has also taught workshops for Christian clergy in continuing education programs at Union/Auburn Theological Seminary in New York and in the United States Navy. Rabbi Wenig has played a major role in moving the Reform movement and the Jewish community toward greater support of GLBT equality and civil rights and toward acceptance of GLBT people in synagogues and among the clergy. She ran the very first symposia in any Jewish institution on medical, legal, and religious issues affecting intersex and transgender people. These were held at the seminaries of the Reform and Reconstructionist movements in 2002 and 2003.

Reuben Zellman will complete his rabbinical studies at the Hebrew Union College – Jewish Institute of Religion in 2010. An educator and activist in the transgender community, he has written many articles and educational materials about gender, sexuality, and Judaism, and has taught at congregations, conferences, and universities around the United States. He currently serves at Congregation Sha'ar Zahav in San Francisco and Congregation Beth El in Berkeley, California.

Permissions and Copyrights

"Judaism and Gender Issues," by Beth Orens, is reprinted here by permission of the author. It appears online at the Web site of Sue Long, http://suelong.tripod.com/tzitz.html.

"Dismantling the Gender Binary within Judaism: The Challenge of Transgender to Compulsory Heterosexuality," by Judith Plaskow, appeared in *Heterosexism in Contemporary World Religion: Problem and Prospect*, edited by Marvin M. Ellison and Judith Plaskow (Pilgrim Press, 2007). Permission to reprint acquired from Daniel C. Maguire.

"Remapping the Road from Sinai," by Judith Plaskow and Elliot Kukla, is reprinted by permission from *Sh'ma: A Journal of Jewish Responsibility*, December 2007. The issue included many essays on the porousness of gender and sexual identities—and how Jewish cultural, religious, and communal life might begin to reflect and address the wider breadth of human experience. For more information, visit www.shma.com.

"Abandonment to the Body's Desire," by Rachel Pollack, is reprinted here with permission from the author. It was first published in the Fall 1992 issue of *Rites of Passage*, the original newsletter of the New Women's Conference, and appears online at the Transsexual Women's Resources Web site at www.annelawrence.com/twr/pollack.html.

"Spiritual Lessons I Have Learned from Transsexuals," by Rabbi Margaret Moers Wenig, was delivered as a sermon at Congregation Beth Simchat Torah, New York, on Rosh Chodesh Nisan 5765 (2005).

"Created by the Hand of Heaven: Making Space for Intersex People," by Reuben Zellman and Elliot Kukla, was published online as a Torah Queery on April 21, 2007, at www.jewishmosaic.org/torah/show_torah/71. Torah Queeries is a project of Jewish Mosaic: The National Center for Sexual and Gender Diversity.